Programming
in BASIC
for Personal
Computers

David L. Heiserman

Research and Development Consultant

Programming in BASIC for Personal Computers

PRENTICE-HALL, INC., Englewood Cliffs, New Jersey 07632

Library of Congress Cataloging in Publication Data

Heiserman, David L date
  Programming in BASIC for personal computers.

  Includes index.
    1. Basic (Computer program language) 2. Minicom-
puters—Programming. 3. Microcomputers—Programming.
I. Title
QA76.73.B3H44   001.64'24   80–15939
ISBN 0–13–730747–0
ISBN 0–13–730739–X (pbk.)

Editorial/production supervision
  by Gary Samartino and Daniela Lodes
Interior design by Gary Samartino
Cover design by Jorge Hernandes
Manufacturing buyer: Joyce Levatino

Printed in the United States of America

10 9 8 7 6 5 4 3 2 1

PRENTICE-HALL INTERNATIONAL, INC., *London*
PRENTICE-HALL OF AUSTRALIA PTY. LIMITED, *Sydney*
PRENTICE-HALL OF CANADA, LTD., *Toronto*
PRENTICE-HALL OF INDIA PRIVATE LIMITED, *New Delhi*
PRENTICE-HALL OF JAPAN, INC., *Tokyo*
PRENTICE-HALL OF SOUTHEAST ASIA PTE. LTD., *Singapore*
WHITEHALL BOOKS LIMITED, *Wellington, New Zealand*

Contents

Preface

Computer power is within the grasp of most people now living in the advanced technological societies of today. Computers are no longer limited to large rooms in industry, business, universities, and military installations. You might even know a youngster down the street who plays with a computer instead of building model airplanes or flying kites. Or maybe you have a computer sitting there on the desk in front of you.

Perhaps computer power has moved into the consumer marketplace a bit too quickly. Many owners of new personal computing systems are not prepared to handle the programming tasks and are thus facing a sort of *computer shock.* Once the novelty of running pre-recorded cassette programs wears off, many people begin wondering if the whole affair was worth the investment.

"I have this dandy new computer at home. Now what can I do with it, and how do I go about doing it?" That's where this book enters the scene.

The BASIC programming language is the overwhelming choice for personal computing systems, and this book is about programming in BASIC. What you can learn here applies to most personal computers on the market—including Radio Shack's TRS–80, Apple II, and the Commodore PET. The notions apply to a number of other brands, but these three happen to be the pace-setters.

There is much more to BASIC programming than simply learning the fundamental expressions. If that were not so, you could learn everything there is to know from the owner's manual supplied with the computer.

Of course, there is a need to master the BASIC language itself, but that is only the tool for fashioning more important things. This book emphasizes the sort of analytical thinking that lets you use the tool—the BASIC language—to transform your own ideas into workable programs.

It isn't easy to learn how to fashion custom programs, no matter what language might be at your disposal. One way to handle the situation is by considering programs from two different viewpoints: (1) Given a prepared program, analyze it to see exactly how it works and, (2) given a basic idea, transform it into a workable program. Both approaches are used in this book, with the latter being the dominant one.

The discussions and examples in this book will be far more useful and meaningful if you have access to a personal computer. Do all of the exercises for yourself and give each of them a lot of careful thought. When you begin feeling confident with a new idea, try it out for yourself, extending the notion as far as your experience will let you.

Exercises in the final section of each chapter are intended to test your understanding of the material in that chapter. Computer programming is a building-block affair, and you will have trouble working the exercises properly if you've been careless about learning the material in earlier chapters.

Learning programming can be a lot of fun. It's frustrating at times, but there is a good answer to every problem you encounter. And if you handle the lessons in the proper spirit, you are likely to learn more from your own tinkering than from the book, itself. When that becomes the case, you'll know you are on your way to becoming a proficient computer programmer—"for fun or for profit," as the old saw goes.

Columbus, Ohio   DAVID L. HEISERMAN

Programming
in BASIC
for Personal
Computers

CHAPTER
1

The System READY Status
and
PRINT Command

Keyboard commands introduced in this chapter:

PRINT   LET

Computers are virtually useless unless there is some means for getting information into them from the outside world. In the case of small personal computers, this generally means entering information from a keyboard, cassette tape machine, or disk operating system (DOS). In some special cases, input devices can also include joystick controls, pushbuttons, and a host of interfacing circuits that translate electrical signals into computer "words."

By the same token, it is important to provide some means for presenting computer information to the outside world in an intelligible fashion. Usually, this is handled by a cathode ray tube (CRT) monitor or, in some instances, a line printer. In the first case, the computer-generated information is presented in the form of *alpha-numeric characters* (combinations of ordinary letters and numerals) and special symbols on the face of the CRT. In the second case, the same sort of information is presented as typewritten *hardcopy* on a sheet of paper.

For our purposes throughout this book, assume the system is operating with the most common input/output (I/O) configuration—a keyboard input linked through the computer assembly to a CRT monitor output. Information is entered into the computer, by hand, from the keyboard, and the results are displayed on a CRT monitor output.

You can, of course, learn about alternative I/O configurations—using cassette tape, disk, and line-printing machines—from the owner's manual for your own computer system. And you can be sure that the BASIC you learn using the keyboard and CRT will apply equally well to the alternative systems.

Figure 1-1 shows the keyboard layout for Radio Shack's TRS–80 home computer. Note that most of the keys are labeled with characters that are identical to those found on a common typewriter. The keyboard, in fact, is normally used as though it were a common typewriter keyboard. There are a few special-purpose keys, though, carrying labels such as BREAK, ENTER, and CLEAR. These represent special computer functions that will be described as the need arises.

Other brands of home computers, such as the Commodore PET and Apple II, have similar kinds of special-purpose keys, but they often carry slightly different labels. When it comes to citing operations that use these special keys, the convention throughout this book will be to cite the Radio Shack TRS–80 key labels. If you are using a different kind of computer, you must consult your user's manual to make the conversions. Describing the possible differences each time they arise in this book would cause needless confusion and defeat one of this book's primary tasks—showing that BASIC is easy to learn and master.

A similar sort of situation arises from the fact that different models of personal computers use a few programming steps that differ slightly from the others. Most of the BASIC programming procedures are completely *portable*; that is, the programs can be carried over directly from one kind of computer to another. But there are slight differences in the BASIC procedures and conventions, and they are going to cause some annoyances if you are not aware of those little differences.

The brand of BASIC used throughout this book is based on something now commonly called Microsoft™ BASIC. It is a slight variation of the original Dartmouth BASIC, and one tailored to the special needs of small computer systems.

Radio Shack's TRS–80 uses Microsoft BASIC, so that will be the convention established in this book. Wherever there is a chance that other machines will not operate exactly as described, you will find a note referring you to your user's manual.

Figure 1-1 Keyboard layout for the Radio Shack TRS–80 personal computer. (Courtesy Radio Shack, a division of Tandy Corporation.)

3

None of this is cause for discouragement, alarm, or even con-fusion. The keyboard and programming differences are important, but rather slight, and it doesn't take long to get accustomed to deal-ing with them. Besides, it all gives you a chance to develop a special knack for dealing with the common problem of portability—a knack that will serve you quite well in the future.

1-1   The System READY Status

Although the exact procedures for turning on and initializing personal computers vary a little from one make and model to another, all schemes include some means for indicating that the system is ready to begin accepting information from the keyboard. The TRS-80, for example, generates the following message:

READY
>_

Other expressions and symbols might precede this particular message when the system is first turned on, but once this message appears on the screen, you know that the system is expecting you to begin entering new data and instructions.

The READY expression is automatically generated from within the system, and it indicates that the system has *just entered the command mode of operation.*

The *greater-than* symbol (>), properly called the *prompt* symbol, also indicates that the system is ready to accept information from the keyboard. But unlike the READY message, which appears only when the system *first enters* the command mode, the prompt symbol appear each time the system is expecting a new line of information, whether that line happens to be the first one or not.

Definition. Command mode—A mode of operation whereby the computer *immediately* executes any valid operation specified by the user from the keyboard.

> *Note.* Not all systems use the *greater-than* symbol as a prompt symbol. Others might use symbols such as # or *.

Every line of information, generally made up of a computer instruction and some data, is typed into the computer one character at a time. The *underline* symbol (_), properly called the *cursor* symbol, indicates where the next keyboard character will appear on the screen. So as you type characters and spaces, the cursor moves to the right, one space at a time.

So in effect, when the computer prints READY on the screen, it is saying, "I have just entered the command mode of operation, and I'm ready to begin accepting information from the keyboard." The prompt symbol means, "I am ready to accept a new line of information." And the cursor symbol means, "Here is where the next character will appear on the screen."

Whenever the system is in the command mode and the operator is entering information, there has to be some provision for telling the computer that the line is completed. The computer itself has no way of telling when you are done entering a line of information—you have to tell it you are done.

On the TRS-80, you signal the end of a line of information by striking the ENTER key. In the command mode, striking the ENTER key signals two things: (1) the end of the command line and (2) time to execute the command.

The system responds by carrying out the specified operation and then returning the READY status message:

```
READY
>_
```

The system is then ready to start all over again. You enter a line of information and strike the ENTER key. The computer does whatever you tell it to do, then returns the READY status message again—and so on, and so on, and so on.

> *Note.* The keyboards for most computer systems have a CR or RETURN key, instead of an ENTER key. The function in any case is exactly the same.

1-2 The PRINT *"expression"* Command

Consider the following set of information and messages on the CRT:

EXAMPLE 1-1

```
READY
>PRINT "DAVID"
DAVID
READY
>_
```

The whole thing began with the system printing READY to indicate it has just entered the command mode of operation. It then printed the prompt symbol at the beginning of the next line.

The operator responded by typing a valid command, PRINT "DAVID", and striking the ENTER key.

Immediately after striking the ENTER key, the system did exactly what it was told to do—print the expression DAVID. It then returned to the command mode.

When the sequence was first started, the screen showed only the READY status message:

```
READY
>_
```

The indication is that the system had just entered the command mode (as signaled by READY) and is prepared to receive some instructions from the keyboard (as signaled by the prompt and cursor symbols).

The user then typed

```
PRINT "DAVID"
```

And before striking the ENTER key, the display looked like this:

```
READY
>PRINT"DAVID"_
```

Note that the prompt symbol remained at the beginning of the second line, but the cursor moved toward the right, still indicating where the next character or space would go. There is no more information to be entered, however.

Striking the ENTER key at this point told the computer that the command sequence from the keyboard was complete and that it was time for the computer to execute that particular command. Here is what the computer did:

```
DAVID
READY
>_
```

What *did* the computer do? It executed the command, PRINT "DAVID". It printed that name enclosed in quotes. And upon executing that command, the system immediately returned to the command mode of operation, generating the

```
READY
>_
```

sequence once again.

Whenever the system is in its command mode, a PRINT command, followed by some sort of expression enclosed in quotation marks, causes the system to reproduce that expression. The quotes are not included in the computer's version; but other than that, the display shows a character-for-character reproduction.

The expression enclosed in quotes doesn't have to make any sense. It can be any combination of keyboard characters and spaces, excluding just one—quotation marks.

Typing something such as PRINT "PRINT NEW @@#2A" works just as well as PRINT "DAVID". Even if the expression enclosed within quotes contains command expressions and other sorts of meaningless characters, the machine won't be confused.

EXAMPLE 1-2

```
READY
>PRINT "DAVID"
DAVID
READY
>PRINT "PRINT NEW @@#2A"
PRINT NEW @@#2A
READY
>_
```

The lines showing PRINT *"expression"* were all entered by the user, followed by an ENTER-key operation. The remainder of the work was done by the computer itself. In one case it PRINT-ed DAVID, and in the other it PRINT-ed nonsense such as PRINT NEW @@#2A.

Attempting to include quotation marks within the PRINT-ed expression causes a problem, however. The machine cannot tell the difference between quotes that are supposed to enclose all PRINT-command expressions and those an unwary user might insert within the expression to be PRINT-ed.

For example, typing the command, PRINT "THE COMPUTER SAYS, "HELLO."" confuses the issue, because the machine will interpret the second quotation mark—the one appearing just before the H in HELLO—as the end of the PRINT *"expression"* command. Characters following that second quotation mark will be reckoned by the machine as something quite different; and the result will be an unwanted computer function or perhaps even an error signal of some sort.

Wherever there is a need to insert a quoted expression within a PRINT *"expression"* command, the programmer has to make a slight compromise as far as punctuation is concerned: namely, using apostrophes in place of the expression quotation marks. Check this example:

```
READY
>PRINT "THE COMPUTER SAYS, 'HELLO.'"_
```

Upon entering this PRINT *"expression"* command and striking the ENTER key, the computer returns

```
THE COMPUTER SAYS, 'HELLO.'
READY
>_
```

> *Principle.* A PRINT *"expression"* command causes the computer to reproduce, in a character-by-character fashion, any expression not containing quotation marks.

Before going on to the next kind of PRINT command, consider several special examples of the PRINT *"expression"* command. Although these examples might appear rather trivial at the moment, they take on special significance later in this chapter. See if you can answer the questions posed here before reading the answers.

EXAMPLE 1-3   How will the computer respond to

```
PRINT "PRINT 'PRINT'"_
```
?

The response will be **PRINT** 'PRINT'. Even a valid computer command, if enclosed in quotes, will be literally reproduced without any regard for its meaning.

EXAMPLE 1-4   How will the computer respond to

PRINT "A"_

?

The response will be simply A, followed by the READY status characters.

EXAMPLE 1-5   How will the computer respond to

PRINT "2+3"_

?

The response will be 2+3, followed by the READY status characters—nothing more, nothing less.

EXAMPLE 1-6   How will the computer respond to

PRINT "A$"_

?

It will return the A$ characters.

Putting together these four examples, the display on the screen looks something like this:

```
READY
>PRINT "PRINT 'PRINT'"
PRINT 'PRINT'
READY
>PRINT "A"
A
READY
>PRINT "2+3"
2+3
READY
>PRINT "A$"
A$
READY
>_
```

> *Note.* With the notable exception of the >_ combination, any
> line preceded by the prompt symbol indicates a line entered by
> the user from the keyboard, and terminated by striking the
> ENTER key. All other information is printed by the computer
> itself.

1-3   The PRINT *numerical variable* Command

In ordinary algebra, letters of the alphabet are often used for terms
that can take on varying numerical values. The expression A+1, for
example, is equal to any desired number, A, plus one.

BASIC has a very nice, built-in algebraic feature that allows the
user to assign numeric values to any letter of the alphabet; and the
PRINT command is used for displaying the numerical values. Consider the following sequence of operations:

EXAMPLE 1-7

```
READY
>A=1Ø
READY
>PRINT A
  1Ø
READY
>_
```

To start, the system is in its command mode. The initial **READY** expression, followed by a prompt character, indicates this fact. The user then sets
the value of A by typing A=1Ø, followed by an ENTER. The system accepted the command and responded with **READY** and another prompt
symbol.

After that, the user typed PRINT A—a PRINT command that clearly does
not have a set of quotation marks around the A. The computer responded
to the command by printing the numerical value of A. That value, in this
example, was set in an earlier operation by typing A=1Ø.

> *Note.* Most computer systems show a zero with a slash through
> it. This "zip zero" is clearly distinguishable from the capital letter
> O ("oh").

PRINT *numerical variable* is thus something quite different from PRINT *"expression"*. Using or not using quotation marks makes all the difference in the world. Consider the following sequence of operations:

EXAMPLE 1-8

```
READY
>A=25
READY
>PRINT A
 25
READY
>PRINT "A"
A
READY
>_
```

In this example, you will find two different PRINT commands: PRINT A and PRINT *"A"*. Although they are quite similar in appearance, they mean two entirely different things. Without enclosing the A in quotes, the command is a request that says, "Print the current numerical value of variable A." Otherwise the request is "Print the letter A."

Note. In Example 1-8, the computer responded to the command PRINT A by printing the numeral 25. Notice that it is indented one space. This is done to allow for the possibility of displaying a minus sign (–) if the value of *A* happens to be a negative number. The number is positive in this example, however, so a space appears in front of the machine-printed version. The plus sign is implied.

Numerical variables can be any desired letter of the alphabet, A through Z. Most personal computing systems also permit the use of double literal expressions, such as AB, AC, DI, and so on. And most even allow the use of a letter followed by a numeral between $\emptyset$ and 9—A1, X2, V4, and the like.

That figures out to a rather large selection of numerical variables. Using single letters A through Z provides 26 variables; combinations AA through ZZ offer 26 X 26, or 626 additional variables; and A$\emptyset$ through Z9 provide 260 more.

This does not mean, however, that you are free to use up to 912 different numerical variables within any one program. Your computer has set aside a certain amount of memory for holding the values of numerical variables, and the size of that memory is often far less than that required for storing 912 separate variables.

You do have the option of choosing from 912 variables in this instance, but the actual number of them you can use at any one time is determined by the machine at hand. Consult your owner's manual to determine the size of your variable memory space.

Some systems also accept numerical variables having more than two characters, but in such cases, only the first two are ever considered. If you enter AAB=1Ø, for example and then call for a PRINT AAA at a later time, the system returns 1Ø. The third character is ignored. Check your manual to see if this situation might be handled differently on your machine.

In the process of describing and demonstrating the PRINT *numerical variable* command, we have actually managed to introduce another kind of command—*numerical variable = numerical value.* When operating in the command mode, typing a numerical variable, an equal sign, a numerical value, and then striking the ENTER key tells the system to assign that particular numerical value to that particular numerical variable.

Principle. Numerical variable = numerical value is a valid keyboard command that sets the value of a variable.

Note. In the original Dartmouth BASIC, the values of numerical variables had to be established by entering LET *numerical variable = numerical value.* The LET expression signaled the computer that a relationship between a variable and a number was forthcoming. In later versions of BASIC, including that used for most personal computers, the use of the LET expression is optional. The LET expression will thus be omitted from most of the examples in this book, although it will be used occasionally to remind you that older systems require it.

The following sequence demonstrates the process of setting some numerical values and printing them. The LET expression is omitted in this case.

EXAMPLE 1-9

```
READY
>A=1
```

```
READY
>B=2
READY
>C=-4
READY
>PRINT A
 1
READY
>PRINT B
 2
READY
>PRINT C
 -4
READY
>_
```

In this instance, the operator used the *numerical variable* = *numerical value* command to preset, or *initialize,* the values of variables A, B, and C to 1, 2, and −4, respectively. The operator then did three PRINT *numerical variable* commands in succession. The computer responded by printing the numerical values that were established in the first three LET commands.

As long as the system remains in the command mode, the computer "remembers" any values assigned to numerical variables. Of course, the values of the variables can be changed at any time—simply do the *numerical variable* = *numerical value* command again, using a different numerical value.

Note. If you make a typing error while entering a line of information, you can "erase" the error by backtracking the cursor with the left-arrow (or "back-arrow") key (←). In a sense, the space bar and left-arrow key move the cursor in opposite directions. The left-arrow, however, erases characters as it moves the cursor along the screen.

1-4 The PRINT *math* Command

As shown in Section 1-3, BASIC seems to lend itself quite readily to manipulating the numerical values of variables. While the usefulness of such a scheme might be questionable to this point, a PRINT *math* command helps bring things together in a more useful way.

Consider this:

```
READY
>PRINT 2+3_
```

This is a PRINT followed by a simple arithmetic function. Note that there are no quotation marks around the expression. How will the computer respond when the operator strikes the ENTER key? It will return the numerical result of the function—the numeral 5. The information on the screen looks something like this:

```
READY
>PRINT 2+3
  5
READY
>_
```

The computer actually calculates the result of the arithmetic function that follows the PRINT command. In BASIC, a computer works exactly like a simple calculator whenever a PRINT command is followed by an arithmetic expression. After calculating the result and PRINT-ing it, the system immediately returns to the command status, as signaled by READY and the prompt symbol.

The math function following PRINT must not be enclosed in quotes. Otherwise, the system will merely reproduce the math statement. Compare the following two operations:

```
READY
>PRINT "2+3"
2+3
READY
>PRINT 2+3
  5
READY
>_
```

The first PRINT operation calls for a literal PRINT-ing of the expression 2+3. The second PRINT operation, however, calls for actually calculating the result and printing it. Note that there is no need for an equal sign following the expression to be calculated.

BASIC usually includes a number of exponential and trigonometric functions, as well as the usual four arithmetic functions: add, subtract, multiply, and divide. Study the following sequence of PRINT *math* commands, using Table 1–1 as a guide to the meaning of some of the special symbols and expressions:

EXAMPLE 1-10

```
READY
>PRINT 2+3
 5
READY
>PRINT 2-3
−1
READY
>PRINT 2*3
 6
READY
>PRINT 2/3
 .666667
READY
>PRINT 2↑3
 8
READY
>PRINT SQR(2)
 1.41421
READY
>PRINT LOG(2)
 .693147
READY
>_
```

Table 1-1 Some BASIC Math Operations

Symbol	Meaning	Function
+	add	$a + b$
−	subtract	$a - b$
*	multiply	$a \times b$
/	divide	a/b
↑	exponent	a^b
SQR(n)	square root of n	$\sqrt{n}$
LOG(n)	natural log of n (base e)	$\log_e n$
ABS(n)	absolute value of n	$\pm n = n$
EXP(n)	natural exponential of n	e^n
SIN(n)	sine of n, where n is in radians	$\sin(n)$
COS(n)	cosine of n, where n is in radians	$\cos(n)$
TAN(n)	tangent of n, where n is in radians	$\tan(n)$

Of course, there is much more to be said about mathematical functions in BASIC—this is merely an introduction. The point is that, in the command mode, the system responds to a PRINT *math* command by printing the numerical result.

The PRINT *math* operation can also be used with literal terms, as long as those terms have some specific numerical values. Look at the following command-mode sequence:

EXAMPLE 1–11

```
READY
>A=10
READY
>B=2
READY
>PRINT A+B
 12
READY
>_
```

In this case, the user first set the values of A and B to 10 and 2, respectively. The next step then calls for summing the values of the two variables and printing the result.

There is another approach available for performing the same sort of operation:

EXAMPLE 1–12

```
READY
>A=10
READY
>B=2
READY
>C=A+B
READY
>PRINT C
 12
READY
>_
```

The result is the same in both cases. Example 1–11 uses a PRINT *math* command that includes a pair of predefined numerical variables. Example 1–12, on the other hand, first solves the math problem, assigning the solution to numerical variable C; and the result is printed by means of a PRINT *numerical variable* command.

In either case, the numerical values of the variables had to be defined before the correct solution could be printed on the screen. What, then, is wrong with the following example?

EXAMPLE 1-13

```
READY
>C=A+B
READY
>A=1Ø
READY
>B=2
READY
>PRINT C
Ø
READY
>_
```

The "solution" is obviously incorrect—10 plus 2 is certainly not zero. The difficulty stems from the fact that the initial values of A and B happened to be zero. They were zero, at least, until the operator defined them as 1Ø and 2, respectively. But the sequence of commands defines the value of variable C first; and since A+B was equal to zero at that time, C was committed to being zero, even after the operator assigned different values as to A and B.

Students of computer programming often wander into such traps, making the assumption the system can somehow figure out what the user means to do. Computers, however, are very literal minded systems, and they cannot second-guess the user.

1-5   The PRINT *string variable* Command

Section 1-4 demonstrates how it is possible to assign numerical values to variables, define a mathematical operation for the variables, and get the system to print the numerical result. BASIC lends itself to a similar kind of situation, using string variables in place of numerical variables.

Beginners often have some trouble grasping the exact definition of a string variable; indeed, the notion of a string variable is something quite different from the usual mathematical scheme of things.

Rather than attempting to form a precise definition at this time, it might be more helpful to look at some specific examples first.

Consider the following sequence of commands and computer responses:

EXAMPLE 1-14

```
READY
>A$="MUGGINS"
READY
>PRINT A$
MUGGINS
READY
>_
```

In this example, A$ is a string variable. A string variable can be viewed as a numerical variable that has one particular quality—it can be assigned nonnumerical "values." In this case, the string variable A$ is assigned the value MUGGINS.

The "value" can then be printed by entering the PRINT *string variable* command. As in the case of numerical variables, the "value" must be established before the machine can do anything meaningful with it.

String variables can be any letter of the alphabet, followed by a dollar-sign symbol ($). A$, E$, X$, and so on, are all legitimate string variables.

The values assigned to a string variable can be any combination of alphanumeric characters, symbols, and spaces that do not include quotation marks. The value of a string variable, in other words, is much the same thing as the *"expression"* portion of a PRINT *"expression"* command (see Section 1-2). And like the PRINT *"expression"*, a string expression should not contain quotes within the quotes.

> **Principle.**   String variables are defined by the *string variable =
> "expression"* command.

A *null string* is a string variable that has no value at all. The following example shows how to create a null string, and it shows what happens if the operator tries to get the system to print a null string:

```
READY
>A$=""
```

```
            READY
            >PRINT A$

            READY
            >_
```

The null string is defined by the operation A$=" ". This is a *string
variable* = *"expression"* command where the expression amounts to
nothing at all—there is nothing enclosed within the quotes. So when
the operator entered the PRINT A$ command, the system printed
nothing. It just left a blank space.

Can you think of any applications of string variables? How about
an instance where the programmer wants to call up printed statements that change under certain circumstances? Suppose that a
certain program calls for printing the name NANCY at one time and
then BILL at some other time?

The same string variable, C$, perhaps, could be inserted into the
program at one particular point. At one time it could be defined as
NANCY, and at a later time it could be defined as BILL.

Working with string variables in the command mode can be a lot
of fun. Take a look at this example:

EXAMPLE 1-15

```
            READY
            >A$="MUGGINS   "
            READY
            >B$="IS SILLY  "
            READY
            >C$="BUT HAPPY  "_
```

If the operator now types the command PRINT B$ and strikes the ENTER
key, the computer returns IS SILLY; and entering the command PRINT C$
makes the computer answer with BUT HAPPY. That's all nice, but let's take
advantage of something else. Suppose that the operator does this:

```
            READY
            >PRINT A$+B$+C$_
```

What is going to happen when the operator hits the ENTER key? Here is
what happens:

```
         MUGGINS IS SILLY BUT HAPPY
         READY

            >_
```

String variables, you see, can be strung together, and that is why they are called string variables. Of course, string variables can be "strung" together in different ways:

EXAMPLE 1-16

```
READY
>PRINT C$+A$+B$
BUT HAPPY MUGGINS IS SILLY
READY
>_
```

The technical term for stringing together string variables is to *concatenate* them. The only valid string operator is the plus sign (+)—attempting to concatenate string variables with any other arithmetic operator results in error codes on the screen.

1-6   A Summary of PRINT Commands

The material in this chapter deals explicitly with the following kinds of PRINT commands:

Command	Example
Print *"expression"*	READY >PRINT "SAM EATS GRASS" SAM EATS GRASS READY
PRINT *numerical variable*	READY >Z=256 READY >PRINT Z 256 READY
PRINT *math*	READY >PRINT 2*16 32 READY

PRINT *string variable*   READY
                                       >F$="NUTS"
                                       READY
                                       >PRINT F$
                                       NUTS
                                       READY

And in the process of demonstrating these PRINT commands, it became necessary to introduce a relational command consisting of two kinds of terms separated by an equal sign:

Command	**Example**
numerical variable = numerical value	READY >V2=3.45 READY
string variable = "expression"	READY >W$="ONE FOR ALL" READY

Here is a list of sample PRINT commands. See if you can determine their exact meaning and the differences between them before reading the explanations.

EXAMPLE 1–17 PRINT "COWS"

EXAMPLE 1–18 PRINT "2+2"

EXAMPLE 1–19 PRINT 2+2

EXAMPLE 1–20 PRINT A

EXAMPLE 1–21 PRINT A+B

EXAMPLE 1–22 PRINT "A+B"

EXAMPLE 1–23 PRINT "A$"

EXAMPLE 1–24 PRINT A$

EXAMPLE 1–25 PRINT A$+U$

Which of the PRINT commands in these examples must be pre-ceded by a relational command? Answer: Examples 1-20, 1-21, 1-24, and 1-25. These four examples rely on variables that must be defined before their PRINT commands have any real meaning. Examples 1-20 and 1-21 presume that some specific numerical values have been assigned to their variables. And in Examples 1-24 and 1-25, the assumption is that an *"expression"* has been assigned to the string variables at an earlier time.

Examples 1-17, 1-18, 1-22, and 1-23 are all examples of the PRINT *"expression"* command. Upon executing these commands, the computer prints the characters enclosed in quotes literally. The commands will print COWS, 2+2, A+B, and A$, respectively—nothing more and nothing less.

Example 1-19 is a simple PRINT *math* command, and the computer responds by printing the result of the addition function, namely a numeral 4.

Example 1-25 concatenates the "values" of string variables A$ and U$.

EXERCISES

1-1 Define the following terms and expressions introduced in this chapter:

(a) DOS

(b) I/O

(c) CRT monitor

(d) prompt symbol

(e) cursor symbol

(f) hardcopy

(g) alphanumeric character

(h) numerical variable

(i) string variable

(j) null string

(k) concatenate

1-2 What is the significance of READY as it appears on the monitor? What is the significance of the prompt symbol as it appears on the monitor? What is the difference in meaning between READY and the prompt symbol?

1-3 What does the cursor indicate? How can it be moved to the right without leaving behind a visible character? How can it be moved to the left, erasing characters as it goes along?

1-4   What is significance of the system being in its command mode?

1-5   Describe the meaning of the following commands:

(a)   PRINT *"expression"*

(b)   PRINT *numerical variable*

(c)   PRINT *math*

(d)   PRINT *string variable*

1-6   Which of the PRINT commands in Exercise 1-5 require prior definition of variables?

1-7   Describe the meaning of the following commands:

(a)   *numerical variable = numerical value*

(b)   *string variable = "expression"*

(c)   PRINT A$+B$

1-8   Assume that you have performed all the operations listed in each example below. Describe what the computer will print immediately after you strike the ENTER key.

(a)   READY
>PRINT "ZZZZZ"_

(b)   READY
>PRINT ZZZZZ_

(c)   READY
>Z=1∅
READY
>PRINT "Z"_

(d)   READY
>Z=1∅
READY
>PRINT Z_

(e)   READY
>Z=2
READY
>PRINT Z–Z–Z_

(f)   READY
>Z$="Z–Z–Z"
READY
>PRINT Z$_

CHAPTER
2

RUN, END
and Some Simple Programs
in Between

Keyboard commands featured in this chapter:
RUN   NEW   LIST

Program statements featured in this chapter:
PRINT   END   CLS

Operating a computer system strictly in its command mode can be fun and instructive, but it doesn't take long to find that the command mode can be cumbersome to use. Aside from some math operations and concatenating some string variables, most of the "thinking" in the command mode must be done by the operator.

There certainly must be something more to operating a computer than running it in the command mode.

2-1 Line Numbers Make the Difference

The way to get a computer doing something on its own is by writing a program for it, entering that program into the machine while it is in its operating mode, and then making the machine execute the program.

A computer program is a list of instructions and data that is intended to perform a series of operations. The computer automatically runs through the program, reading the instructions and carrying out the specified operations.

> *Definition.* A *computer program* is a list of instructions and data the computer can execute automatically.

Before any program can be run, or executed, it must be entered into the system's program memory, either directly from the keyboard or in an automatic fashion from a cassette tape player or disk machine. Throughout this chapter, we will assume all programs are entered directly from the keyboard, however.

Programs can be entered into the machine only while it is in the command mode of operation. This means that the task of entering a program can begin only after seeing the READY status signal on the screen—READY followed by the prompt and cursor symbols.

Computer programs are entered into the machine one line at a time; and in BASIC, every line in a program must begin with a line number. Look at this example:

EXAMPLE 2-1

```
READY
>10 PRINT "PAUL"
>_
```

After noting that the system is in the command mode, the operator typed a one-line program. The program line in this case begins with line 10, followed by the program statement, PRINT "PAUL".

> *Principle.* Every line in a BASIC program must begin with a line number.

Line numbers are positive integers between zero and some very large number. The largest allowable line number is determined by the specifications for the computer at hand; and in the case of Radio Shack's TRS-80, that number happens to be 32767. But line numbers, no matter how large they might be, must never contain commas. For example, a system will not know what to do with a line number entered as 1,024. Line number one-thousand-four must be entered as 1024.

As a matter of fact, commas should never be inserted into large numbers, no matter what the purpose of those numbers might be. As shown in a later chapter, commas serve a very special purpose in computer programs, and that purpose has nothing at all to do with separating place values in very large numbers.

Line numbers serve several important purposes; and to appreciate the significance of one of those purposes, consider what would happen if the one-line program just cited did not include a line number.

```
READY
>PRINT "PAUL"
PAUL
READY
>_
```

Does that look familar? It should, because it is a PRINT *"expression"* command of the kind described in Chapter 1. After typing PRINT *"PAUL"*, the operator struck the ENTER key, and the computer responded by printing PAUL and immediately returning to the command mode of operation.

Typing a line number just before entering PRINT *"PAUL"* completely changes the situation. The line number, you see, informs the computer that a program *statement,* rather than a *command,* is coming next. Upon seeing the line number, the system does not immediately execute the operation that follows the line number—not even after the operator strikes the ENTER key.

Rather, the system stores the line number and program line in its memory and returns a prompt and cursor, but no READY expression. The prompt and cursor informs the operator that the system is ready for the next line of program information.

Compare the differences between the two examples cited thus far in this section. In the first instance, the operator enters a line number, followed by the program statement, PRINT *"PAUL"*. Upon striking the ENTER key, the computer returns the prompt and cursor, but does not execute the PRINT *"PAUL"* instruction—it is waiting for another instruction.

In the second example, however, the operator enters PRINT *"PAUL"* as before, but without preceding it with a line number. Upon striking the ENTER key, the system immediately executes the command, printing PAUL and returning the READY expression, prompt, and cursor.

Whether or not you begin a line with a line number determines how the machine will respond to the line of information. And the responses are vastly different.

> *Principle.* *Commands* are entered without line numbers, and upon striking the ENTER key, the computer immediately executes the command. Program *statements* are preceded by a line number, and upon striking the ENTER key, the computer merely stores the line number and statement in the program memory—the statement is not executed.

A program—even a one-liner—isn't much good until it is somehow executed; and in BASIC, a program is executed immediately after typing RUN and striking the ENTER key. RUN is a command expression that causes an immediate response, and it is never to be preceded by a line number.

The following example shows how the screen appears when the operator enters a one-line program and runs it:

```
READY
>10 PRINT "PAUL"
>RUN
PAUL
READY
>_
```

In this case the operator entered a one-line program, PRINT "PAUL". When the computer accepted the program line and returned the prompt symbol, the operator then typed RUN and struck the ENTER key. RUN is a command, so the system immediately responded by doing just that—running the program. It printed PAUL, and then automatically returned to the command mode of operation.

This simple one-line program can be run any number of times by typing the RUN command and striking the ENTER key:

```
READY
>RUN
PAUL
READY
>RUN
PAUL
READY
```

```
>RUN
PAUL
READY
>_
```

Here the programmer ran the one-line program PRINT "PAUL" three more times in succession. As long as the program remains intact in the computer's memory, it can be RUN any number of times. This is something quite different from operating strictly in the command mode. In the command mode, PRINT "PAUL" would have to be typed each time:

```
READY
>PRINT "PAUL"
PAUL
READY
>PRINT "PAUL"
PAUL
READY
>PRINT "PAUL"
PAUL
READY
>PRINT "PAUL"
PAUL
READY
>_
```

Before going on to bigger and better things, take a look at a two-step program:

EXAMPLE 2-2

```
READY
>10 PRINT "PAUL"
>20 PRINT "JUDY"
>_
```

In this case, the computer is being programmed to do two PRINT operations in succession—PRINT "PAUL" followed by PRINT "JUDY". The fact that the line number for PRINT "PAUL" is smaller than the line number for PRINT "JUDY" makes certain PAUL will always be printed before JUDY is.

When the operator types RUN and strikes the ENTER key, the computer responds this way:

```
>RUN
```

```
                              PAUL
                              JUDY
                              READY
                              >_
```

After studying this little demonstration, you should be able to see a second important feature of program line numbers: The computer executes statements in numerical order, beginning with the statement having the lower line number and then going to the statement having the larger line number.

> *Principle.* The computer executes a program according to the order of the line numbers, beginning with the lowest line number and moving toward the highest line number.

Actually, the operator doesn't have to enter program lines in numerical succession. The operator can scramble the line numbers during the programming phase of the operation. BASIC, however, will automatically put the operations into numerical succession in the program memory. Check this example:

EXAMPLE 2–3a

```
                    READY
                    >20 PRINT "JUDY"
                    >10 PRINT "PAUL"
                    >RUN
                    PAUL
                    JUDY
                    READY
                    >_
```

In spite of the fact that the operator programmed line 20 before entering line 10, the system straightened things out; and upon running the program, the machine executed the lower-numbered line first.

> *Note.* Program lines do not have to be entered in numerical sequence. The computer, however, will execute the lines in numerical sequence.

This is a good place to introduce a special program statement,

END. Many programmers make a habit of ending every program with the END statement, although it isn't always absolutely necessary to do so. For instance:

EXAMPLE 2-3b

```
READY
>10 PRINT "PAUL"
>20 PRINT "JUDY"
>30 END
>_
```

It is probably obvious that the END statement in line 30 tells the computer that it has reached the end of the current program sequence. Normally, running this program produces the same result as running without the END statement. END is really important only when there are other programs having larger line numbers residing elsewhere in the memory and the operator doesn't want the system to execute them.

The computer continues executing a series of program statements until one of two things happens; either it executes the highest-numbered program line or it encounters an END statement. It responds to whichever of these two conditions occurs first, ending all automatic operations and returning READY, followed by the prompt and cursor symbols. Consider this example:

EXAMPLE 2-3c

```
READY
>10 PRINT "PAUL"
>20 PRINT "JUDY"
>30 END
>40 PRINT "MUGGY"
>_
```

Upon typing and entering the RUN command, the display shows

```
>RUN
PAUL
JUDY
READY
>_
```

Line 40 in the program is never executed because the system is told to END the program at line 30.

> *Principle.* END is a program statement that tells the system to cease executing the program and return to the command mode of operation.

2-2 Patching Up Programs

Experienced programmers, as well as beginners, generally spend more time devising and correcting programs than actually running them. Making mistakes is a way of life for programmers, especially when working from the keyboard; and if you have been working with a computer system while studying the material presented thus far in this book you've probably made your share of mistakes already.

It is thus quite important to know how to patch up mistakes and modify programs already stored in the computer's memory. The purpose of this section is to examine a couple of procedures for changing programs, either to fix errors or to extend operations in a program already written.

The most drastic sort of "fix" is executing the NEW command. Whenever the system is in its command mode, the operator can type NEW and strike the ENTER key. Since NEW is a command operation, the system executes it immediately.

What does the NEW command do? NEW wipes out all existing programs and sets all variables to zero. String variables are often set to the null string as well. That's pretty drastic, but it's a good way to start things all over from scratch.

Entering the NEW command also does some housekeeping chores, such as clearing all information from the screen and setting the prompt and cursor symbols to the upper left-hand corner.

> *Principle.* NEW is a keyboard command that clears all programs from the computer memory, sets all numerical variables to zero, sets all string variables to the null string, clears the screen, sets the cursor and prompt symbols to the "home" position, and returns the system to the command mode.

Sometimes, however, it is more desirable to take less drastic action—clearing the CRT screen without wiping out the programs and initializing all the variables. This can be done by striking the CLEAR key. In the command mode, striking the CLEAR key neatens up the CRT display without affecting the programs or changing the values of any variables.

Although there is no program statement corresponding to the NEW command, it is possible to clear the screen as part of a program. The statement in this instance is CLS. The CLS statement is a programmable counterpart of striking the CLEAR key while in the command mode.

Whenever the computer is executing a program and comes across a line number followed by the CLS statement, the machine automatically clears the CRT screen and goes on from there.

> *Principle.* Striking the CLEAR key in the command mode or programming a CLS statement clears all information from the screen without affecting the program memory or changing the value of any variables.

An excessive amount of information printed on the CRT monitor can be confusing at times, and the CLEAR command and CLS statement can go a long way toward relieving some of that sort of confusion.

But what if the operator clears the screen and wants to inspect the program? The program still resides in the memory, but it is no longer visible. Here's how to get the program listed on the screen again: type LIST and strike the ENTER key.

In the command mode, typing LIST and striking the ENTER key tells the system to print out all programming resident in the program memory. So if the screen is cleared for some reason or another, or the original program lines have been *scrolled* off the top of the screen, the LIST command calls up and prints the programs on the screen for you.

> *Principle.* LIST is a keyboard command that calls up and displays programs listed in the memory.

Now let us apply some of these principles to a particular programming situation.

To get things started, the operator types NEW and strikes the ENTER key. That operation clears out all old programs, sets variables to their zero or null values, and clears the screen. Everything is nice and tidy.

Now suppose that the programmer enters the following program sequence:

EXAMPLE 2–4

```
READY
>10 CLS
>20 A$ ="I AM DOING  "
>30 B$="A GOOD JOB"
>40 PRINT A$+B$
>50 END
>_
```

This program is complete, but the operator hasn't done a RUN command yet. When the program is run, the first thing the machine will do is clear the screen, as prescribed by line 10. Then it will print the concatenated string variables I AM DOING and A GOOD JOB, and end.

The screen looks like this after doing the RUN command:

```
I AM DOING A GOOD JOB
READY
>_
```

The program can then be recalled to the screen by typing LIST and striking the ENTER key:

```
I AM DOING A GOOD JOB
READY
>LIST
10 CLS
20 A$="I AM DOING  "
30 B$="A GOOD JOB"
40 PRINT A$+B$
50 END
READY
>_
```

Now suppose the operator types NEW and strikes the ENTER key. All the text will be erased from the screen, and READY, following by a prompt-cursor line, will appear in the upper left-hand corner of the screen. Can the program be run now?

```
READY
>RUN
READY
>_
```

The operator entered the RUN command; but since NEW wipes out the program memory, there is no program to run. So the system responds immediately with another READY status.

But is the program *really* gone? Maybe the PRINT statement in line 40 simply got lost somewhere along the line. So the operator tries a LIST command:

```
READY
>RUN
READY
>LIST
READY
>_
```

No; the program is gone. Doing a LIST when the program memory is empty merely causes the READY status to appear again.

Note. Whenever there are no program statements residing in the computer memory, doing RUN or LIST commands cause the system to respond immediately with the READY status.

So the NEW command wipes out everything, and the CLEAR key is responsible for just clearing the screen while the system is in the command mode. A CLS statement written into a program clears the screen, leaving the memory intact; and programs residing in the memory can be printed out on the monitor by entering the LIST command.

Now suppose you are in the process of writing a program into the system, and somewhere along the way you decide that one of the lines has to be changed. Perhaps the program looks like this:

EXAMPLE 2-5a

```
READY
>10 A=10
>20 B=2
>30 C=A*B
>40 PRINT C
>50 END
>_
```

But you really wanted to sum variables A and B, instead of multiplying them as indicated by the asterisk (*) in line 30. Line 30 has to be changed before running the program. How can you fix it?

One way to correct the error is by entering the NEW command and starting all over again. It doesn't take a whole lot of imagination, however, to realize this is a rather drastic step—especially if the program contains perhaps a hundred steps.

A more attractive alternative is to retype line 30 by itself. In BASIC, it is possible to "write over" any program line by simply typing the line number and entering the revised version of the command. In this particular instance, you can correct line 30 by doing

```
>30 C=A+B
>_
```

anywhere along the way.

To make sure the line is entered properly, you can then do a LIST command. Here is the whole procedure as it would appear on the monitor:

```
READY
>10 A=10
>20 B=2
>30 C=A*B
>40 PRINT C
>50 END
>30 C=A+B
>LIST
10 A=10
20 B=2
30 C=A+B
40 PRINT C
50 END
>RUN
 12
READY
>_
```

In this particular case, the operator discovered the error in line 30 just after entering program line 50. The line was rewritten after that; and doing a LIST command confirmed that the system accepted the correction.

The operator ran the program after inspecting the listing; and by that time, the screen was getting cluttered. So wouldn't it have been nice to include a CLS at the beginning of the program? Is it too late to add the CLS operation?

No, of course not. A CLS operation can be inserted before line 10 in the program by typing

```
>5 CLS
>_
```

A new program line can be inserted at any place in the program and at any time the system is in the command mode. Simply pick a line number that will make the statement fall wherever you want it. In this example the idea is to get the CLS operation at the beginning of the program; so the line number could actually be any integer between zero and 9 inclusively.

Upon doing a LIST command, the new statement will be found in its proper sequential position:

EXAMPLE 2-5b

```
>LIST
5 CLS
10 A=10
20 B=20
30 C=A+B
40 PRINT C
50 END
READY
>_
```

Although it is often desirable to add a new program line, it is often necessary to delete a line—not just change it, but wipe it out. The NEW command wipes out everything, but maybe you want to wipe out just one line. That's easy: Simply type the line number and strike the ENTER key. Doing a LIST after that will show that the line is missing altogether.

So you can wipe out the entire program by entering NEW, or you can wipe out one line of the program by typing its line number and striking the ENTER key.

Then bear in mind that a line can be revised by typing its line number, followed by the revised statement; and also that a line can be inserted by typing an appropriate line number and the desired instruction.

The fact that new lines can be written into a program explains why all of the program examples shown thus far have line numbers specified at intervals of 10. It is entirely possible to write programs with line numbers 1, 2, 3, and so on; but doing so leaves no room for inserting new lines. And you might be surprised how often you might want to insert a new line.

Thus programmers habitually leave space between each line number. Numbering the lines in multiples of 10 is probably the most common practice, but intervals of 5 or 20 would work just as well.

2-3 Running from Different Places

In all of the examples presented thus far in this chapter, the operator initiates the execution of a program by entering the RUN command. The assumption is that the computer will begin executing the program with the lowest-numbered line and work its way up to the highest-numbered line.

Indeed, that is what happens when the operator enters the RUN command. It is not absolutely necessary to begin the execution of a program from the very beginning, however; and a slightly modified form of the RUN command forces execution to begin at any desired program line.

Before seeing how this can be done, take a look at this little math program:

EXAMPLE 2–6a

```
READY
>10 CLS
>20 A=10
>30 B=2
>40 C=A+B
>50 PRINT A"+"B"="C
>60 C=A*B
>70 PRINT A"X"B"="C
>80 END
>_
```

Can you figure out what this program will do? Well, line 10 calls for clearing the screen, while lines 20 and 30 set the numerical values of variables A and B. After that, variables A and B are summed, and the solution is assigned to variable C (line 40).

Line 50 is a little bit different from anything we have done so far, but the idea shouldn't be too confusing. Line 50 is basically a PRINT statement that combines three PRINT *"numerical variable"* and two PRINT *"expression"* statements. Reading line 50 from left to right, it is saying: PRINT the numerical value of A, literally reproduce the plus-sign character, PRINT the numerical value of B, literally reproduce the equal sign character, and PRINT the value of variable C.

Note. A single PRINT line can contain any combination of PRINT statements, including *"expression"*, *numerical variable*, *math,* and *string variable.*

37

Perhaps this is getting a bit ahead of the story, but when line 50 is executed, the computer will respond by printing 10 + 2 = 12.

Line 60 in the program redefines variable C, making it equal to the product of variables A and B. Line 70 calls for another combination of two kinds of PRINT statements, and line 80 ends the program.

Upon entering RUN, the screen will look something like this:

```
10 + 2 = 12
10 X 2 = 20
READY
>_
```

Now that's a nice little arithmetic sequence. Its appearance on the screen is enhanced by clearing away the program in line 10.

Look over the program again, comparing it with the results appearing on the screen after running it. Make sure you understand the little trick of doing more than one kind of PRINT operation in a single command line.

Suppose that you now clear the screen by striking the CLEAR key, and then enter the LIST command. The screen looks like this:

```
>LIST
10 CLS
20 A=10
30 B=2
40 C=A+B
50 PRINT A"+"B"="C
60 C=A*B
70 PRINT A"X"B"="C
80 END
READY
>_
```

Then take advantage of the fact you left room for inserting new statements between the existing program lines. Type and enter this:

```
>55 END
```

That line is automatically inserted between lines 50 and 60 in the program. It won't appear that way on the screen until you do another list command, but the program memory already sees that line in its designated position.

Now what happens when the program is run? Things are going to come to a halt at line 50. Right?

```
10 + 2 = 12
READY
>_
```

Inserting END into the program at line 55 allowed the system to do only the first part of the program. The remainder of the program is just hanging there, completely closed off from execution by the new END statement.

But it is possible to get access to the second part of the program by doing a different sort of RUN command, RUN 6∅.

Principle. It is possible to begin execution of a program at any desired line by entering the command RUN *n,* where *n* is the starting line number.

So type RUN 6∅ and watch what happens:

```
READY
>RUN 60
 ∅ X ∅ = ∅
READY
>_
```

Oh-oh, something went wrong. Program execution began at line 60 all right—you know that because the computer printed the X (times) symbol from line 70 in the program. But where did those zeros come from?

Beginning program execution from line 60, you can see that the values of variables A and B are not set. Most home computer systems automatically set the values of numerical variables to zero everytime a RUN command is executed. So doing a RUN 6∅ started execution at line 60; but at the same time, it reset the values of A and B back to zero.

Again, you must take advantage of the numerical spacing between the program lines, and insert some commands that reinitialize the values of A and B ahead of line 60. Try this:

```
READY
>57 A=1∅
>58 B=2
>_
```

Then enter RUN 57, and you will see this added to the existing display on the screen:

```
>RUN 57
 1∅ X 2 = 2∅
READY
>_
```

There it is! Everything is put back into good order. Enter the RUN command, and you will see this:

```
10 + 2 = 12
READY
>_
```

Then enter RUN 57, and the overall display looks something like this:

```
10 + 2 = 12
READY
>RUN 57
 10 X 2 = 20
READY
>_
```

The first part of the program, the summing part, is executed by entering RUN. You could do the same thing by entering RUN 10. In either case, execution begins with line 10 in this particular example.

The second part of the program, the multiplication part, is then executed by entering RUN 57. There are no options in this case: Execution of the second part of the program must begin with a RUN 57.

To take a look at the program as it stands now, enter LIST. You should see the following information added to the current display:

EXAMPLE 2-6b

```
>LIST
10 CLS
20 A=10
30 B=2
40 C=A+B
50 PRINT A"+"B"="C
55 END
57 A=10
58 B=2
60 C=A*B
70 PRINT A"x"B"="C
80 END
READY
>_
```

This listing actually represents two separate programs: lines 10 through 55 is one of them, and lines 57 through 80 is the other. One or the other can be executed by entering the appropriate RUN *n* command.

Incidentally, you can neaten up the second program by inserting 56 CLS. That will clear the screen so that the information from line 70 will appear without a lot of other printing above it. But, of course, inserting line 56 as part of the second program means that it should be executed by doing a RUN 56. The second program will run in response to RUN 57, but the screen will not be cleared.

It is possible to stack any number of programs in this fashion. Each one must be terminated by an END statement, however. Otherwise, the system will simply execute the entire listing.

Running any one of the programs is a matter of entering RUN *n*, where *n* is the first line number of the desired program.

2-4 Tightening Up a Program

The real skill in computer programming is not so much a matter of knowing a lot of different statements and commands as it is a matter of finding ways to write efficient programs. Efficient programs are those that do their intended task with the fewest possible lines of information.

Look at the program listing in Example 2–6b. That program uses 11 statement lines. Is it possible to tighten up this program? Try this sequence of editing operations:

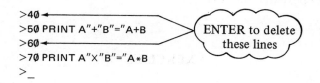

```
>40
>50 PRINT A"+"B"="A+B
>60
>70 PRINT A"X"B"="A*B
>_
```

ENTER to delete these lines

Assuming that the 11-line program in Example 2–6b is still residing in the computer's program memory, the operator edits the program by typing 40 and striking the ENTER key. Recall from Section 2–2 that this kind of command-mode operation erases the designated line. In effect, the operator deletes line 40 from the program.

The operator then rewrites line 50, replacing numerical variable C with the *math* operation A+B. Numerical variable C is now completely eliminated from the first part of the program.

The operator performed the same kind of surgery on the second part of the program, deleting line 60 and rewriting line 70 to eliminate variable C again.

Doing a LIST command displays the revised program:

EXAMPLE 2-6c

```
>LIST
10 CLS
20 A=10
30 B=2
50 PRINT A"+"B"="A+B
55 END
57 A=10
58 B=2
70 PRINT A"x"B"="A*B
80 END
>_
```

It turns out that the computer returns the same display as the earlier version. This revised version, however, uses only nine program lines and contains one less variable. That isn't a remarkable reduction in program complexity, but the example illustrates that it is indeed possible to do a task at least two different ways.

There is rarely one "correct" way to handle a computing task—most jobs can be done any number of ways, ultimately yielding the same results. There are always just a few "better" ways to do a computing job, however; and that is where a programmer's knowledge, skill, and experience pay off.

EXERCISES

2-1 In the context of computer programming, what is the difference between a *command* and a *statement*?

2-2 Classify each of the following as a statement, command or both a statement and command:

(a) PRINT *"expression"*

(b) PRINT *math*

(c) RUN

(d) CLEAR

(e) CLS

(f) NEW

(g) LIST

(h) END

(i) ENTER

2-3 Name at least two functions performed by a line number.

2-4 Describe how it is possible to correct a command line or program state-ment *before* terminating it by striking the ENTER key.

2-5 Describe the procedure for deleting an entire line from a program.

2-6 Describe the procedure for inserting a new program line into an existing program.

2-7 Describe the procedure for changing an existing program line *after* it has already been committed to the program memory.

2-8 Compare NEW and CLEAR, describing both their similarities and dif-ferences.

2-9 Under what conditions is it possible to omit the END statement without affecting the execution of a program?

2-10 Suppose that the lowest-numbered line in a program is line 100. What is the difference between executing the program with RUN and RUN 1ØØ?

2-11 In each of the following examples, describe how the computer will respond upon entering RUN 1Ø:

(a) 10 CLS
      20 PRINT 2*8
      30 END

(b) 10 CLS
      20 PRINT 2*8
      30 CLS
      40 END

(c) 10 CLS
      20 A=2
      30 B=8
      40 PRINT "THE ANSWER IS" A*B
      50 END

(d) 10 CLS
      20 A=2
      30 B=8
      40 PRINT A "TIMES" B
      50 PRINT "THE ANSWER IS" A*B
      60 END

2-12 How will the computer respond to the programs in Exercise 2-11 upon entering RUN 2Ø? RUN 3Ø?

CHAPTER 3

INPUT and GOTO
for
Interaction and Automation

Keyboard commands introduced in this chapter:
BREAK   CONT

Program statements introduced in this chapter:
INPUT   GOTO   STOP

The short programs described in Chapter 2 showed how it is possible to get the computer to do some arithmetic and present the solutions in an automatic fashion. The scheme was a little awkward and limited in its application, however. The trouble was that the necessary numerical values had to be assigned as specific program lines. In order to get the computer to solve a slightly different problem, it was necessary to rewrite the program lines that set the numerical values and then run the program all over again.

There just has to be a more convenient way to get the machine to solve different arithmetic problems!

3-1 Getting Yourself into the Program
with INPUT

An INPUT statement inserted into a program tells the computer to stop all ongoing operations and wait for some information from the keyboard. It gives you, the operator, an opportunity to set numerical values and enter string expressions.

Consider the following program:

EXAMPLE 3-1

```
10 CLS
20 PRINT "WHAT IS 'A'"
30 INPUT A
40 PRINT "WHAT IS 'B'"
50 INPUT B
60 CLS
70 PRINT A"+"B"="A+B
80 END
```

Upon entering RUN, the computer will first clear the screen of any information (CLS statement in line 10) and then print the expression WHAT IS 'A'. Nothing new so far. When the system encounters the INPUT A statement in line 30, all operations come to a halt, and the screen looks like this:

```
WHAT IS 'A'
?_
```

Note the question mark. The computer always prints a question mark when it is halted by an INPUT statement. In effect, it is asking the question: What value do you want assigned to variable A?

How do you, as the operator, respond to this? Answer the machine's question. Type a numerical value and strike the ENTER key to let the machine know the value is ready.

Upon entering a numerical value and striking the ENTER key, the computer resumes executing the program—in this case, it goes on to line 40 and prints WHAT IS 'B', followed by another question mark. It's doing another INPUT halt, waiting for you to type in the numerical value of variable B.

After you type the numerical value of B and strike the ENTER key, operations resume again at line 60. But take a look at the screen just before you strike the ENTER key:

```
WHAT IS 'A'
? 2
WHAT IS 'B'
? 4_
```

In this instance the operator responded to WHAT IS 'A' by typing 2 and striking the ENTER key. The system then printed WHAT IS 'B' by typing 4. The system remains halted until you strike the ENTER key. The computer is very, very patient—it will wait forever, remaining stuck on line 50 until you type in a valid numerical value and strike the ENTER key.

So strike the enter key. Operations then resume at line 60, first clearing the screen and then printing the line specified in line 70:

> 2 + 4 = 6
> READY
> >_

The program is finally executed in its entirety.

Now you can do another RUN command, responding to the two INPUT *numerical value* statements with any numbers you choose. You can play around as long as you want—even doing some command-mode operations—and the program will not resume execution until you strike the ENTER key.

Comparing this program with the summing programs cited in Chapter 2, you can see a clear advantage here. By using INPUT *numerical value* statements in the program, there is no longer any need to specify specific numerical values as part of the program itself. The numerical values are all entered from the keyboard as part of the program execution process.

Of course, you can experiment with this particular program as long as it resides in the program memory. Just enter RUN whenever you want to start the program again, then respond to the INPUT question marks with valid numerical values.

INPUT statements can also handle string variables. Think about this:

EXAMPLE 3-2

```
10 CLS
20 PRINT "FIRST PHRASE"
30 INPUT A$
40 PRINT "SECOND PHRASE"
50 INPUT B$
60 CLS
70 PRINT A$+B$
80 END
```

This program is essentially the same as the first one. The only differences are that the system is expecting string expressions at lines 30 and 50, and it concatenates them (rather than adding them) at line 70. Suppose that the operator runs this program, responding to the question marks as follows:

> FIRST PHRASE
> ? MUGGINS IS
> SECOND PHRASE
> ?A SILLY CAT_

Entering the second phrase, A SILLY CAT, the computer might respond with this:

```
MUGGINS ISA SILLY CAT
READY
>_
```

Before dealing with the obvious problem of having the words IS and A run together, note that it is not necessary to enclose the responses to INPUT *string* commands within quotes.

> *Note.* Keyboard responses to INPUT *string variable* commands need not be enclosed in quotation marks. If such responses are enclosed in quotes, the quotes are ignored by the computer.

String expressions entered from the keyboard, in response to an INPUT *string variable* statement, can be any combination of keyboard characters, including numerals, spaces, and any of the special symbols.

In fact, it is possible to respond with the null string by simply striking the ENTER key. Entering the null string in response to an INPUT *string variable* command in the program can be a handy little trick. This trick will be demonstrated later in this chapter.

Now deal with the problem of having the IS and A words run together when the two string variables are concatenated in line 70. There are at least two ways to handle the problem in this particular case: Either put a space at the end of your first input response or put a space at the beginning of the second response.

The INPUT *string variable* statement accepts spaces as well as any other keyboard character. So if you run the program again, inserting a space in one of the two places just described, the result looks much nicer:

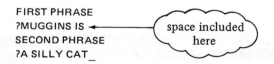

```
FIRST PHRASE
?MUGGINS IS ◄──────   space included
SECOND PHRASE                 here
?A SILLY CAT_
```

Then striking the ENTER key, you see:

```
MUGGINS IS A SILLY CAT
READY
>_
```

Later you will discover a more suitable way to make certain that concatenated string statements are not run together. At that time, you will be able to build the space into the program, eliminating the need to think about it every time you enter a string expression.

Considering the same program, what do you suppose will happen if you respond to the question marks with numerals instead of string expressions? For instance:

```
FIRST PHRASE
?10
SECOND PHRASE
?20_
```

Will the system show an error condition? Will the system sum the two numerals at line 70? It will do neither of these things. Numerals are valid string expressions, and the system will concatenate them in a literal fashion:

```
1020
READY
>_
```

Principle. Whenever the computer encounters an INPUT *numerical variable* command, it prints a question mark and waits for a numeral to be entered from the keyboard. The computer will then treat that input as a number value through all operations that follow.

Whenever the computer encounters an INPUT *string variable* command, it prints a question mark and waits for a string to be entered from the keyboard. The computer will then treat that input as a string expression through all operations that follow.

The practical value of INPUT statements is that they allow the operator to set the values of variables *after* execution of the program begins. The values of those variables then remain unchanged until the program is run from the beginning or another INPUT statement allows the operator to change the values.

Using INPUT commands represents a marked improvement over the variable-setting procedures used in Chapter 2.

3-2 Jumping Around with GOTO

A GOTO *line number* statement in a program tells the computer to interrupt the normal sequence of execution and go directly to the specified line number. This can be a powerful programming tool, as demonstrated in the following example. Note the GOTO 1Ø statement in line 90.

Here is a slightly modified version of the two-variable arithmetic program already discussed in Section 3–1:

EXAMPLE 3-3

```
10 CLS
20 PRINT "WHAT IS 'A'"
30 INPUT A
40 PRINT "WHAT IS 'B'"
50 INPUT B
60 CLS
70 PRINT A"+"B"="A+B
80 INPUT A$
90 GOTO 1Ø
100 END
```

If you have studied Section 3-1 carefully, you should have no trouble following the program down to line 80—that's where a couple of different things begin happening.

At line 80, the system encounters an INPUT *string* command. It responds by printing a question mark and waiting for the operator to strike the ENTER key. You can input any string expression you want; but in this particular application, you will see the value of entering the null string.

Suppose that you do enter the null string in response to line 80. What happens then? The following line, line 90, is a GOTO statement accompanied by a valid line number—line number 10, in this case.

Upon encountering line 90, the computer obeys the statement and jumps up to line 10, effectively starting the program all over again. Work through the entire program, beginning with a RUN command.

Operation begins at line 10 and the computer clears the screen. Immediately after that, it prints WHAT IS 'A', followed by a question mark. Suppose, for the sake of discussion, that the operator responds by typing 15 and striking the ENTER key.

After that, the system prints WHAT IS 'B' and a question mark. Suppose that the operator responds with a 12. Before hitting the enter key, the display looks something like this:

WHAT IS 'A'
?15
WHAT IS 'B'
?12_

When the operator strikes the ENTER key, execution resumes at line 60 and the computer clears the screen. Now here is where things are a bit different from the example in Section 3-1:

15 + 12 = 27
?_

Line 70 calls for printing this nice little arithmetic format; but then line 80 tells the system to expect a string expression from the keyboard. That's why the question mark is appearing just ahead of the cursor.

In the context of this program, the question mark might be interpreted as saying, "Let me know when you are ready to go on."

Now the operator can respond by typing anything at all and striking the ENTER key. But notice that A$ is never acted upon in the program, so anything typed as a response to the INPUT A$ statement in line 80 will never be used. So why not keep things simple, and enter the null string. In other words, respond to that statement by striking the ENTER key.

Program execution will then resume at line 90; and since line 90 tells the system to jump back to line 10, the apparent response is a clearing of the screen and the question, WHAT IS A.

The operator can now assign some different numerical value to A and go on from there. The whole program can be executed any number of times, using any desired combinations of A and B values. All of this takes place in response to just one initial RUN command.

In a sense, this program makes the computer work as a simple calculator that sums any two numbers.

Note. The INPUT *string variable* command in line 80 is absolutely vital to the proper operation of this program scheme. Without it, the system would display the information from line 70 for only a fraction of a second before GOTO 10 would cause the screen to be cleared by the statement in line 10. This illustrates the inherent value of inserting INPUT *string variables* and responding to them with the null string—simply striking the ENTER key after having time to see the results of any previous operations.

Using GOTO *line number* statements can set up looping situations where certain operations can be performed again and again. But this technique, as applied in Example 3–3, can give rise to a certain kind of problem. The program, in this case, has no ability to end itself. To be sure, there is an END statement in line 100; but the fact that a GOTO 1∅ precedes it means that the END statement will never be encountered.

Maybe things have gotten a little *too* automatic. As it is, the program never ends, and the machine is tied up with it until the power is turned off.

Well, actually there is a way out of this sort of GOTO loop—strike the BREAK key.

Striking the BREAK key interrupts any ongoing program and returns the system to the command mode. Most systems also respond to a BREAK by printing the number of the last program line it executed.

So a good way to get out of a looping program is by striking the BREAK key. After that, you can modify the program, do PRINT commands to see the values of variables, write a new program, or start the old one from the beginning by entering RUN.

Programmers sometimes create GOTO loops inadvertently, thereby causing the computer to "buzz" around through several program lines. In that case, BREAK acts as a panic button for ending the vicious circle of events, and gives the programmer a chance to iron out the bug. There is more to be said about BREAK and other "program stoppers" at the conclusion of this chapter.

Right now, you only need to know that BREAK lets you get out of a looping program created by the GOTO *line number* statement.

> **Principle.** While the computer is executing a looping or very long program, striking the BREAK key halts the program and returns the system to the command mode of operation.

One of the exciting features of computers is getting them to print out personalized text. If you have not worked with this personalizing feature on a firsthand basis, you have probably received a "personalized" form letter from a firm that is trying to sell you something.

The following program illustrates how such personalizing schemes work; and in the process of going through this program, you will have a chance to see all the principles of INPUT statements and GOTO's at work.

EXAMPLE 3-4

```
10 CLS
20 PRINT "PRINT YOUR NAME, PLEASE."
30 INPUT N$
40 A$="HELLO,"
50 PRINT A$+N$
60 PRINT "STRIKE THE 'ENTER' KEY TO CONTINUE,"
70 PRINT N$
80 INPUT D$
90 PRINT
100 PRINT "HOW ARE YOU, "N$"?"
110 PRINT "IAM FINE, THANK YOU."
120 PRINT
130 PRINT "STRIKE THE 'ENTER' KEY TO DO THIS AGAIN."
140 PRINT "OR HIT THE 'BREAK' KEY IF YOU DON'T"
150 PRINT "WANT TO PLAY WITH ME ANY MORE"
160 PRINT "(YOU JERK, "N$")"
170 PRINT D$
180 PRINT "YOU'RE A SWELL PERSON, "N$
190 GOTO 20
```

Before examining the line-by-line operation of this program, let us go through the actual running assuming that your name is Sally.

Upon entering RUN, the screen will clear and you will see this:

```
        PRINT YOUR NAME, PLEASE
        ?_
```

Type SALLY and strike the ENTER key. The display then takes this form:

```
        PRINT YOUR NAME, PLEASE.
        ?SALLY
        HELLO, SALLY
        STRIKE THE 'ENTER' KEY TO CONTINUE,
        SALLY
        ?_
```

After striking the ENTER key, you see:

```
        PRINT YOUR NAME, PLEASE.
        ?SALLY
        HELLO, SALLY
        STRIKE THE 'ENTER' KEY TO CONTINUE,
        SALLY
        ?
```

HOW ARE YOU, SALLY?
I AM FINE, THANK YOU.

STRIKE THE 'ENTER' KEY TO DO THIS AGAIN.
OR HIT THE 'BREAK' KEY IF YOU DON'T
WANT TO PLAY WITH ME ANY MORE
(YOU JERK, SALLY)
?_

Now you have the option of either playing the program all over again from the beginning, or being a coward and ending the whole affair. If you decide to play some more and respond by striking the ENTER key, the computer responds by printing YOU'RE A SWELL PERSON, SALLY, followed by PRINT YOUR NAME, PLEASE. In this particular case, the screen is not cleared when the sequence is restarted.

Text games such as this one can be a lot of fun and they are highly instructive. We will leave it up to you to do the "fun" things with your computer, however, and work here with the "instructive" phase.

First take note of the fact that this is a looping program. If things ever get to the point where the computer encounters line 190, everything starts over from line 20. The GOTO 2∅ statement in line 190 forces this condition to occur.

A second point of particular importance at this time is the use of INPUT *string variable* statements. These statements are used in two different ways: to set the "value" of variable N$ in line 30 and to resume program execution by entering the null string at lines 80 and 170.

The value of a third string variable, A$, is set by the program itself in line 40.

The remaining steps all use some variation of PRINT statements.

Now for a line-by-line analysis.

When the operator does a RUN command, the system executes line 10, clearing the screen. Immediately after that, line 20 calls for printing PRINT YOUR NAME, PLEASE. This is a standard sort of PRINT *"expression"* statement.

Line 3∅ is an INPUT *string variable* statement that halts program execution until the user enters some string variable and strikes the ENTER key. Presumably, the variable in this case will be the operator's name. It can be any sort of nonsense, however. In any event, the string is assigned to N$.

After accepting the value of N$, the value of A$ is established by the program. Remember: Whenever a string is assigned as a program statement, it must take the form, *string variable = "expression"*. The *expression* must be enclosed in quotation marks. Establishing the string expression for INPUT N$ does not require quotation marks. What is the essential difference between these two situations? Answer that one for yourself.

Line 50 then uses the established values of A$ and N$ to concatenate the expressions and print HELLO, SALLY.

Line 60 is another ordinary PRINT *"expression"* statement, and line 70 is an example of a PRINT *string variable* statement.

The purpose of INPUT D$ in line 80 is to let the user continue the program by entering the null string. Execution of the program is halted until the user responds by striking the ENTER key. Since string variable D$ is never acted upon anywhere in the program, the user can actually enter any combination of keyboard characters, however.

Line 90 is not a printing error in this book. A PRINT statement followed by nothing at all results in a blank line on the display. It's a handy trick for separating lines of text on the screen.

> **Principle.** A PRINT standing alone in a program produces a blank line on the screen when it is executed by the computer.

So line 90 creates a blank line above the text generated by line 100. Line 100 is an example of a PRINT statement followed by a *string variable* inserted between a pair of *"expression"* forms. This line combines two different kinds of PRINT statements into one. The portions to be literally reproduced are enclosed in quotes, while the variable expression is not.

Lines 110 through 180 are all examples of various PRINT and INPUT statements already described in this particular discussion. You might want to give line 160 some special consideration, however, because it includes some rather tricky formatting.

3-3   Building a Text-and-Math Program

One of the problems with reading and trying to understand someone else's BASIC computer program is that it isn't always obvious why things are done the way they are. Programmers, you see, tend to develop a certain programming style—a style that is as peculiar to a programmer as his or her handwriting.

The examples and discussions in this section show how a program can be constructed from scratch, assembled in a skeletal fashion, tested, and then polished. And in the process of doing all this, you will have a chance to use just about all the commands and statements described so far in this book.

Here's the hypothetical situation: The owner of a building materials supply firm wants a computer program that will calculate the weight of bulk materials (sand, gravel, concrete, and so on) required for covering a given rectangular area at some specified average depth. Some text should accompany the calculations, informing the operator which figures are to be entered at any given time and spelling out the meaning of the results in a clear fashion.

Before starting to write such a program, it is important to define the exact nature of the task. It is necessary to assemble the necessary mathematical equations, assign variables, and come up with a step-by-step calculation procedure. On a larger scale, this phase of the work would be handled by a system analyst.

Ultimately, this program should show the total weight of the material to be shipped, and that is a matter of working this equation:

$$WT = V \times WB \qquad (1)$$

where: WT is the total weight of the shipment in tons;
V is the volume of the material in cubic feet;
WB is the weight of the material in pounds per cubic foot.

This equation must be adjusted somewhat, because there is a conflict of units—WT is in tons and WB is to be entered in pounds per cubic foot. This is easily handled, however, by recalling that there are 2000 pounds in 1 ton. So Equation (1) can be adjusted to read

$$WT = V \times \frac{WB}{2000} \qquad (1a)$$

Presumably, WB will still be entered in pounds per cubic foot and the computer will take care of converting that figure to tons.

The volume of material required is not normally known from the outset, so it is necessary to calculate that value as well:

$$V = X \times Y \times D \qquad (2)$$

where: X and Y are the rectangular measurements of the area to be covered in feet;
D is the average depth of the material in inches.

Again, there is a conflict of units—X and Y in feet and D in inches. Equation (2a) shows how the depth can be converted into units of feet.

$$V = X \times Y \times \frac{D}{12} \qquad (2a)$$

Equations (1a) and (2a) can be combined to yield a single equation for the job at hand:

$$WT = X \times Y \times \frac{D}{12} \times \frac{WB}{2000} \tag{3}$$

If this equation is programmed into the computer, the operator enters:

the X dimension in feet

the Y dimension in feet

the D (depth) in inches

the WB (basic weight) in pounds per cubic foot

And the result is the total weight of the material in tons.

This is really a very simple programming task, and it could be done on paper in its entirety. But for the sake of making an important point, assume that the task is much, much more involved.

When beginning a large programming task that involves mathematical equations, it is a good idea to test the equations on the computer. You might want to test Equation (1a) this way:

```
10 CLS
20 INPUT V,WB
30 PRINT V*WB/2000
40 INPUT A$
50 GOTO 10
```

Before trying this test, note a new feature in line 20. The INPUT statement in line 20 shows two different numerical variables separated by a comma. This is a matter of combining two INPUT *numerical variable* statements into one. When the computer first encounters line 20, it will print a question mark and wait for a numerical value for V from the keyboard. When the operator enters that value and strikes the ENTER key, the system prints another question mark (or two of them if you are using a TRS–80). Now the system is waiting for a numerical value for variable WB.

In this particular example, the system expects two numerical values at line 20; and it won't go on to line 30 until the two values are entered from the keyboard, each followed by an ENTER.

Line 20, in effect, does something equal to this:

```
20 INPUT V
21 INPUT WB
```

Using INPUT V, WB, however, saves one programming line.

Principle. Any number of variables can be entered from a single INPUT line by listing the variables and separating them with commas. Such a multiple INPUT line can include combinations of numerical and string variables.

The values of the variables, however, must be entered in the same sequence as they appear on the INPUT line.

So test Equation (1a) by running the program just described, using some values for V and WB that will yield a known solution. For instance, entering V=2000 and WB=1 should work out to an answer, 1.

Upon loading this program and entering the RUN command, the screen is cleared by line 10 and a question mark and cursor appear in the upper left-hand corner. Respond to this first INPUT request by entering 2000 (for variable V).

```
?2000
??_
```

The system has accepted your numerical value for V and is now waiting for a value for WB. Respond by entering the numeral 1:

```
?2000
??1
1
?_
```

Upon entering 1 in response to the second input request, the system printed the solution specified by line 30. Line 40 calls for entering a string variable; but since its real function is to let the operator restart the program, the null string is appropriate. In other words, the equation can be tested again by striking the ENTER key.

Try the equation with a couple of other critical values for V and WB—zeros, for instance. Work with this little test program until you are sure the equation is being solved properly.

It is then necessary to check out Equation (2a). So hit the BREAK key to get out of the ongoing test program and then enter NEW to wipe it out of the program memory. You don't want that first test program interfering with the next one:

```
10 CLS
20 INPUT X, Y, D
30 PRINT X*Y*D/12
40 INPUT A$
50 GOTO 10
```

This program checks Equation (2a) as expressed in BASIC in line 30. Note the use of a three-variable INPUT statement in line 20. Upon entering RUN, the system will clear the screen and then expect the three variables to be assigned values in the sequence X, Y, and D. After picking up the three values from the keyboard, the system goes on to line 30, where it calculates the volume and prints it on the screen.

Test the operation of the equation with a few carefully selected values for X, Y, and D.

After you are convinced that Equation (2a) is being solved properly, it is time to begin putting things together. Do a BREAK to get out of the last looping program, and then enter NEW to clean up the memory.

As the analyst/programmer, you have been able to use multiple-variable INPUT lines; but the actual user should not have to keep in mind which variable to enter at a particular time. And that means your program should include some text that specifies which variable should be evaluated from the keyboard. Such a scheme might take this form:

EXAMPLE 3-5a

```
10 CLS
20 PRINT "WHAT IS THE X DIMENSION IN FEET"
30 INPUT X
40 PRINT "WHAT IS THE Y DIMENSION IN FEET"
50 INPUT Y
60 PRINT "WHAT IS THE AVERAGE MATERIAL DEPTH IN INCHES"
70 INPUT D
80 V=X*Y*D/12
90 PRINT "WHAT IS THE BULK WEIGHT IN POUNDS PER CUBIC FOOT"
100 INPUT WB
110 CLS
120 PRINT "THE NET WEIGHT REQUIRED IS "V*WB/2000 "TONS"
130 PRINT
140 PRINT "STRIKE THE 'ENTER' KEY TO RESTART"
150 INPUT A$
160 GOTO 10
```

Test the overall program by entering RUN and responding to the plain-text questions with the appropriate numerical values. This is what the display looks like if you enter 100 for X, 100 for Y, 8 for D, and 85 for WB.

```
WHAT IS THE X DIMENSION IN FEET
? 100
WHAT IS THE Y DIMENSION IN FEET
? 100
WHAT IS THE AVERAGE MATERIAL DEPTH IN INCHES
? 8
WHAT IS THE BULK WEIGHT IN POUNDS PER CUBIC FOOT
? 85_
```

That takes the program through line 100. Upon striking the ENTER key now, line 110 clears the screen and the display takes this general form:

```
THE NET WEIGHT REQUIRED IS 283.333 TONS

STRIKE THE 'ENTER' KEY TO RESTART
?_
```

The program is stopped at line 150, waiting for a null string from the keyboard. (Note the line space between the two lines of text. It is created by the PRINT *nothing* statement in line 130.)

When the operator strikes the ENTER key in response to the final line of text, the program picks up at line 160, and its GOTO *line number* statement carries operations all the way back to line 10.

The only way to get out of the program is by either striking the BREAK key or turning off power to the computer.

For all intents and purposes, the programming job is done. The program performs its intended task. But consider this matter of programming "style."

The example shown here is just one of many different ways to accomplish the same task. A certain programming style is reflected at a couple of points.

For instance, the program includes two CLS statements. Neither of them is essential to the execution of the program, but the programmer deemed them important for avoiding needless confusion on the screen. The PRINT *nothing* statement in line 130 falls into that same general category.

What is even more telling, in terms of programming style, is the way the equations are handled. The mathematical function in line 80, for example, could be eliminated and its terms included in the function in line 120. Such a modification would eliminate one program line and one numerical variable (V). If you choose to make this modification, get the system back into the command mode and type the following:

```
80
120  PRINT "THE NET WEIGHT REQUIRED IS"X*Y*D/12*WB/2000"TONS"
```

Recall that typing a line number and striking the ENTER key effectively deletes that line from the program. So the first step deletes line 80. The next step is to rewrite line 120 so that it includes the composite equation [Equation (3)].

After making these two modifications, the program seems to run exactly as it did before. Only the programmer knows that anything has changed.

Now suppose that the programmer demonstrates the scheme to the ultimate user—the owner of the building materials company. The individual is impressed with the basic idea but objects to the fact that the original parameters (dimensions, cubic-foot weights, and so on) are erased from the screen before the final result is displayed. In this case, the CLS statement in line 110 is causing the programmer some trouble with the customer.

So what can be done to please the customer? Of course, the programmer could delete line 110, but that leaves a mess. A satisfactory alternative would be to reprint the original parameters, in a neat fashion, above the final result. So go to the command mode and insert these lines:

```
112 PRINT "WITH X ="X"FEET"
114 PRINT "WITH Y ="Y"FEET"
116 PRINT "WITH THE AVERAGE DEPTH ="D"INCHES"
118 PRINT "WITH THE BULK WEIGHT ="WB"POUNDS PER CUBIC FOOT"
119 PRINT
```

Running the revised version, using the same input parameters as before, the screen ends up looking something like this:

```
WITH X = 100 FEET
WITH Y = 100 FEET
WITH THE AVERAGE DEPTH = 8 INCHES
WITH THE BULK WEIGHT @ 85 POUNDS PER CUBIC FOOT

THE NET WEIGHT REQUIRED IS 283.333 TONS
```

STRIKE THE 'ENTER' KEY TO RESTART
?_

Now that ought to satisfy the customer. But maybe you, as a program consultant, feel the customer might be a little disturbed about having to tell you to do something differently. So why not add some icing to the cake? At no extra charge, you can have the computer work out some handy figures that might enhance the customer's view of your genius. Insert these lines:

```
115 PRINT "THE AREA IS" X*Y "SQUARE FEET"
117 PRINT "THE MATERIAL VOLUME IS" X*Y*D/12"CUBIC FEET"
```

Let us see what the final display looks like now. Then take a look at the entire program.

```
WITH X = 100 FEET
WITH Y = 100 FEET
THE AREA IS 10000 SQUARE FEET
WITH THE AVERAGE DEPTH = 8 INCHES
THE MATERIAL VOLUME IS 666.67 CUBIC FEET
WITH THE BULK WEIGHT = 85 POUNDS PER CUBIC FOOT

THE NET WEIGHT REQUIRED IS 283.333 TONS

STRIKE THE 'ENTER' KEY TO RESTART
?_
```

Returning to the command mode and entering LIST, the revised program looks like this:

EXAMPLE 3–5b

```
10 CLS
20.PRINT "WHAT IS THE X DIMENSION IN FEET"
30 INPUT X
40 PRINT "WHAT IS THE Y DIMENSION IN FEET"
50 INPUT Y
60 PRINT "WHAT IS THE AVERAGE MATERIAL DEPTH IN INCHES"
70 INPUT D
90 PRINT "WHAT IS THE BULK WEIGHT IN POUNDS PER CUBIC FOOT"
100 INPUT WB
110 CLS
112 PRINT "WITH X ="X"FEET"
114 PRINT "WITH Y ="Y"FEET"
```

```
115 PRINT "THE AREA IS" X*Y "SQUARE FEET"
116 PRINT "WITH THE AVERAGE DEPTH ="D"INCHES"
117 PRINT "THE MATERIAL VOLUME IS" X*Y*D/12"CUBIC FEET"
118 PRINT "WITH THE BULK WEIGHT ="WB"POUNDS PER CUBIC FOOT"
119 PRINT
120 PRINT "THE NET WEIGHT REQUIRED IS"X*Y*D/12*WB/2000"TONS"
130 PRINT
140 PRINT "STRIKE THE 'ENTER' KEY TO RESTART"
150 INPUT A$
160 GOTO 10
```

3-4 More about Breaking into Programs

Section 3–2 introduced the notion of striking the BREAK key to get out of a program loop and force the system into its command mode of operation. This section deals with BREAK in a bit more detail and describes two closely related operations, CONT and STOP.

BREAK is used under three different kinds of conditions. First, it can be a legitimate, routine way to get the operator out of one kind of GOTO looping program, into the command mode, and then into another program residing elsewhere in the program memory. Second, BREAK can serve as a "panic button" in cases where a program "blows up" and starts running out of control. Third, it serves as a debugging tool for working the wrinkles out of programs under development.

Consider the following example that shows how BREAK can be used for exiting one program and getting to another one:

EXAMPLE 3-6

```
10 CLS
20 PRINT "THIS IS A MATH PROGRAM"
30 PRINT "IF YOU WANT TO ADD, FIRST STRIKE THE 'BREAK' KEY"
40 PRINT "AND THEN TYPE 'RUN 100.'"
50 PRINT "IF YOU WANT TO MULTIPLY, FIRST STRIKE THE 'BREAK' KEY"
60 PRINT "AND THEN TYPE 'RUN 200.'"
70 PRINT
80 INPUT A$
90 PRINT "YOU GOOFED UP. TRY AGAIN"
91 PRINT
92 PRINT
95 GOTO 20
100 CLS
```

```
110 PRINT "THIS IS AN ADDITION PROGRAM"
120 PRINT "WHAT IS THE FIRST NUMBER"
130 INPUT A
140 PRINT "GOOD. WHAT IS THE SECOND NUMBER"
150 INPUT B
160 CLS
170 PRINT A"+"B"="A+B
180 PRINT
190 PRINT "IF YOU WANT TO DO ANOTHER ADDITION PROBLEM,"
191 PRINT "STRIKE THE 'ENTER' KEY. OTHERWISE STRIKE THE"
192 PRINT "'BREAK' KEY AND ENTER 'RUN.'"
195 INPUT A$
196 GOTO 100
197 END
200 CLS
210 PRINT "THIS IS A MULTIPLICATION PROGRAM"
220 PRINT "WHAT IS THE FIRST NUMBER"
230 INPUT A
240 PRINT "GOOD. WHAT IS THE SECOND NUMBER"
250 INPUT B
260 CLS
270 PRINT A"x"B"="A*B
280 PRINT
290 PRINT "IF YOU WANT TO DO ANOTHER ADDITION PROBLEM,"
291 PRINT "STRIKE THE 'ENTER' KEY. OTHERWISE STRIKE THE"
292 PRINT "'BREAK' KEY AND ENTER 'RUN.'"
295 INPUT A$
296 GOTO 200
297 END
```

This is actually three different programs. Lines 10 through 95 make up the program's *header*—the introductory comments and instructions. In this case the header tells the user that there is an option of running either an addition or a multiplication program, and it says exactly how to get to them. The header looks like this whenever the operator does a RUN command from the system's command mode:

```
THIS IS A MATH PROGRAM
IF YOU WANT TO ADD, FIRST STRIKE THE 'BREAK' KEY
AND THEN TYPE 'RUN 100.'
IF YOU WANT TO MULTIPLY, FIRST STRIKE THE 'BREAK' KEY
AND THEN TYPE 'RUN 200.'
?_
```

This text is the result of running program lines 10 through 80. If the user fails to handle the situation properly (a BREAK, followed by entering RUN

1ØØ or RUN 2ØØ), the INPUT A$ statement in line 80 picks up any other sort of operation that is followed by striking the ENTER key. The result is

YOU GOOFED UP. TRY AGAIN

followed by a repeat of the header statements.

The only way to get out of the header program in lines 10 through 95 is by striking the BREAK key.

Lines 100 through 197 make up the addition portion of the program. Upon entering RUN 1ØØ, the display looks like this:

THIS IS AN ADDITION PROGRAM
WHAT IS THE FIRST NUMBER
?4Ø
GOOD. WHAT IS THE SECOND NUMBER
?2Ø_

To this point, program execution is down to line 150. After entering that second number, line 160 clears the screen. Then the user sees

4Ø + 2Ø = 6Ø

IF YOU WANT TO DO ANOTHER ADDITION PROBLEM,
STRIKE THE 'ENTER' KEY. OTHERWISE STRIKE THE
'BREAK' KEY AND ENTER 'RUN.'

If the user elects to do another addition problem, striking the ENTER key carries program operation down to line 196, which, in turn, causes the system to go to line 100. The screen is thus cleared and the addition routine is started all over again. Doing a BREAK, however, returns the system to the command mode, and if the user then types RUN and strikes the ENTER key, program execution picks up at line 10, and the header is printed on the screen once again. (Remember that entering a RUN without a line-number suffix automatically runs the program from the lowest-numbered line.)

Doing a BREAK, followed by entering RUN 2ØØ, causes the system to run the multiplication routine in lines 200 through 297. The program steps are virtually identical to those used in the addition routine—only line 270 is different.

Although this particular program is rich in examples of programming procedures and tricks, the main point is that the BREAK key can allow the user to move from one kind of program to another. In this case, BREAK is used as a normal keyboard operation.

BREAK can also be used as a panic button to break up a program that is getting out of hand—running out of control for one reason or another. Consider the following example of a "runaway" program:

1Ø A=Ø
2Ø PRINT A

30 A=A+1

40 GOTO 20

Line 10 in this little, innocent-looking program merely initializes the numerical value of A at zero. In line 20, the value of A is printed on the screen.

Now step 30 is a little different from anything done so far in this book. In effect, line 30 establishes a new numerical value for A by adding one to the "old" value. If A happens to be zero upon encountering line 30, it will be 0 plus 1 (or 1) upon leaving it. Line 30, in other words, causes the current value of variable A to increase by one.

Line 40 then carries the program back to line 20, where the new value of A is printed on the screen. Then A is incremented, printed, incremented, printed, ... The operator sees an endless stream of numbers running up the screen. Without any outside interference, the program will continue counting indefinitely.

The cycle can be broken by striking the BREAK key, thereby pulling the system out of the program and setting up the command mode of operation.

Although it might be fun and instructive to run such wild looping programs, they sometimes occur inadvertently when setting up a new program. In either case, the operator regains control of the matter by hitting the BREAK.

Finally, there is the matter of using BREAK as a debugging tool. Programs of any significant size are bound to have some flaws in them, either because the programmer's initial plans have a defect in them or because of some typing errors. *Debugging* is an accepted buzz word that applies to the process of working flaws out of a program.

When a program is run and a flaw (or bug) is found, the programmer can stop the operation with a BREAK and fix the trouble while the system is in the command mode.

Suppose that you are debugging a program and strike the BREAK key to halt operations. Maybe you decide that nothing has to be changed after all, and you would like the program to resume where it left off. It is possible to resume the program by entering CONT (CONTinue).

> *Principle.* After halting a program by striking the BREAK key, it is possible to resume from that point by typing and entering the command CONT.

During a BREAK, you can check the values of numerical and string variables by doing PRINT *numerical variable* or PRINT *string variable*. You can also set the values of variables from the keyboard by doing *numerical variable = numerical value* or *string variable = expression*. Any of these command-mode operations can be followed by CONT to resume execution of the program after doing a BREAK. You cannot, however, expect the program to continue if you have changed any of the program text. In the latter case, you must restart the program with a RUN command.

So it is possible to BREAK an ongoing program, do just about anything except alter the program itself, and then resume operations from the BREAK point by entering CONT.

Most programs are executed very rapidly, however; and it is thus difficult to halt a program at one particular point. In that case, the programmer has access to a program-statement version of BREAK. A STOP statement inserted into a program causes it to break at that point, automatically returning the system to the command mode.

> *Principle.* The STOP statement works as a programmable BREAK, halting execution of the program at the STOP line and returning the system to its command mode.

After responding to a STOP statement, the program can be restarted from that line by entering CONT; or, of course, it can be restarted from the beginning by entering a RUN command.

STOP statements are normally inserted into a program for debugging purposes; and once they have served that function, the programmer normally deletes them.

Suppose that you are working with the following program:

```
10 A=100
20 A=A-1
30 GOTO 20
```

This is a simple down-counting routine—one calling for counting backward from 100. The value of A is initialized by line 10, decremented by line 20, and immediately returned to line 20 again by the GOTO statement in line 30. The system "buzzes" between lines 20 and 30 for an indefinitely long period of time.

None of the values of A are ever printed on the screen, making it virtually impossible for the operator to know whether or not the program is actually working. One way to check the operation is by inserting a STOP statement as line 25:

```
10 A=100
20 A=A-1
25 STOP
30 GOTO 20
```

Upon entering RUN, the operator almost immediately gets this sort of response on the screen:

```
>RUN
BREAK IN 25
READY
>_
```

Now the program has been executed down to line 25. To see if the down-counting operation is actually taking place, the programmer can enter the command, PRINT A. If all is going well, the computer should respond by printing 99. Execution can then be resumed by entering CONT. Study the following sequence of operations:

```
>RUN
BREAK IN 25
READY
>PRINT A
 99
READY
>CONT
BREAK IN 25
READY
>PRINT A
 98
READY
>CONT
BREAK IN 25
READY
>A=1
READY
>CONT
BREAK IN 25
READY
>PRINT A
 0
READY
>_
```

In this particular case the operator allowed the program to cycle twice, noting that the value of A was automatically decremented to

99 and then 98. After doing the next CONT and getting the BREAK IN 25 signal, the programmer decided to set the value of A to 1— note the A=1 command from the keyboard. Doing a CONT let the program resume from that point, and it responded by decrementing the value of A to 0.

It thus appears that the program is working rather well, and after noting the system stopping at line 25 again, the operator can delete the STOP statement by typing 25 and striking the ENTER key.

Deleting the STOP statement amounts to a change in the program, however; and that means that it cannot be resumed by entering CONT. Whenever the program itself is altered in any way after BREAK or STOP, it can be restarted only by entering a RUN command.

EXERCISES

3-1 An INPUT statement tells the computer to expect information from the keyboard. Describe, in each of the following situations, the exact sort of information the computer is expecting:

(a) INPUT A

(b) INPUT D$

(c) INPUT A, CA

(d) INPUT A$, X$

(e) INPUT D$, Z$, AB, C

3-2 Describe how the computer will respond to the following PRINT statements:

(a) PRINT A

(b) PRINT D$

(c) PRINT

3-3 Suppose that a program includes the following sequence:

50 INPUT X$
60 PRINT X$

What will the computer print in response to line 60 if the operator replies to line 50 by entering:

(a) DAD

(b) "DAD"

(c) 200

(d) "200"

   (e) nothing—just striking the ENTER key

3-4 Describe how the computer will respond to the following GOTO loops:

   (a)
```
10 PRINT "FOOEY"
20 CLS
30 GOTO 10
```

   (b)
```
10 CLS
20 PRINT "FOOEY"
30 GOTO 10
```

   (c)
```
10 PRINT "FOOEY"
20 CLS
30 GOTO 20
```

   (d)
```
10 CLS
20 PRINT "FOOEY"
30 GOTO 20
```

   (e)
```
10 CLS
20 PRINT "FOOEY"
30 GOTO 30
```

3-5 Describe what the following program will do:

```
10 CLS
20 A=0
30 PRINT A
40 INPUT B$
50 A=A+1
60 CLS
70 GOTO 30
```

Can you devise a way to do the same thing, using fewer program lines?

3-6 Describe what the following program will do:

```
10 CLS
20 PRINT "ENTER YOUR FULL NAME"
30 INPUT N$
40 CLS
50 PRINT "ENTER TODAY'S DATE (M/D/Y)"
60 INPUT D$
70 CLS
80 PRINT "DEAR "N$":                "D$
90 PRINT
100 PRINT "AS OF THIS DAY, "D$", YOU ARE FIRED!!!"
110 PRINT
120 PRINT "HAVE A NICE DAY, "N$"."
130 PRINT "                SINCERELY,"
140 PRINT "                    YOUR COMPUTER"
150 GOTO 150
```

CHAPTER 4

Looping with Conditional Statements

Statements introduced in this chapter:

IF ... THEN   FOR ... TO   NEXT

If you think RUN *line number* and GOTO *line number* are nifty statements for jumping around in programs, wait until you have a chance to try IF ... THEN, FOR ... TO, and NEXT statements.

4-1 Loops: Unconditional versus Conditional

A *loop operation* is one that causes program execution to cycle around and around through a particular set of program statements. The GOTO *line number* statement introduced in Chapter 3 is sometimes used for setting up program loops. Check the following example:

EXAMPLE 4-1

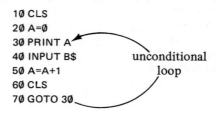

```
10 CLS
20 A=0
30 PRINT A
40 INPUT B$          unconditional
50 A=A+1                  loop
60 CLS
70 GOTO 30
```

70

When the user enters the RUN command, the computer first executes the program lines in numerical order. Line 10 clears the screen, 20 sets the initial value of A, and line 30 prints the value on the screen. All operations come to a halt at the INPUT statement in line 40, waiting for the user to enter a string statement—presumably a null string because the B$ value is never used.

After that, the computer resumes running the program, incrementing the value of A at line 50, clearing the screen, and then returning to line 30 in response to the GOTO statement in line 70.

This is an example of a loop operation, because the same sequence of operations take place in a cyclic fashion: always running lines 30 through 70 in sequence, and then returning to line 30.

Definition. A *loop* is a set of program statements that are executed in an orderly and cyclic fashion.

Furthermore, this is an example of an *unconditional loop.* In other words, there are no conditions placed upon the return from line 70 to line 30. The looping operation can take place an indefinite number of times. As long as the user is willing to continue striking the ENTER key in response to the question mark generated by the INPUT statement in line 40, the screen continues showing incrementing values of A.

Definition. An *unconditional loop* is one that has no conditions or limitations placed upon its execution.

However, it is possible, and often more desirable, to work with *conditional loops*—program loops that are executed only as long as certain conditions are met. Compare Example 4–1 with this one:

EXAMPLE 4-2

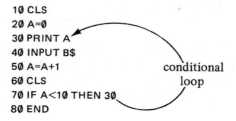

```
10 CLS
20 A=0
30 PRINT A
40 INPUT B$
50 A=A+1            conditional
60 CLS              loop
70 IF A<10 THEN 30
80 END
```

This program is identical to Example 4-1 through line 60. Line 70, however, is a *conditional statement* that places a limit on how many times the loop can be executed. As long as A is less than 10, line 70 returns operations back to line 30, creating the same effect on the screen as Example 4-1.

But when line 70 sees a value of A that is greater than 10, its condition is no longer satisfied and program execution proceeds to the next line. The program, in other words, counts 0 through 9 and then ends. The loop is broken as soon as line 70 sees A greater than 10.

Definition. A *conditional loop* is one that has a well-defined limit or condition placed upon its execution.

4-2 The IF . . . THEN Conditional Statement

Line 70 in Example 4–2 uses a powerful conditional statement—a statement that is either satisfied (true) or not satisfied (untrue), depending upon conditions prevailing at the time. BASIC includes a number of different conditional statements, but most are built around the IF . . . THEN idea.

Expressing the IF . . . THEN conditional statement in a formal way:

IF *expression*–relation–*expression* THEN statement.

Basically, this is saying, "If some relation between two expressions is satisfied, then do whatever the statement calls for doing." IF, for instance, numerical variable A is greater than numerical value 10, THEN go to line 30. If the condition is not satisfied, program execution goes to the next line.

Principle. If the conditions of an IF . . . THEN statement are satisfied, the computer responds to the THEN portion of the statement. If the conditions are not satisfied, the computer goes to the program line that follows.

Table 4–1 lists the *relational operators* that can be used as the "relation" part of IF . . . THEN conditional statements. Table 4–2 shows a fairly complete list of possible *"expression"* terms in that same kind of conditional statement.

Table 4-1 Relational Operators for IF ... THEN Statements

Symbol(s)	Literal Meaning
=	... is equal to ...
>	... is greater than ...
<	... is less than ...
>=	... is greater than or equal to ...
<=	... is less than or equal to ...
<>	... is not equal to ...

Table 4-2 Some Valid Expressions for IF ... THEN Statements

IF *numerical variable*–relation–*numerical value* THEN ...

    Examples: IF A>1Ø THEN ...
                   IF X2 = 470 THEN ...

IF *numerical variable*–relation–*numerical variable* THEN ...

    Examples: IF A=B THEN ...
                   IF XY>=C THEN ...

IF *math*–relation–*math* THEN ...

    Examples: IF X+1 = Y*2 THEN ...
                   IF 2*(X+Y) = Z↑2 THEN ...

Combinations of the Above

IF *numerical variable*–relation–*math* THEN ...
IF *math*–relation–*numerical value* THEN ...
IF *math*–relation–*numerical variable* THEN ...

The consequence of satisfying an IF ... THEN condition can be just about any sort of program statement. The most commonly used consequence, however, is a GOTO *line number* statement. In this instance, the GOTO portion is assumed and the consequence takes the form of a line number. For instance:

IF A>1Ø THEN 3Ø   implies   IF A>1Ø THEN GOTO 3Ø.

The GOTO can be included, but it isn't necessary.

Other consequential statements can be used to terminate an IF ... THEN conditional; but more often than not, they give rise to some programming troubles. Consider the following statement:

IF X=2 THEN PRINT "TWO"

73

Whenever X is equal to 2, the computer will print TWO on the screen. It works, but you will see later in this chapter that such a statement must be used with care. The safe thing, for the time being, is to limit the consequences of satisfying an IF . . . THEN conditional to a line-number statement—they never cause logical problems.

Before running the risk of getting lost in a lot of general theory, take a look at some programs that use IF . . . THEN statements.

Example 4–3a

```
10 CLS
20 A=0
30 PRINT A↑2
40 A=A+1
50 IF A<=10 THEN 30
60 PRINT "DONE"
70 END
```

This program lists the squares of integers between 0 and 10, and then prints DONE before returning to the command mode. The value of A is initialized at zero by line 20. Line 30 calculates and prints the square of A, and line 40 increments the value of A.

The conditional statement in line 50 is responsible for looping the squaring, printing, and incrementing cycle as long as A is less than or equal to 10. The moment this condition is no longer satisfied (specifically, when A is incremented to 11), the system leaves the loop and resumes program execution at line 60.

This happens to be an example of a program using an IF . . . THEN statement of the form:

IF *numerical variable*-relation-*numerical value* THEN *line number.*

The program in Example 4–3a is limited to printing out the squares of numbers from 0 to 10. It is possible to extend the range of computations and, at the same time, demonstrate the application of a slightly different form of the IF . . . THEN statement.

EXAMPLE 4–3b

```
10 CLS
20 PRINT "TERMINAL NUMBER"
30 INPUT B
40 A=0
50 PRINT A↑2
60 A=A+1
```

```
70 IF A<=B THEN 50
80 PRINT "DONE"
90 END
```

This program now prints the values of squared integers between 0 and any specified value, B. The user specifies the value of variable B at the INPUT statement in line 30. And after initializing variable A at zero, the program begins looping through a calculate-print-increment sequence. The looping continues until line 70 is no longer satisfied—A is incremented beyond the value of B.

Line 70 is an example of an IF . . . THEN statement of the form

IF *numerical variable*-relation-*numerical variable* THEN *line number.*

There is a practical problem inherent in the program in Example 4-3b: If the user-specified value of B is larger than 15, there is not enough line space on the screen for displaying all the values of A squared. After the fifteenth value is printed, the column of figures begins scrolling upward and off the top of the screen.

One nice way to get around the problem is by restructuring the program so that it prints no more than 10 values at a time.

EXAMPLE 4-3c

```
10 CLS
20 PRINT "INITIAL VALUE"
30 INPUT B
40 A=B
50 PRINT A↑2
60 A=A+1
70 IF A<=B+10 THEN 50
80 PRINT "DONE"
90 END
```

In this instance, the user specifies the initial value at the INPUT statement in line 30. Variable A is then set to that value by the equality statement in line 40; and after that, it is squared, printed, and incremented.

The conditional statement in line 70, in essence, asks this question: Is the value of A presently less than 10 units greater than at the start? If the current value of A is indeed less than its initial value plus 10, the looping action continues. The program concludes only after A exceeds B+10.

Here we have an application of an IF . . . THEN statement of the form

IF *numerical value*-relation-*math* THEN *line number.*

It's a neat way to pick up the squares of integers, although the formatting (form of the presentation on the screen) leaves something to be desired. You will have a chance to improve the format in a later lesson.

4-3 Sequences of IF . . . THEN Statements

The programming examples cited in Section 4-2 contained only a single IF . . . THEN conditional statement. But look at this:

EXAMPLE 4-4

```
10 CLS
20 A=0
30 PRINT "ZERO"
40 INPUT C$
50 CLS
60 A=A+1
70 IF A=1 PRINT "ONE"
80 IF A=2 PRINT "TWO"
90 IF A=3 PRINT "THREE"
100 IF A=4 PRINT "FOUR"
110 IF A=5 PRINT "FIVE"
120 IF A<=5 THEN 40
130 GOTO 10
140 END
```

This is another of those counting programs that increment the value of a variable whenever the user strikes the ENTER key. In this case, however, the numerical values are translated into their corresponding literal expressions. Instead of printing 1, 2, 3, . . . , it prints the words ONE, TWO, THREE, ...

The translation takes place in a series of successive IF . . . THEN conditionals. To see how the conditional sequence works, suppose that the value of variable A has already been incremented to 5. Now that would take place in line 60; and immediately after that, the program calls for, "If the value of A is 1, print the word 'one'." But that condition (line 70) is not satisfied, because we have said A is equal to 5 at the moment; so control goes to the next line, "If the value of A is 2, print the word 'two'."

But that condition isn't satisfied either, so the system continues running down through the list of conditionals until one of two things happens: it either comes across a condition that it can meet or it runs out of conditional statements.

Since we have said that A is equal to 5 at the moment, the conditional in line 110 is satisfied. The system responds by carrying out the consequential statement PRINT "FIVE".

> *Note.* When using consequential statements other than *line number* in an IF . . . THEN conditional, the THEN expression is usually not included. THEN can be included, but it is not necessary.

So now the conditional statement in line 110 has been satisfied, and the computer has responded by printing FIVE on the screen. What happens after that?

Since the conditional does not specify a line number, the computer assumes that it is supposed to go to the next program line—line 120 in this case.

Now line 120 is a different sort of IF . . . THEN conditional statement, but it should be no stranger. It is one of the basic conditionals already described in Section 4-2.

Variable A is still equal to 5 by the time the system gets down to line 120. As a result, the condition A<=5 is satisfied, so control is picked up at line 40—the operation loops at least one more time.

Line 40 calls for a null string input from the keyboard. And when the user strikes the ENTER key to enter that particular string value, the screen is cleared by line 50, A is incremented to 6, and the series of conditional statements test that value again.

This time, however, none of the conditional statements, including the one in line 120, is satisfied; so by *default,* the computer leaves the conditional loop and goes to line 130.

Now line 130 is an unconditional GOTO statement that forces the system up to line 10—the very beginning of the program. Shortly after that, the word ZERO appears on the screen, and the whole scheme starts over.

So this program counts around between ZERO and FIVE, and then back to ZERO, and so on. The main point of interest, however, is the application of a series of IF . . . THEN statements. The system runs through the list until it finds a condition that can be satisfied or runs out of conditional statements. In the former case, the program loops back to line 40. In the latter case, the loop is broken and line 130 is executed by default.

Incidentally, this program is also an example of one having a nested loop—a loop within a larger loop. The "inside" loop is being executed as long as one of the conditionals is satisfied. In that instance, operation loops around between lines 40 and 120. But when the system finds that none of the conditionals is satisfied, the large loop comes into play. That one runs between lines 130 and 10.

There's more to be said about nested loops in Section 4-4.

For the moment, consider another program having a short sequence of IF . . . THEN conditional statements.

EXAMPLE 4-5

```
10 CLS
20 PRINT "ENTER A NUMBER BETWEEN 1 AND 10"
30 INPUT A
40 IF A<1 THEN 80
50 IF A>10 THEN 110
60 PRINT "GOOD SHOT. YOU SEEM TO KNOW WHAT YOU'RE DOING."
70 END
80 PRINT "THAT NUMBER IS TOO SMALL."
90 PRINT "TRY AGAIN."
100 GOTO 20
110 PRINT "THAT NUMBER IS TOO LARGE."
120 GOTO 90
130 END
```

Programs of this kind are often used in programmed, computer-aided instruction. The user is asked to enter any number between 1 and 10. If that is done properly, neither of the conditional statements in lines 40 and 50 is satisfied; so, by default, control goes to line 60, where the user's good work is rewarded with a complimentary statement, GOOD SHOT. YOU SEEM TO KNOW WHAT YOU'RE DOING. Line 70 then returns the system to the command mode.

If, on the other hand, the user enters a number less than 1, the condition in line 40 is satisfied, and control is carried down to line 80. The comment is, THAT NUMBER IS TOO SMALL. And after printing that statement, line 90 is responsible for the comment, TRY AGAIN. The unconditional GOTO statement in line 100 then takes the whole operation back to line 20, where, in effect, the user is prompted to try all over again.

Responding with a number larger than 10 does not satisfy the condition in line 40, so the computer moves on to the next line; and in this case, the conditional is satisfied.

Entering a number larger than 10 satisfies the IF . . . THEN condition in line 50, and control is sent to line 110. The computer prints THAT NUMBER IS TOO LARGE. After that, the system does a GOTO 90 (line 120). The user sees the comment TRY AGAIN, followed by the opening statement printed by line 20.

The only way to get out of the loops in this program is by doing the job right: entering a number between 1 and 10. Of course, striking the BREAK key will interrupt the loops, too; but the user doesn't have to know that!

A clever application of a series of conditional IF . . . THEN statements brings up the possibility of creating program passwords. The program in Example 4-6 is set up to work something like a combination lock.

EXAMPLE 4-6

```
10 CLS
20 INPUT A,B,C
30 IF A<>3 THEN 100
40 IF B<>3 THEN 100
50 IF C<>8 THEN 100
60 PRINT "YOU MADE IT!!"
70 END
100 PRINT "YOU BLEW IT, KLUTZ"
110 GOTO 100
120 END
```

The "secret combination" in this example is the sequence 3, 3, 8. Line 20 is a multiple INPUT statement that expects numerical values for variables A, B, and C. It assigns the values from the keyboard in that order—A, B, C.

Lines 30 through 50 are "not equal" conditionals. If the value of variable A has not been set to 3, the condition is satisfied and control goes down to line 100. If variable A *is* 3, on the other hand, the condition in line 20 *is not* satisfied and control goes to line 40. The only way to pass from one of the conditional statements to the next is if they are not satisfied; and in this particular instance, the user is presumably hoping to satisfy none of them and get down to the default operation, PRINT "YOU MADE IT", in line 60.

If the user does not select the 3-3-8 combination, at least one of the conditional statements will be satisfied; and the first one to be satisfied sends the system down to line 100. That's an embarrassing situation because the unconditional GOTO 100 causes YOU BLEW IT, KLUTZ to appear as an endless list, streaming up the screen until the user manages to strike the BREAK key.

4-4 Some Nested Loops and Timing Programs

There are all kinds of ways to illustrate nested loops—programs having loops within loops; but one of the more enjoyable ways to handle the matter is with timing programs. The examples in this section all use a timing loop, or time-delay routine.

How about this?

EXAMPLE 4-7

```
10 CLS
20 A=0
30 A=A+1
40 IF A<100 THEN 30
50 PRINT "DONE"
60 END
```

This program actually contains a loop that forces the value of the variable A to increment, or count, from zero to 100. At the conclusion of that operation, the computer is told to print DONE on the screen.

Here is a chance to appreciate the fact that a computer carries out the program steps, one at a time; and that each step occupies some amount of time. Depending upon the kind of computer system you are using, this program might take about 1 second to show the DONE expression. It takes about 1 second to count from 0 to 100.

What makes the system stop looping and counting? Why, the conditional statement in line 40. As long as the condition, A less than 100, is satisfied, control continues looping around between lines 30 and 40. Only after the count reaches 100 does the system get out of the loop.

But Example 4-7 does not have a loop within a loop. So try putting the timing loop within a larger control loop.

EXAMPLE 4-8

```
10 CLS
20 A=0
30 A=A+1
40 IF A<100 THEN 30
50 IF B=1 THEN 90
60 B=1
70 GOTO 10
90 PRINT "* * * *"
100 B=0
110 GOTO 20
120 END
```

Run this program and you will find a set of four asterisks flashing on and off in the upper left-hand corner of the screen. In the context of what has been discussed to this point, this example might seem rather hard to understand—there are too many conditionals for most novice programmers to follow.

Give it a try, anyway. After that, you will come across an important tool for analyzing tricky, loopy programs such as this one.

For one thing, you ought to be able to pick out the timing loop between lines 30 and 40. It is basically the same loop as the one in Example 4-7. But then line 50 is a conditional that carries operations down to line 90 whenever it is satisfied—satisfied by having variable B somehow set to 1.

And then after getting down to line 90, the computer is told to print four asterisks on the screen, set B=1, and then go back to line 20, where the timing loop starts all over again.

If the conditional in line 50 is not satisfied, however, variable B is set to 1 (so that's how it's done!), and line 70 sends the computer to line 10, where the screen is cleared and the next timing loop begins.

Now take a look at Fig. 4-1. It should help clarify the whole matter. This type of diagram is technically called a *flowchart*. A flow-

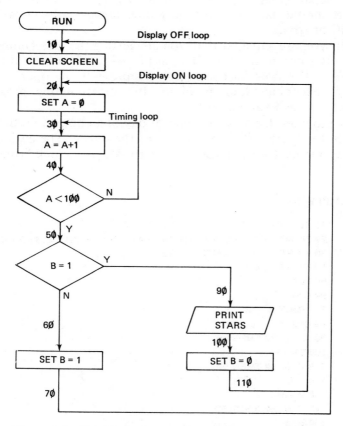

Figure 4-1 Flowchart for the flashing-asterisk program in Example 4-8.

chart is a convenient way to present the operation of a computer program. By convention, the "rounded" rectangle represents the program's starting (or ending) point, the trapezoids represent INPUT or PRINT functions, and the rectangles represent any sort of relevant operation within the computer itself.

For our immediate purposes, however, the diamond-shaped figures are most important. They represent conditional statements. If the condition specified within the diamond is satisfied, the program flow leaves via the Y (yes) arrow. If, on the other hand, the condition is not satisfied, the flow is from the N (no) arrow.

One of the nice things about flowcharts is that the loops show up rather clearly.

Compare the flow of operations in the flowchart and its associated program (Fig. 4-1 and Example 4-8). Every location on the flowchart should have one, and only one, corresponding position on its BASIC program.

When you are satisfied that you are getting the idea behind reading and interpreting the flowchart in Fig. 4-1, take a look at the one in Fig. 4-2. The flowchart in Fig. 4-2 represents the operation of a simple timekeeping clock program. Its corresponding program is presented here as Example 4-9.

This program displays the time of day in an hour:minute:second format in the upper left-hand corner of the screen. The current time is initially set by the operator; but after that, the "clock" runs all on its own.

EXAMPLE 4-9

```
10 CLS
20 PRINT "ENTER CURRENT TIME AS HOUR, MINUTE, SECOND"
30 PRINT "FOR EXAMPLE - - 10, 15, 48."
40 INPUT H,M,S
50 CLS
60 C=0
70 PRINT H":"M":"S
80 C=C+1
90 IF C<100 THEN 80
100 S=S+1
110 IF S<60 THEN 50
120 S=0
130 M=M+1
140 IF M<60 THEN 50
150 M=0
160 H=H+1
170 IF H<=12 THEN 50
180 H=1
```

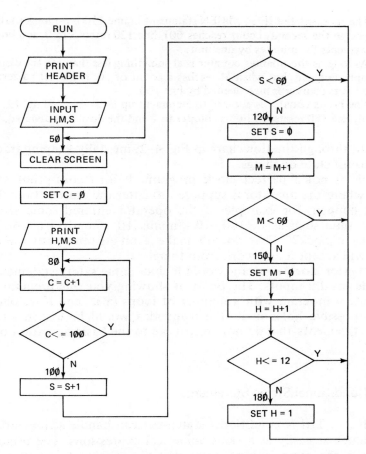

Figure 4-2 Flowchart for the real time clock program in Example 4-9.

190 GOTO 50
200 END

The looping operations can be sorted out and studied much easier from the flowchart than from the program itself. There is, for instance, a little conditional loop between statements 80 and 90. The purpose of this loop is to slow down the computer's natural counting rate; and until variable C is incremented from 0 to 101, the "seconds" display is not changed.

Incidentally, if your clock seems to be running a bit fast, you can slow it down by increasing the value of the *numerical value* in the IF . . . THEN statement in line 90. If the clock seems slow, try decreasing the value of that *numerical value* in line 90.

Seconds counting takes place at line 100; and as long as S is less than 60, the conditional statement in line 110 loops the operation directly back to line 50, where the display is updated.

The moment the IF . . . THEN statement in line 110 is no longer satisfied (because the seconds count reaches 60), line 120 resets S to 0, and line 130 increments the minutes by one unit.

As long as the minutes counter is at something less than 60, the display is simply updated; but when M reaches a count of 60, it is reset to zero and the hours counter is incremented by line 160.

The hours counter is allowed to increment up to, and including, 12. After that, line 180 resets the hours counter to 1 and the display is updated.

Run through the flowchart in Fig. 4–2, mentally keeping track of the current state of things.

This is not a perfect clock program. It isn't goof-proof at the point where the operator is supposed to enter the current time. What would happen, for example, if the operator entered some strange, invalid time such as 66,1∅∅,–1∅–"minus 10 seconds after 66 one-hundred o'clock?" That doesn't make a bit of sense, but the computer will accept it and work from there.

A better clock program would include some safety statements to exclude invalid inputs. The point of showing you this program is to illustrate a program with a number of loops in it; and if we plugged up all possible holes in it, the main idea would be lost in a lot of other statements that do not contribute to the basic operation of the thing.

4-5 Conditional String Statements

The IF . . . THEN conditional statement can handle string variables and values as easily as it does numerical expressions. The principles are quite the same in both cases, but the relational operators have different meanings.

Table 4–3 lists the IF . . . THEN relational operators as they apply to string values and variables. Check your manual if you find you are having some trouble running these string conditionals—not all systems work exactly the same way.

String-oriented IF . . . THEN statements can be fun to use, and of course they can also prove to be very useful.

EXAMPLE 4-10

```
1∅ CLS
2∅ PRINT "ENTER YOUR FIRST NAME"
3∅ INPUT N$
4∅ IF N$ = "GEORGE" END
5∅ PRINT "NOPE. TRY AGAIN"
```

```
6Ø GOTO 2Ø
7Ø END
```

Upon entering RUN, line 10 clears the screen and line 20 prints a request for the user's first name. That string is input at line 30.

In essence, line 40 checks to see if the name is George. If the user typed GEORGE in response to the opening statements, the IF . . . THEN condition in line 40 is satisfied and the program is terminated by the END consequences. But if the user enters anything other than GEORGE, the conditional line line 40 is not satisfied, and program control picks up at line 50, printing NOPE. TRY AGAIN and looping back to line 20.

Table 4-3 Relational Operators for String IF . . . THEN Statement

Symbol(s)	Meaning
=	. . . is identical to . . .
>	. . . follows alphabetically . . .
<	. . . precedes alphabetically . . .
>=	. . . follows (alphabetically) or is identical to . . .
<=	. . . precedes (alphabetically) or is identical to . . .
<>	. . . is not identical to . . .

I'm sure you can think of some ways to use the "is identical to" relational operation and its negated form, "is not identical to." But it is sometimes a bit harder to come up with some practical (and simple) applications of the other operators—the ones conditioning according to alphabetical order. Anyway, here is a simple (if not practical) application.

EXAMPLE 4-11

```
1Ø CLS
2Ø PRINT "ENTER ANY WORD"
3Ø INPUT A$
4Ø PRINT "ENTER ANOTHER WORD"
5Ø INPUT B$
6Ø IF A$<B$ THEN 12Ø
7Ø IF A$>B$ THEN 14Ø
8Ø IF A$=B$ PRINT "SAME"
9Ø PRINT "ENTER TO DO AGAIN"
1ØØ INPUT C$
11Ø GOTO 1Ø
12Ø PRINT A$,B$
```

```
130 GOTO 90
140 PRINT B$,A$
150 GOTO 90
160 END
```

The program in Example 4–11 arranges two user-specified words in alphabetical order. If the words happen to be identical, however, the computer simply prints SAME. In any event, the "game" is restarted from line 10 when the user responds to the request, ENTER TO DO AGAIN.

The flowchart for Example 4–11 appears in Fig. 4–3.

4-6 Simplifying Counting Loops with FOR . . . TO . . . STEP and NEXT

Whenever people in this business of computers and computer programming find that they have to do the same series of steps over and over again, they tend to invent a tidy package for handling the operation as a single unit. The case in point is a set of two statements, FOR . . . TO . . . STEP and NEXT.

EXAMPLE 4-12

```
10 CLS
20 A=0
30 PRINT A
40 A=A+1
50 IF A<=10 THEN 30
60 END
```

EXAMPLE 4-13

```
10 CLS
20 FOR A=0 TO 10
30 PRINT A
40 NEXT
50 END
```

These two programs do precisely the same job: They clear the screen and print integers 0 through 10. Example 4–12 does the job using the conditional procedures already outlined a number of times in this chapter. Example 4–13, on the other hand, uses a FOR . . . TO statement in line 20 and a NEXT statement in line 40.

Given the choice, most BASIC programmers would opt for the program in Example 4–13—not because it uses significantly fewer program lines, but because it is so much easier to set up. For instance, there is no need for carefully thinking through the conditional operators—being concerned about

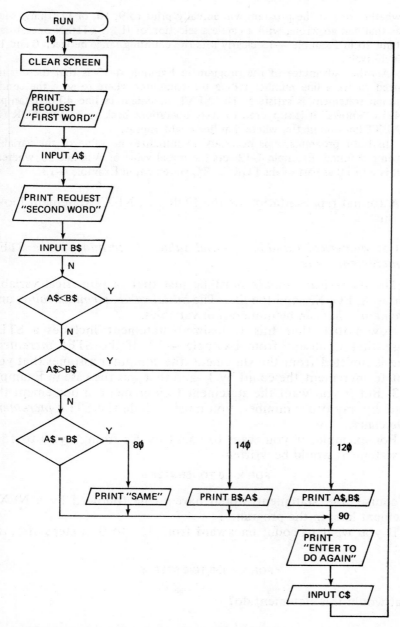

Figure 4-3 Flowchart for the word-organizing program in Example 4-11.

whether or not the program will actually print to 9, 10, or 11 (things such as that can go wrong with a careless selection of IF . . . THEN operators). Line 20 in Example 4-13 clearly sets the counting range between 0 and 10 inclusively.

Another advantage of the program in Example 4-13 is that there is no need to fix a line number telling the computer where to go if the conditional statement is satisfied. The NEXT statement in line 40 of Example 4-13 "knows" it is supposed to carry operations back to its own FOR . . . NEXT line—no matter where that line might appear.

In both programs, it is necessary to initialize the value of the variable being counted. Example 4-12 sets the initial value of A in line 20, whereas it is set to 0 as part of the FOR . . . TO statement in Example 4-13.

A formal representation of the FOR . . . NEXT statement looks like this:

For *numerical variable* = *initial value* TO *terminal value* STEP *increment value.*

The *numerical variable* must be just that: a numerical variable such as A, FO, X3, and the like. The *initial value, terminal value,* and *increment value* can be numerals or variables.

Now notice that this formalized statement includes a STEP clause that is absent from Example 4–13. If the STEP *increment value* is omitted from the statement, the computer assumes that you want to increment the count by 1—and that was the case in Example 4–13. But if you want the statement to increment or decrement the count by any other number, you must include the STEP *increment value* clause.

For example, if you want to count by 5's from, say, 0 to 155, the statement would be written

FOR X = 0 TO 155 STEP 5.

Of course, the statement would have to be followed by a NEXT statement later in the program.

If you want to count backward from 155 to 0 in steps of 5, try this:

FOR X = 155 TO 0 STEP –5.

What would this statement do?

FOR D = 0 TO 1 STEP .001.

If followed later in the program by a NEXT or NEXT D statement, the value of D would increment from 0 to 1 in steps of 0.001.

> *Principle.* Every FOR . . . TO statement must have a corre-
> sponding NEXT statement appearing later in the program.

The NEXT statement is wholly responsible for looping operations back to the originating FOR . . . TO statement. NEXT statements can take the form NEXT or NEXT *numerical variable,* where
the *numerical variable* clause matches the clause of that same name
in the originating FOR . . . TO statement.

Here is an example of a simple time-delay program:

EXAMPLE 4-14

```
10 CLS
20 FOR T = 0 TO 100
30 NEXT
40 PRINT "BLAM!!"
50 END
```

EXAMPLE 4-15

```
10 CLS
20 PRINT "TIMING INTERVAL"
30 INPUT T0
40 CLS
50 FOR T=0 TO T0
60 NEXT
70 PRINT "BLAM!!!"
80 END
```

Both of these examples use the FOR . . . TO and NEXT statements for
executing a time-delay scheme. In Example 4-14, the time delay is fixed
at the interval required for counting by 1's from 0 to 100. Example 4-15
has the special advantage of allowing the user to adjust the time-delay
interval. In that case, the user enters some numerical value for T0 at the
INPUT statement in line 30. The FOR . . . TO, NEXT counting interval is
then from 0 to whatever value T0 might have.

Example 4-15 also illustrates the notion of using a numerical variable
as the *terminal value* in a FOR . . . TO statement.

4-7 Nested FOR . . . TO and NEXT Loops

FOR . . . TO and NEXT loops can be neated quite easily. In other
words, there is no real difficulty with the notion of building loops
within loops. Compare the programs in Examples 4-16 and 4-17:

EXAMPLE 4-16

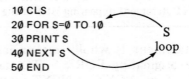

```
10 CLS
20 FOR S=0 TO 10
30 PRINT S
40 NEXT S
50 END
```

EXAMPLE 4-17

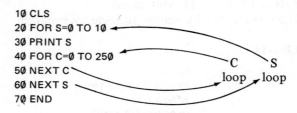

```
10 CLS
20 FOR S=0 TO 10
30 PRINT S
40 FOR C=0 TO 250
50 NEXT C
60 NEXT S
70 END
```

Both of these programs first clear the screen and then list numerals 0 through 10. The program in Example 4-16 does the job very rapidly, however, whereas the one in Example 4-17 prints the numerals at a rate of about one per second.

Example 4-16, you see, contains only one FOR . . . TO, NEXT loop, which, according to line 20, causes variable S to increment from 0 to 10. The counting takes place at a rate determined by the execution time of lines 20, 30, and 40—and that rate can be very high.

In Example 4-17, the programmer decided to insert a time delay between the printing of each new value of S. There are two FOR . . . TO, NEXT loops in this program; and the C loop is nested within the S loop.

Having the C loop nested within the S loop means that variable S cannot be incremented until C goes through its entire looping cycle. C cycles 0 to 250, and then S is incremented by one. C is set to zero and allowed to cycle from 0 to 250 again, but S cannot increment until that cycle is completed.

Looking at the situation from a slightly different view: For every complete, 250-step cycle of the C loop, the S loop is executed just one time. The whole process is complete only after the 10-step cycle of the S loop is finished.

It might be helpful to bear in mind that a NEXT statement works like a GOTO. Whenever C in Example 4-17 is somewhere between 0 and 250, NEXT C means, "Go to the FOR C in line 40." So as long as the value of C is less than 250, the program "buzzes" between lines 40 and 50.

By the same token, NEXT S might be interpreted as saying, "If S is less than 10, go to line 20." *Here is an important point:* If the NEXT S tells the system to return to line 20, that means the system will print the S value in line 30 and then restart C from 0 at line 40.

Every time the outer loop is executed (loop S), the inner loop goes through its entire counting cycle (loop C).

Nested FOR . . . TO, NEXT loops are executed from the innermost to the outermost. Each loop must complete its entire cycle before the one just outside it can be executed one time. Figure 4-4 illustrates this principle with a diagram.

Figure 4-4a shows a set of four nested loops labeled A through D. Loop A is the innermost one, followed by B, C, and D. Since loop execution is from the innermost to the outermost loop, A loop will have to be satisfied (or "cycled out") before B loop can be executed one time. Executing the B loop resets the A loop; and the A loop then has to be satisfied again before the B loop can undergo another execution.

The C loop rests in its initial condition until the cycling action of the A loop finally satisfies the B loop. Then the C loop is executed one time. But running the C loop causes all the inner loops—A and B—to be reset to their initial conditions; and that means the C loop won't be executed again until the B loop is satisfied once more.

All this is going on, and the D loop has not done a thing. It won't until the C loop is satisfied.

If you are getting the right perspective on this situation, you can see that it is possible to tie up the computer for a long time before the D loop is finally satisfied.

> ***Principle.*** Unless stated otherwise, nested FOR . . . TO, NEXT loops are executed and satisfied from the innermost to the outermost.

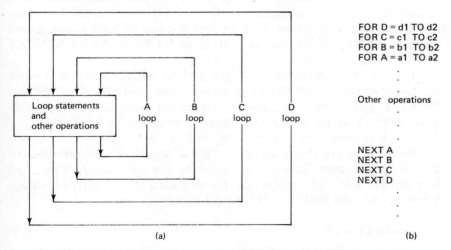

(a)   (b)

Figure 4-4   Nesting FOR . . . TO, NEXT loops. (a) Four nested loops shown in a diagram fashion. (b) General programming sequence for four nested loops.

The principle of running loops from the inside to the outside is so firmly established that the computer assumes that is the case. This being the situation, there is really no need to attach a loop specifier to the NEXT statement. The computer knows what it is supposed to do. For instance, the two-loop program in Example 4–18 could be written this way:

```
10 CLS
20 FOR S=0 TO 10
30 PRINT S
40 FOR C=0 TO 250
50 NEXT
60 NEXT
70 END
```

Lines 50 and 60 need not be written as NEXT C and NEXT S, respectively. A simple NEXT statement is sufficient, because the computer assumes line 50 refers to the FOR . . . TO statement in line 40, and that line 60 refers to the FOR . . . TO statement in line 20.

Returning to Fig. 4–4, note the general flow of statements in Fig. 4–4b. The FOR . . . TO statements are listed from the outermost to the innermost. The corresponding NEXT statements, however, are listed in the opposite order—from the innermost to the outermost.

The NEXT statements in Fig. 4–4b do not really have to be "pointed" to their respective FOR . . . TO statements. The loop specifiers can be omitted, leaving just a series of NEXT statements (NEXT, NEXT, NEXT, NEXT instead of NEXT A, NEXT B, NEXT C, NEXT D).

In fact, loop specifiers are attached to NEXT statements more for the convenience of the programmer than anything else. Seeing a NEXT Y statement in a program leaves no room for confusion on your part. You know the statement is pointing to a FOR Y . . . TO . . . statement earlier in the program.

Before closing this chapter, let's put together another time-of-day clock program. This one is similar to the one already illustrated in Example 4–9; but in this case the awkward IF . . . THEN routines are replaced with FOR . . . TO, NEXT loops.

EXAMPLE 4-18

```
10 CLS
20 FOR H=1 TO 12
30 FOR M=0 TO 59
```

```
40 FOR S=0 TO 59
50 FOR C=0 TO 250
60 NEXT C
70 CLS
80 PRINT H":"M":"S
90 NEXT S
1001 NEXT M
110 NEXT H
120 GOTO 10
```

Note the hierarchy of nested loops: C is the innermost loop (the one that cycles most often), and H is the outermost loop (the one that cycles least often).

Now compare Examples 4–9 and 4–18, noting specifically the different counting ranges for the C-loop variable. In Example 4–9, the counting range for the C variable is between 0 and 100; while in Example 4–18 it is between 0 and 250. The C variable performs exactly the same "slowing down" function in both examples. Why, then, are the counting ranges different?

One of the important advantages of a FOR . . . TO, NEXT loop is its higher execution rate. In Example 4–9, it takes about 1 second to run variable C from 0 to 100; but in Example 4–18 it takes 1 second to increment variable C from 0 to 250. Obviously, the FOR . . . TO, NEXT cycle runs about 2½ times faster. The implication is that one would select a FOR . . . TO, NEXT loop over an IF . . . THEN sequence in cases where speed is of importance.

> *Note.* FOR . . . TO, NEXT loops can be executed much faster than an IF . . . THEN sequence. And faster operation means doing more operations in the same period of time.

Unfortunately, the program in Example 4–18 does not include provisions for setting the right time when the program is started. Doing so with the FOR . . . TO loops would confuse the issue of nested loops. Rest assured, you will have a chance later to slick up the clock program.

EXERCISES

4-1 Define the following terms:
   (a) loop
   (b) unconditional loop

(c) conditional loop

(d) unconditional statement

(e) conditional statement

(f) relational operator

(g) consequential statement or, as some call it, "action clause"

(h) default condition

(i) satisfied conditional statement

(j) flowchart

4-2 Classify the following program statements as *conditional* or *unconditional* statements:

(a) GOTO *line number*

(b) IF A=2 THEN 20

(c) IF X=1000 END

(d) NEXT *loop specifier*

4-3 For each of the following programs, specify the numeral appearing on the screen when the program ends:

(a)
```
10 CLS
20 A=0
30 A=A+1
40 IF A<10 THEN 30
50 PRINT A
60 END
```

(b)
```
10 CLS
20 A=0
30 A=A+1
40 IF A<10 THEN 60
50 GOTO 30
60 PRINT A
70 END
```

(c)
```
10 CLS
20 A=0
30 A=A+1
40 IF A>10 THEN 30
50 PRINT A
60 END
```

(d)
```
10 CLS
20 A=0
30 A=A+1
40 IF A>10 THEN 60
50 GOTO 30
60 PRINT A
70 END
```

(e)
```
10 CLS
20 A=0
30 A=A+1
40 IF A>=10 THEN 30
50 PRINT A
60 END
```

(f)
```
10 CLS
20 A=0
30 A=A+1
40 IF A<=10 THEN 60
50 GOTO 30
60 PRINT A
70 END
```

(g)
```
10 CLS
20 A=0
30 A=A+1
40 IF A<>10 THEN 30
50 PRINT A
```

(h)
```
10 CLS
20 A=0
30 A=A+1
40 IF A>=10 THEN 60
50 GOTO 30
```

```
        60 END                              60 PRINT A
                                            70 END
(i)   10 CLS                    (j)   10 CLS
      20 FOR A=0 TO 10                20 FOR A=0 TO 10
      30 NEXT                         30 NEXT
      40 PRINT A                      40 PRINT A-1
      50 END                         50 END
```

4-4   The following statements represent a portion of some program. Assuming that the variables are defined before reaching the specified portion of the program, describe the conditions necessary for going from line 50 to line 60:

(a)   50 IF X=100 THEN 20
      60 PRINT X

(b)   50 IF X=10 THEN 20
      60 PRINT X

(c)   50 IF X<> 100 THEN 20
      60 PRINT X

(d)   50 IF B$="SICK" THEN 20
      60 PRINT S$

4-5   Under what circumstance can the THEN word be omitted from an IF . . . THEN conditional statement? Give at least two specific examples. Are there any circumstances where the THEN word must be omitted from an IF . . . THEN conditional statement? If so, give one example.

4-6   Describe the literal meaning of the following string statements:

(a)   IF A$=B$ THEN . . .
(b)   IF A$>B$ THEN . . .
(c)   IF A$<B$ THEN . . .
(d)   IF A$<=B$ THEN . . .
(e)   IF A$>=B$ THEN . . .
(f)   IF A$<>B$ THEN . . .

4-7   Describe the literal meaning of the following statements:

(a)   IF A=N+1 THEN . . .
(b)   IF A↑2>3*B/2 THEN . . .

4-8   Describe the effect this program will have on the screen:

```
            10 CLS
            20 B=0
            30 FOR T=0 TO 200
            40 NEXT
            50 IF B=1 THEN 100
            60 CLS
```

```
70 PRINT "TICK"
80 B=1
90 GOTO 30
100 CLS
110 PRINT
120 PRINT "TOCK"
130 GOTO 20
```

4-9   Compare the operation of the following two programs:

(a)
```
10 CLS
20 INPUT A,B,C
30 FOR X=A TO B STEP C
40 PRINT X, SQR(X)
50 NEXT
60 END
```

(b)
```
70 CLS
80 INPUT A,B,C
90 FOR X=A TO B STEP C
100 INPUT X$
110 PRINT X, SQR(X)
120 NEXT
130 END
```

What is the meanng of FOR X=A TO B STEP C?

4-10   Using the same line numbers as in Exercise 4-9, combine the two programs by inserting:

```
0 PRINT "AUTO OR STEP"
2 INPUT A$
4 IF A$="AUTO" THEN 10
6 IF A$="STEP" THEN 70
8 GOTO 0
```

As far as the user is concerned, what is the effect of combining the programs in Exercises 4-9 and 4-10? Write a composite program (one complete listing). Prepare a flowchart for the composite program. Can you devise a way to combine these three programs and end up with fewer lines?

4-11   Write a clock program, using FOR . . . TO and NEXT loops, for a computerized "stopwatch"—show tenths of seconds, seconds, minutes, and hours. What would the flowchart look like?

CHAPTER
5

Some Formatting Hints
and
Programming Shortcuts

Statement introduced in this chapter:

PRINT TAB (. . .)

Control characters introduced in this chapter:

comma   ,   semicolon   ;   colon   :

You have covered a lot of new material in the first four chapters of this book. You have learned something about getting a computer wound up, programmed, and running in BASIC. There is a lot more material to cover before you can begin claiming to be something of an expert in the BASIC language; but this is a good place to take stock of everything that has gone before, look at just one new program statement, learn some techniques for making neater looking displays on the CRT, and consider some ways to make the programming job a bit easier.

After that, it will be time to get back to the heavier stuff.

5-1   A Closer Look at the Layout
of the CRT Screen

You have probably noticed by now that the screen on your video monitor can display just so many characters at one time. In fact, it has room for 64 characters on each line and for just 16 lines down the screen. That provides a total of 1024 characters that can be visible at any given moment.

To check the line capacity of your video screen, clear the screen and get into the command mode by typing and entering the command NEW. That should leave a READY status appearing in the upper left-hand corner of the screen.

Now begin striking the "greater than" key (>) until the line is filled and overflowing to the next line. The number of greater-than symbols on the full line should be 64. Continue striking the > key until you are convinced that each line can hold just 64 characters. Choose any other keyboard character and you will find the same result.

Now clear the screen by either striking the CLEAR key or entering NEW. Then begin striking the ENTER key. Each time you hit the ENTER key in the command mode, the prompt symbol should appear at the beginning of each new line. You will find that you cannot get more than 16 of these prompt symbols lined up vertically along the left-hand edge of the screen. The system can display only 16 lines of characters at one time.

Of course, the system will accept more than 16 lines; but after the sixteenth is displayed, attempting to enter yet another line causes the entire display to scroll upward. The new line is entered at the bottom of the screen, and the top line is effectively lost from view as it "pops" off the top.

All printing on the screen is done within this 16 × 64 graphic format; *formatting* is the term applied to the process of setting up displays within the 16-line, 64-characters-per-line format on the screen.

Some special systems, especially those designed for high-quality video graphics, can handle larger amounts of information on the screen at one time. The 16 × 64 format is standard for conventional computer systems.

Principle. Most CRT monitors are designed to display up to 64 characters per line and 16 lines per frame. All printing operations take place within this 16 × 64 format.

Definition. *Formatting* is any programming process intended to set up a custom display within the system's 16 × 64 character format.

Through the first four chapters of this book, the computer system itself has handled most of the formatting. It automatically starts a new line when one is overflowed by anything that causes more than 64 characters and spaces to appear in sequence. And the system automatically scrolls the display whenever the line count overflows.

5-2   Formatting with Semicolons

As mentioned earlier, the ENTER key on the Radio Shack TRS–80 personal computer is more often called the *carriage-return* or CR key on other systems. In the command mode of operation, striking this ENTER or CR key causes the display to terminate one line and begin a new one at the left-hand side of the screen. This is an example of a manual carriage-return operation. (The expression *carriage return* is a carryover from typewriter and Teletypewriter technology—it refers to the operation that begins a new line of printed text.)

When the system is executing a program that calls for printing information on the CRT screen, the carriage-return operation can be wholly automatic and under the control of the computer. In fact, the computer, unless instructed to do otherwise, will execute a carriage return after each and every PRINT statement. Try the following program:

EXAMPLE 5-1

```
10 CLS
20 PRINT "$"
30 GOTO 20
```

Basically, this example is one of those endless looping programs that can be terminated only by striking the BREAK key. The point of the demonstration, however, is to show that the computer does a carriage-return each and every time it executes line 20. What appears on the screen is a single string of dollar signs along the left-hand edge. (Note that there are just 16 of them on the screen at once. Why is that?)

Principle.   Unless instructed otherwise, the system automatically does a carriage return after executing a PRINT statement.

Now, what is this "unless instructed otherwise" business? Is it possible to suppress the automatic carriage return? Try this program:

EXAMPLE 5-2

```
10 CLS
20 PRINT "$";
30 GOTO 20
```

The only difference between this program and the one in Example 5-1 is
that line 20 in this example has a semicolon at the end of it. That semicolon instructs the computer to suppress its natural desire to do a carriage
return after every PRINT statement.

Run the program and you will find the display looking quite different
from that generated by Example 5-1. The screen is literally filled with
dollar signs—64 in a row and 16 rows of them. That one little bit of punctuation in line 20 makes all the difference in the world. The system still
does an automatic carriage-return operation when a line is filled, however.

If you are now convinced that it is possible for you, as the programmer, to suppress the system's automatic carriage-return feature
after a PRINT operation, consider this little wrinkle:

EXAMPLE 5-3

```
10 CLS
20 PRINT "NAME"
30 INPUT A$
40 PRINT
50 PRINT A$
60 END
```

EXAMPLE 5-4

```
10 CLS
20 PRINT "NAME";
30 INPUT A$
40 PRINT
50 PRINT A$
60 END
```

Again, the only difference between these two programs is the presence of
a semicolon at the end of the PRINT statement in line 20 of Example 5-4.

Upon running the program in Example 5-3, this blurb appears immediately on the screen:

```
NAME
?_
```

The question mark and cursor appear as a result of the INPUT A$ statement in line 20. Now you can enter a name such as HERMAN, and complete the program execution:

```
NAME
?HERMAN

HERMAN
READY
>_
```

The line space between ?HERMAN and HERMAN is generated by the PRINT *nothing* in line 40. That is an example of formatting a blank line by having the system print nothing and execute its normal carriage return.

The real point of this demonstration is not clear until you try running the program in Example 5-4 and comparing the results. Upon running the program in Example 5-4, the following information appears on the screen:

```
NAME?_
```

Note that using the semicolon after the PRINT statement in line 20 suppressed the normal carriage return, causing the question mark and cursor to appear on the same line as the printed word NAME.

Typing and entering HERMAN in response to this INPUT request, the overall display looks like this:

```
NAME? HERMAN

HERMAN
READY
>_
```

In Example 5-4, the printed request and INPUT-generated question mark appear on the same line—and so does the operator's response. Although the difference between this program and the one in Example 5-3 might seem trivial at this point, this demonstration clearly shows the effect of following a PRINT statement with a semicolon.

Using the semicolon in this fashion gives you some measure of control over the formatting on the screen.

Principle. A semicolon following any PRINT statement in a program suppresses the automatic carriage return and causes the next printed information to appear on the same line.

Generally speaking, a semicolon is used after a PRINT statement whenever it is important to print information in horizontal succession, as opposed to vertical succession. The following program concludes this part of the formatting discussion.

EXAMPLE 5-5

```
10 CLS
20 FOR N=0 TO 100
30 PRINT N;
40 NEXT
50 END
```

In this case numerals 0 through 100 will be printed on the screen in horizontal rows. Zero through 17 will appear on the first line, 18 through 30 on the next, and so on. Without the semicolon in line 30, the numerals would appear vertically, one on a line.

5-3 Formatting with the PRINT TAB (. . .) Statement

It is possible to do some pretty fancy formatting with the return-suppressing semicolon and PRINT *nothing* statements; but the complexity of the task gets out of hand rather quickly. And when things start getting too complicated, it is time to consider the PRINT TAB statement.

Recall that each line on the CRT screen has room for exactly 64 characters. Think of each of the available spaces as a little rectangle having a number assigned to it—specifically 0 through 63. (That is 64 numbers, isn't it?)

The PRINT TAB statement allows you to print any valid keyboard character into one of those little numbered rectangles. Or better yet, PRINT TAB lets you begin printing a line of characters at any one of the rectangles.

For starters, put the system into the command mode and clear the screen. Then enter PRINT TAB(10) *"#"*. Lo! there is a # character in rectangle number 10 on the next line. The display might look something like this:

```
>PRINT TAB(10) "#"
          #
READY
>_
```

You can confirm that the # symbol is in the space for imaginary rectangle number 10 by using the PRINT command about it as a reference. The cursor on that command line occupies position 0, the P in PRINT occupies position 1, the R is in position 2, and so on. Count it out, and you will find that the # on the second line is directly below the number-10 character—(—on the line above.

Figure 5-1 shows the imaginary grid of TAB numbers on the screen. There are 64 TAB positions, labeled 0 through 63. Having convenient access to such a grid can be invaluable when formatting lines of text on the screen.

As described thus far, the TAB statement takes the following form:

$$\text{PRINT TAB}(\textit{tab number})\ \textit{"expression"}$$

where *tab number* is any number between 0 and 63, inclusively. The larger the tab number, the farther to the right the *"expression"* is printed on the line.

Actually, the TAB statement is simply a modified PRINT statement; and anything you can do with PRINT you can do with PRINT TAB(*tab number*). For example:

```
PRINT TAB (tab number) numerical variable
PRINT TAB(tab number) numerical value
PRINT TAB(tab number) math
PRINT TAB(tab number) string variable
PRINT TAB(tab number) string value
```

In fact, you can terminate a PRINT TAB statement with a semi-colon to suppress the carriage return, presumably to print several TAB statements on the same line.

Let's look at the formatting power you now have at your disposal.

EXAMPLE 5-6

```
10 CLS
20 PRINT "A";
30 PRINT TAB(12) "A SQUARED";
40 PRINT TAB(28) "SQUARE ROOT";
50 PRINT TAB(47) "LOG A"
60 PRINT TAB(30) "OF A"
70 FOR N=0 TO 63
80 PRINT "-";
90 NEXT
```

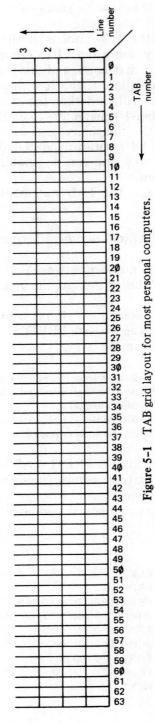

Figure 5-1 TAB grid layout for most personal computers.

```
100 FOR A=1 TO 10
110 PRINT A;
120 PRINT TAB(15)A↑2;
130 PRINT TAB(30) SQR(A);
140 PRINT TAB(45) LOG(A)
150 NEXT
160 END
```

Running this program produces a format similar to that shown in Fig. 5-2. This material is printed one line at a time, beginning at the top of the screen and working down toward the bottom. With the programming tools presently at hand, there is no way to back up and add something after a line is finished.

The program itself can be divided into two distinctly different parts: printing the column headings and doing the math. The column headings and dashed line are specified and formatted by program lines 20 through 90. Lines 100 through the end take care of the math.

The first line in the display is made up of words A, A SQUARED, SQUARE ROOT and LOG A. See lines 20 through 50 in the program; and note that all but the last one is terminated with a semicolon.

Since the A label is to be printed at TAB($\emptyset$), there is no need to specify a tab—the system assumes printing is to begin at TAB $\emptyset$ if nothing specifies otherwise. That line must end with a semicolon, however, to prevent the system from doing a carriage return and printing A SQUARED on the next line down.

So the system works its way across the first line of the display heading, printing the designated expressions at the designated TAB points. Line 50 does not conclude with a semicolon, however. It shouldn't carry a return-suppressing semicolon, because you then want the next expression to appear on the following line.

A	A SQUARED	SQUARE ROOT OF A	LOG A
1	1	1	$\emptyset$
2	4	1.41421	.692147
3	9	1.732$\emptyset$5	1.$\emptyset$9861
4	16	2	1.38629
5	25	2.236$\emptyset$7	1.6$\emptyset$944
6	36	2.44949	1.79176
7	49	2.64575	1.94591
8	64	2.82843	2.$\emptyset$7944
9	81	3	2.19722
1$\emptyset$	1$\emptyset\emptyset$	3.16228	2.3$\emptyset$259
READY			
>-			

Figure 5-2 CRT display as a result of running the tabular program in Example 5-6.

By selecting an appropriate TAB number, the OF A term appears directly under SQUARE ROOT. This is all determined by line 60 in the program. And since that is the only piece of text on the second line of the display heading, it should not end with a semicolon.

The next line in the display consists of 64 dashes in sequence across the screen. Lines 70 through 90 in the program take care of this particular job. The FOR . . . TO, NEXT sequence, in effect, counts the number of dashes to be printed; and the PRINT "-"; statement tucked in between causes all 64 of them to be printed in a single line on the screen.

Line 100 then limits the calculating range of the table to integers between 0 and 100 inclusively. Line 110 is an example of a PRINT TAB(*tab number*) *numerical variable* statement, while lines 120, 130, and 140 are PRINT TAB (*tab number*)*math* statements. All of these lines, except the last one, conclude with a semicolon, the idea being to print the four items on a single line across the screen.

It often takes some playing around to format a table such as this one. Don't be ashamed to try some tab numbers and change them if things don't work out as you would like. Actually, this program was originally set up by writing the math portion first—lines 100 through 160. It's rather easy to specify evenly spaced TAB numbers for numerical data. Once that part of the program was written and checked by running it, I tagged on the heading-printing portion, using the TAB numbers for the data as guides. The TAB numbers for the columns of data can give you a very good idea about TAB numbers for the column headings.

Who ever said you must write all programs from the very beginning?

While on this subject of writing programs in a piecemeal fashion, you might become aware of the fact that programmers tend to establish personal styles and ways of approaching programming situations. Some will carefully plan everything in minute detail before approaching the keyboard. Such people will have the program all written out and "tried" on paper.

Other programmers take a more casual approach, getting a few key ideas programmed into the machine right away, and then mold it into shape much as an artist creates a statue or oil painting.

There are arguments, pro and con, for both approaches. So don't worry about the "right way" to approach this matter of building computer programs in BASIC. You will be developing your own style as you gain more knowledge, understanding, and experience.

5-4 Getting Fancy with PRINT TAB (*math*)

All of the PRINT TAB statements in Section 5-3 were fixed numerical values—an integer somewhere between 0 and 63. But it is altogether possible, and a lot of fun, to substitute some math functions for the *tab number* portion of the statement.

What that does is change the tab setting for each line; and if that tab number happens to change according to some rational pattern (specifically a math function) you end up with some interesting patterns, and even some animation, on the screen.

Study this example; or, better yet, try it on your computer:

EXAMPLE 5-7

```
10 CLS
20 FOR N=0 TO 14
30 PRINT TAB(N) "#"
40 NEXT
50 GOTO 50
```

As the value of N increments from 0 toward 14, the tab position of the # figure increments one space farther to the right with each line. Each # appears on a different line because there is no semicolon at the end of line 30 to suppress the carriage returns. What you see on the screen is something like the figure in Fig. 5-3a.

Incidentally, line 50 might seem to be a rather peculiar operation. All it does is tell the line to go to itself. So when the computer encounters line 50, it just "buzzes" there until the operator strikes the BREAK key to return to the command mode of operation.

Having a line return to itself is a popular trick when drawing pictures on the screen. Without it, the computer would return the ready status charac-

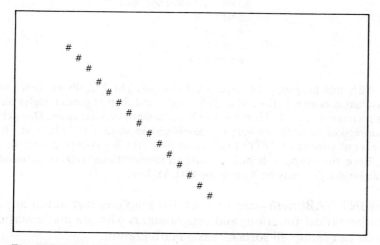

Figure 5-3 A bit of TAB graphics using the program in Example 5-7.

ters, mess up the picture, and maybe even shift everything upward by one line. So you get the computer busy with some nonsense task so it won't mess up the image.

Now if you want to get a shallower slope than the program generates, simply modify line 30 to read

30 PRINT TAB(4*N) "#"

That statement sets the tab four times farther to the right with each line, creating an image much like the one in Fig. 5-3b.

Of course, you can enclose any character or combination of characters within the quotes in line 30. Maybe # figures don't interest you much. So how about this?

30 PRINT TAB(4*N) "ZZZIP"

Put whatever you want inside those quotes.

Or maybe you think you are ready to try your hand at some computer animation—making that line wiggle around a little bit. Then try this:

EXAMPLE 5-8

```
10 CLS
20 FOR A=0 TO 4 STEP .5
30 FOR N=0 TO 14
40 PRINT TAB(N*A) "ZZZIP"
50 NEXT N
60 CLS
70 NEXT A
80 GOTO 20
```

With this program, the angle itself changes. The ZZZIPs are first printed straight downward, then at a slight angle, and then at greater angles until A is incremented to 4. Then the whole cycle starts all over again. One gets the impression of a funny sort of searchlight in action. It (whatever "it" is) fires out streams of ZZZIP's (whatever they are) in a sweeping pattern.

Since the program is built around an unconditional GOTO statement, it can be stopped only by hitting the BREAK key.

PRINT TAB(*math*) can be used for graphing just about any sort of mathematical function; and programmers who are mathematically inclined can set up all sorts of basic math graphs.

Consider, for instance, the basic exponential function $A = x^2$.

There are a couple of different ways to set up this graph on the screen, both using PRINT TAB(*math*).

EXAMPLE 5-9a

```
10 CLS
20 FOR X=0 TO 7
30 PRINT TAB(X↑2) "*"
40 NEXT
```

EXAMPLE 5-9b

```
10 CLS
20 X=0
30 A=X↑2
40 IF A>63 END
50 PRINT TAB(A) "*"
60 X=X+1
70 GOTO 30
```

Both of these programs generate the same exponential curve on the screen; and there is only one thing wrong with it: the conventional X and Y axes are reversed (see Fig. 5-4).

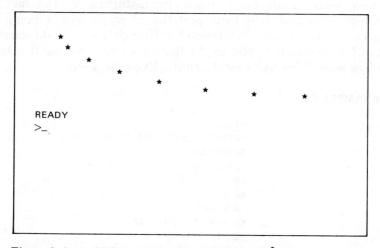

```
READY
>_
```

Figure 5-4 A CRT plot of the equation $A = x^2$. Both programs in Example 5-9 can do this job. Note the unfortunate fact that the graph is rotated so that the independent variable (x) is plotted along the vertical axis, while the dependent variable (A) is plotted along the horizontal axis.

Note. When graphing mathematical functions with PRINT TAB (*math*), the graph is always rotated so that the independent variable is along the vertical axis and the dependent variable is along the horizontal axis. In other words the conventional X and Y axes are reversed, and the function is drawn from the top to the bottom, rather than from left to right.

The program in Example 5–9a is certainly simpler than its counterpart in Example 5–9b. What we are dealing with here is the fact that the tab value should not exceed 63; and using the shorter program puts the burden of limiting the values of X on the programmer—the programmer must know that allowing X to increment to a value of 8 will cause the tab value in line 30 to exceed 63, thereby overflowing the information onto the next line and messing up the graph.

Example 5–9b is a longer program, but the programmer need not be concerned about limiting the value of the X. Line 40 in that program does all the "thinking" and brings the program to a stop when the tab value exceeds 63.

It is the "style" of many programmers to write goof-proof programs such as the one in Example 5–9b.

Now some math buffs might be disturbed by the fact that Examples 5–9a and 5–9b both plot the x^2 graph with x being only integers between 0 and 7. Wouldn't it be nice if you could select the interval? For instance, you might like to see x^2 plotted at intervals of 0.5 or something like that. Examine Example 5–9c.

EXAMPLE 5-9c

```
10 CLS
20 PRINT "WHAT INTERVAL";
30 INPUT I
40 CLS
50 X=0
60 NL=0
70 A=X↑2
80 IF A>63 GOTO 140
90 PRINT TAB(A)"*"
100 NL=NL+1
110 IF NL>14 GOTO 140
120 X=X+I
130 GOTO 70
140 GOTO 140
```

In this program, lines 10 through 30 handle the matter of the x-plotting interval, variable I. After that, the screen is cleared (line 40), the initial value of X is fixed at zero (line 50), and another variable, NL, is introduced.

Ultimately, NL is going to prevent vertical overflow on the screen—it will limit the number of plotted points to 15 lines. Recall that the program in Example 5-9b prevents horizontal overflow by limiting the upper value of A. NL does the same sort of thing, but limits the number of lines to one full frame and avoids the possibility of having the entire display scroll upward. But that is all a bit more of the goof-proofing stuff. The main point of this example is to plot the x^2 curve at selectable intervals of I.

So once I is entered at line 30, the computer plots the first point (line 90), keeps track of the line in use (line 100), and finally increases the value of X by interval I (line 120).

As long as everything is still fitting onto the screen, the program cycles between lines 130 and 70. The operations come to a conclusion when either A or NL exceed the values specified in lines 80 and 110, respectively. At that time, control goes down to line 140; and since that line simply calls itself, the computer "buzzes" on that line, doing essentially nothing at all until the operator breaks up the whole routine by striking the ENTER key. Line 140 is inserted merely to prevent the ready status characters from messing up an otherwise pretty graph.

It would be possible to make even further improvements in this program, doing things such as inputting and starting the value of X at something other than zero. You might also have the system print the values of A and X that exist the moment there is a line or screen overflow. But all of that sort of thing has little to do with the main point of this section—applying PRINT TAB(*math*).

The fact that tab values must be limited to the range 0 to 63 can cause the unwary math programmer some problems. We have already dealt with the matter of tab numbers exceeding the value of 63—that causes an overflow condition that prints the tabbed expression somewhere else on a longer line. But what about tab-number values that are negative—less than zero? Well, that will prompt an error condition every time.

This matter of negative tab numbers comes to a head when working with trig functions such as sin X [or something such as Y=SIN(X) in BASIC]. If the values of X are allowed to exceed $\pi/2$, sin X is bound to swing negative, making a statement such as PRINT TAB(SIN(X)) virtually useless.

The problem of dealing with negative tab values can be eliminated in this case by translating the whole graph so that its baseline is running vertically near the center of the screen. Make the statement look like this: PRINT TAB(SIN(X)+31)"*". Now the function cannot swing negative, no matter what the value of X might be. The tab value will swing between 30 and 32—and there are no more problems.

And if you want to amplify the size of the graph, do this: PRINT TAB(3∅*SIN(X)+31)"*". In this case the graph swings between tab values 1 and 61.

All that remains for graphing this function are some values for X and a few housekeeping chores.

EXAMPLE 5-10

```
10 CLS
20 FOR X=0 TO 6.28 STEP .4
30 PRINT TAB(30*SIN(X)+31)"*"
40 NEXT
50 GOTO 50
```

This program prints a nice sine-wave form on the screen. Line 20 is responsible for setting the range and plotting interval of angle X. The range, 0 to 6.28, represents the full sine-plotting interval of 0 to 2π radians. The STEP interval .4 was selected so that the program would draw the curve on 15 lines, thereby preventing a scrolling effect that would move part of the graph off the top of the screen ($6.28/15 \cong .4$).

Programmers with a special knack for math can do more work with this sort of program—altering the amplitude, frequency, and so on. The main point of the discussion, however, is that the *math* expression in a PRINT TAB(*math*) statement can be quite complex.

While considering some graphing programs using PRINT TAB(*math*), bear in mind a couple of points. First, the scheme can print only *integers* between 0 and 63 inclusively. Yes, *integers* only. The system automatically does an integer-rounding operation before plotting a tab value.

Another important point is that the TAB scheme always plots from left to right on any given line. For instance, the system cannot handle the sequence. PRINT TAB(20) followed by a PRINT TAB(10) on the same line. Add to that the fact that the lines are always printed from the top toward the bottom, and you can see how difficult it would be to plot some of the conic expressions—circles, ellipses, and the like.

Finally, there is the little problem of having all the graphs printed sideways. Of course, you could fix that by setting the CRT monitor on its side. (That's supposed to be funny.)

All things considered, PRINT TAB(*math*) can be a powerful tool for graphing equations and doing some simple and interesting animated graphics on the computer. One additional advantage is that it is a "universal" scheme that can be applied to virtually any computer system. Although most personal computers feature their own special graphics statements, they share the same TAB statements.

Then, too, TAB statements can be output on a line printer to produce permanent *hardcopy* of the pictures. This is not at all the case for special graphics commands that are devised for CRT outputs only.

5-5 Automatic TAB(16) with a Comma

Tabulating data is such a common application for computers that the designers of BASIC built in a simple tab scheme. What it amounts to is inserting a comma between the information to be printed. In effect, the comma says, "Print the next bit of information 16 spaces farther to the right."

By way of a direct demonstration, compare the following operations while the system is in the command mode:

```
>PRINT 1234
 1234
READY
>_
```

That should come as no big surprise. The system was instructed to print 1234, and that is what it did.

But then try this:

```
>PRINT 1,2,3,4
 1              2              3              4
READY
>_
```

Inserting the commas between these numerals told the system to separate the numerals by 16 tab spaces. Instead of having to program a long TAB sequence such as PRINT TAB($\emptyset$) . . ., PRINT Tab(15) . . . , PRINT TAB(31) . . . , and so on, the simple commas take care of it.

EXAMPLE 5-11

```
10 CLS
20 FOR X=1 TO 10
30 PRINT X, X↑2,SQR(X), LOG(X)
40 NEXT
50 END
```

This program prints the value of X, the square of X, the square root of X, and the log of X in four columns on the screen. Attempting to do the same job with TAB statements would call for three additional program lines; and, more important, a lot of planning concerning the values of the tab numbers.

PRINT statements that include a serial string of data separated by commas certainly make life easier. Compare the program in Example 5-6 with this one:

EXAMPLE 5-12

```
10 CLS
20 PRINT "A","A SQUARED","SQUARE ROOT","LOG A"
30 PRINT ,,"OF A"
70 FOR N=0 TO 63
80 PRINT "-";
90 NEXT
100 FOR A=1 TO 10
110 PRINT A, A↑2, SQR(A) ,LOG(A)
150 NEXT
160 END
```

The programs in Examples 5-6 and 5-12 essentially do the same thing; but you will have to agree that the latter one is much easier to set up. So why not use the comma to set up columns of data whenever possible?

Before moving on to the next topic, you ought to take a close look at line 30 in Example 5-12. The purpose of the line is to place an OF A comment directly below the SQUARE ROOT comment in the first line of the heading. The OF A is placed into its proper position by means of two commas in succession. Without using any commas at all in line 30, the OF A comment would appear under the A heading. Using just one comma would place the comment under A SQUARED; but using two commas in a row places it right where it belongs.

Note. Commas can be used in succession in a PRINT statement to TAB a character at multiples of 16.

5-6   Simplifying INPUT Routines

So far in this chapter you have seen how semicolons and commas affect the formatting of PRINT statements. It so happens that the same two punctuation marks can be applied to INPUT statements to make the programming job a whole lot easier.

Let's suppose you are in a programming situation that calls for inputting three different values in succession. Until now, you would probably handle the situation in this sort of way:

                    100 INPUT A
                    110 INPUT B
                    120 INPUT C

Of course, there is some programming that comes before and follows these INPUT lines, but the idea is that each INPUT request is handled separately.

The same thing can be accomplished in a much simpler way:

                    100 INPUT A, B, C

In both instances, the computer would first print a question mark and halt all operations until the user typed in the value for variable A. Then the computer would print another question mark, waiting for a value for variable B. Finally, it would print another question mark, and go on with the program only after receiving a value for C from the keyboard. The computer works just as hard in both cases, but the programmer doesn't.

For that matter, the operator doesn't have to work as hard either. When using a program that is set up with three separate INPUT statements, the user has to respond to each one of them by typing in the desired value and striking the ENTER key. When using the single-line version with commas, the operator enters the value for A, inserts a comma, inputs the value for B, types another comma, types the value for C, and *then* strikes the ENTER key.

Look at a specific example:

EXAMPLE 5-13

        10 CLS
        20 PRINT "TYPE THE NAME OF THE MONTH, DAY, YEAR"
        30 PRINT TAB(20) "EXAMPLE: MAY, 10,1979"
        40 INPUT A$,A,B
        50 CLS
        60 PRINT "TODAY IS "A$;A ","B
        70 END

Running this program, the operator first sees

TYPE THE NAME OF THE MONTH, DAY, YEAR
EXAMPLE: MAY, 10,1979

?_

Now the system is expecting three different pieces of information separated by commas: a string value spelling out the name of the month, a
numerical value for the day, and a second numerical value for the year.
Suppose the operator types JULY,11,198∅. That being the case, after
striking the ENTER key, the operator sees on the screen:

JULY 11, 198∅
READY
>_

> *Principle.* A single INPUT statement can handle a number of
> string and numerical values as long as they are separated by
> commas. And when the values are entered from the keyboard,
> they, too, must be separated by commas.

Take a good look at line 60 in Example 5–13. This is a multiple
PRINT line containing three different kinds of PRINT commands.
If you have trouble understanding the rationale behind the punctuation in that line, recall this note from Section 2–3: A single PRINT
line can contain any combination of PRINT variables or quoted
phrases as long as each one is separated from the preceding one by a
comma, semicolon, or quotation mark. All three kinds of punctuation
are used for a specific purpose on that particular PRINT line.

There is yet another way to simplify the routines for inputting
information from the keyboard. Until now, all INPUT statements
following some sort of explanatory PRINT command have been programmed on at least two lines: one for the explanatory statement
and one for the INPUT statement.

For example, if you want to tell the operator to input a value for
the numerical variable X, you would probably handle the programming this way:

```
2∅ PRINT "ENTER THE VALUE OF A"
3∅ INPUT A
```

The scheme certainly works, but it so happens there is an easier way
to do the same thing:

```
2∅ INPUT "ENTER THE VALUE OF A";A
```

Stated in a formal fashion:

INPUT *"expression"* ;*variable value*

In other words, you can insert a printed statement within an INPUT program statement. There are just a couple of rules, however. First, the quoted expression must follow the INPUT statement; and second, the *variable value* must be separated from the quoted expression by a semicolon.

Here is a simple example:

EXAMPLE 5-14

```
10 CLS
20 INPUT "WHAT DAY IS THIS";D$
30 CLS
40 PRINT "TODAY IS"D$
```

Running this program, the operator first sees

WHAT DAY IS THIS?_

Maybe the operator responds by typing TUESDAY and striking the ENTER key. Line 30 then clears the screen, and line 40 prints the final result:

```
TODAY IS TUESDAY
READY
>_
```

The more "traditional" way to handle the program would be:

```
10 CLS
20 PRINT "WHAT DAY IS THIS";
30 INPUT D$
40 CLS
50 PRINT "TODAY IS"D$
```

The original program is shorter and it occupies less memory space. Program execution is also a lot faster, but that's a trivial point when working with programs that are as short as these.

Now, let's put together all the ideas introduced in this chapter. The problem is one of calculating the value of the equation $Ax^2 + Bx + C = D$, where the operator inputs the values of A, B, C, and x from the keyboard.

EXAMPLE 5-15

```
10 CLS
20 INPUT "ENTER VALUES A,B,C,X";A,B,C,X
30 PRINT
40 PRINT "D="A*X↑2+B*X+C
```

After entering RUN, a complete routine might look like this:

```
ENTER VALUES A,B,C,X? 1,2,3,-2

D=3
READY
>_
```

What would the program look like if it were not possible to place printed expressions within an INPUT statement and fit more than one variable into the statement? Well, in part, it would look something like this:

```
10 CLS
20 PRINT "ENTER THE 'A' VALUE"
30 INPUT A
40 PRINT "ENTER THE 'B' VALUE"
50 INPUT B
```

and so on, and on, and on . . .

5-7 Using Colons for Multiple-Statement Lines

There is one more scheme for simplifying some of the programming routines. This one pays off sometimes, but at other times it's more trouble than it's worth. For the sake of its positive value, let's give it a bit of consideration.

It is possible to include more than one program statement on a single program line, provided the statements are separated by a colon. Suppose, for example, you want to skip four lines in succession on the screen (a formatting scheme you think is appropriate). There is actually a choice of two different ways to handle the situation:

```
10 PRINT          10 PRINT:PRINT:PRINT:PRINT
20 PRINT
30 PRINT
40 PRINT    or
```

Take your pick. The computer does the same thing in either case.

Using multiple-statement lines, Example 5-15 could be rewritten as:

```
10 CLS:INPUT "ENTER VALUES A,B,C,X";A,B,C,X
20 PRINT:PRINT "D="A*X↑2+B*X+C
```

The only disadvantage inherent in using multiple-statement lines is that it becomes more difficult to change a statement within such a line. Unless the computer system happens to have a moderately sophisticated EDIT mode, changing just one character in a line means wiping out the whole thing and starting all over again. A related problem is specifying GOTO statements: If a GOTO statement carries operations to a multiple-statement line, the entire line will be executed.

5-8   Tightening Up Programs—In Retrospect

By way of a summary for this chapter, it is quite instructive to go back to earlier chapters and see how it is possible to tighten up some of those programs.

Try the program in Example 4-3b:

```
10 CLS: INPUT"TERMINAL NUMBER";B
40 A=0
50 PRINT A↑2
60 A=A+1:IF A>=B THEN 50
80 PRINT "DONE": END
```

Actually, this program could be rewritten quite a few different ways, many of them perhaps better than this one. Again, that is where a programmer's personal style begins showing through.

Example 4-4 appears rather lengthy. Try tightening it up:

```
10 CLS:A=0:PRINT "ZERO"
40 INPUT C$
50 CLS:A=A+1
70 IF A=1 PRINT "ONE";IF A=2 PRINT "TWO"
90 IF A=3 PRINT "THREE":IF A=4 PRINT "FOUR"
110 IF A=5 PRINT "FIVE"
120 IF A<=5 THEN 40: GOTO 10
140 END
```

The only thing to watch out for in this example is making certain that the THEN and GOTO statements in line 120 carry the program back to a valid point. For example, you would be in trouble if INPUT C$ from line 40 were tacked onto the end of line 10—there would be no way to get to that statement without executing all the statements preceding it; and you don't want to do that in this case.

Example 5–5 could look more like this:

```
10 CLS
20 FOR N=0 TO 100:PRINT N;:NEXT
50 END
```

And Example 5–9c like this:

```
10 CLS
20 INPUT"WHAT INTERVAL";I
40 CLS:X=0:NL=0:A=X↑2
80 IF A>63 THEN 140
90 PRINT TAB(A)"*":NL=NL+1
110 IF NL>14 THEN 140
120 X=X+I: GOTO 70
140 GOTO 140
```

EXERCISES

5–1 What will the following programs do?

(a) `10 PRINT "A";: GOTO 10`

(b) `10 PRINT "A": GOTO 10`

(c) `10 PRINT "A",: GOTO 10`

(d) `10 PRINT TAB(32)"A"; GOTO 10`

5–2 A certain programming task calls for setting up five columns of numbers. If each number has five digits in it, and their columns are tabbed at 0, 10, 20, 30, and 40, what are the tab numbers for column headings A, B, C, D, and E? The letter headings must be centered over their respective columns.

5–3 What is the difference between INPUT A$ and INPUT A$;?

5–4 Devise a program that will print a character or string at TAB(31) all by itself, 10 lines down from the top of the screen.

5–5 Using Exercise 5–4 as a starting point, devise a program that will allow you to print any character or string at some X, Y coordinate on the screen. You ought to be able to specify the nature of the character or string, The Y coordinate (line number), and the X coordinate (the TAB number).

5-6 See if you can devise a program that uses TAB statements as tools for building this figure on the screen:

```
        #########
        #  -  -  #
       &#  *   *  #&
        #   ' '   #
        #  -O-   #
        ( ( ( ( ) ) ) )
           ( ( ) )
```

CHAPTER 6

Sorting with ON...GOTO
and
Scrambling with RND(n)

Statements introduced in this chapter:

ON . . . GOTO   RND(n)   RANDOM

The BASIC statements introduced in this chapter are studies in contrasts. The ON . . . GOTO statement can be a powerful tool for sorting and decoding information, and RND(n) and RANDOM provide ways for scrambling things.

6–1 The ON n GOTO line numbers Statement

To get a feeling for how the ON n GOTO line numbers statement works, consider the following example:

EXAMPLE 6–1

```
10 CLS
20 INPUT "ENTER A NUMBER, 1 THRU 5";N
30 ON N GOTO 50, 60, 70, 80, 90
40 PRINT "YOU GOOFED IT. TRY AGAIN": GOTO 20
50 PRINT "*":GOTO 20
60 PRINT "**":GOTO 20
```

```
70 PRINT "***":GOTO 20
80 PRINT "****":GOTO 20
90 PRINT "*****"GOTO 20
100 END
```

There is nothing new in the first two lines. Line 10 merely clears the screen, and line 20 instructs the user and allows a numerical value for N to be entered from the keyboard.

Line 30 is the case in point here. This single line says this:

```
IF N=1 THEN 50
IF N=2 THEN 60
IF N=3 THEN 70
IF N=4 THEN 80
IF N=5 THEN 90
```

The line actually says more than that, but the example will suffice for the time being. The point is that an ON *n* GOTO *line numbers* statement permits you to select one of any number of GOTO branching statements, depending upon the integer value of *n*.

Upon picking up a value for *n* the system counts that number of designated line numbers, and causes control to shift to that particular line number.

Principle. An ON *n* GOTO *line number, line number* . . . statement permits the execution of any one of a number of possible GOTO *line number* branches. The one that is executed is determined by the integer value of *n*; and the system goes to the *n*th line number in the designated sequence of line numbers.

Suppose, for example, the operator using the program in Example 6–1 enters the numeral 2 in response to the INPUT statement in line 20. In that case N=2, and the system counts the line numbers designated in line 30 until it comes to the second one. The line number designated there is 60, so the system does a GOTO 60.

Line 60 then tells the system to print two asterisks and then return to line 20 to pick up another value for N. In essence, this little program translates numerals 1 through 5 into an equal number of asterisks printed on the screen.

As one more example, suppose the operator enters the numeral 5. N=5 in that case; and upon seeing line 30 of the program, the system counts over to the fifth line-number designation, which is line 90.

The computer then does a GOTO 90, which calls for printing five asterisks and returning to line 20 again.

It is really a rather simple sort of routine once you catch on to it. But as promised earlier in this discussion, there is more to the statement than these examples might lead you to believe there is.

For one thing, you should be able to see that the ON n GOTO *line numbers* statement involves some internal counting operation—counting designated line numbers out to the nth one. That fact implies that n ought to be an integer, a whole number. It doesn't make a whole lot of sense to try counting out to the 2.5th line number.

The inventors of this statement were apparently sympathetic to this idea and built in an automatic roundoff feature. So if the value of n is specified as something other than an integer, the system automatically figures the least-integer value and adjusts n accordingly.

So if the operator using the program in Example 6–1 happens to enter 2.16678 as a value for N, the system automatically does a greatest-integer operation on the number, setting n to 2. So entering a numeral such as 2.16678 (or in fact any numeral between 2 and 2.99999) will result in an n value of 2, and the system prints two asterisks (by line 60).

The program in Example 6–1, then, can actually handle values of N between 1 and 5.99999 without any difficulty at all.

The meaning of line 30 in Example 6–1 can thus be represented by

```
IF N=1 through 1.99999 THEN 50
IF N=2 through 2.99999 THEN 60
IF N=3 through 3.99999 THEN 70
IF N=4 through 4.99999 THEN 80
IF N=5 through 5.99999 THEN 90
```

(The lowercase letters are not legitimate parts of a program statement, but are shown here to clarify the explanation.) In any event, that's a lot of ideas tied up in a single-line statement. But there is even more to the matter—look at line 40.

Line 40 is a default statement that is used only when the value of n exceeds the number of designated GOTO lines in the ON n GOTO *line numbers* statement. In Example 6–1, entering a value of N that is equal to 6 or more causes the system to count through all of the designated line numbers and, in effect, "drop off the end." Whenever that happens, the system ignores the ON n GOTO *line numbers* statement and goes on to the next line, line 40 in this case.

Upon going to line 40 by default in Example 6–1, the system is instructed to print YOU GOOFED IT. TRY AGAIN and then return to line 20 to start over.

Bearing in mind that the execution of an ON *n* GOTO *line numbers* statement involves an integer counting operation, one might wonder what the system will do with a *n* value of zero or between zero and 0.99999. That is a good question, because the response might well vary from one kind of personal computer BASIC to another. In the case of Radio Shack's TRS-80, *n* values from 0 through 0.99999 are treated as 1 through 1.99999. A zero, in other words, is treated as a 1; but the 1 is still treated as a 1, and that can cause some confusion. The moral of the story is to check a current version of your own manual to see how the system treats *n* values between 0 and 0.99999 in these ON *n* GOTO *line numbers* statements.

While on the subject of *n* values between 0 and 1, it must be said that BASIC cannot handle *n* values less than zero—that is, negative values. Counting out to the (-2)nd line does not make any sense to people or to computers.

Don't be discouraged about the fact that your system will have trouble working with *n* values that are less than 1 or negative. There is a way around it.

First consider a good way to resolve the ambiguity surrounding a need for dealing with an *n* value of 0 through 0.99999:

EXAMPLE 6-2

```
10 CLS
20 INPUT "ENTER A NUMBER BETWEEN 0 AND 4";N
30 ON N+1 GOTO 50, 60, 70, 80, 90
40 PRINT "YOU BLEW IT. TRY AGAIN":GOTO 20
50 PRINT "ZERO": GOTO 20
60 PRINT "ONE": GOTO 20
70 PRINT "TWO": GOTO 20
80 PRINT "THREE ":GOTO 20
90 PRINT "FOUR":GOTO 20
100 END
```

This program can deal with an INPUT value of zero because 1 is added to N before the count-out operation in line 30 begins. Entering a 0 at line 20 actually makes the system look for the 0+1, or first GOTO line number. Entering a 1 makes it look for the 1+1, or second line number; and so on.

In essence, line 30 in Example 6-2 demonstrates the application of an ON *math* GOTO *line numbers* statement, where *math* is any mathematical function that generates a numerical value of 1 or greater.

As far as the operator is concerned, the range of legitimate input values in Example 6–2 is between 0 and 4.99999. In this case, entering a value of 5 or more would cause the default, error statement to appear on the screen (from line 40).

What about negative numbers entered at line 20? Well, that is still a problem. It can be resolved only by structuring the program differently. If the operator shouldn't be entering any negative values in the first place, you can goof-proof the program by inserting

25 IF N<∅ THEN 4∅

That being the case, entering a negative number (a number less than zero) will satisfy this new line 25, causing the error text in line 40 to appear on the screen.

But if negative numbers are supposed to be legitimate entries, the *math* portion of ON *math* GOTO *line numbers* must be written so that it creates a numerical value of 1 or more.

At this point in your experience with BASIC, applications of the ON . . . GOTO statements are pretty much limited to decoding or encoding operations of the kind already illustrated in Examples 6–1 and 6–2. Used in this fashion, the statements replace a series of sequential conditionals with a single-line statement calling for a GOTO line number *n* or line number *math*.

The real power of the notion becomes quite apparent in the more advanced topics, which, in essence, deal with running through a sequence of operations amid a host of alternatives.

The following note summarizes the special features of ON . . . GOTO.

Note. When using the ON *n* GOTO *line number, line number* statement, *n* is ideally an integer between 1 and *k,* where *k* is the number of line numbers designated in the statement. But . . .

1. When *n* is less than 1 or negative, the system usually generates an error signal of its own and returns to the command mode of operation (check your manual for specific details).

2. When *n* is not an integer, the number is rounded off to its greatest-integer value (all numerals to the right of the decimal point are dropped).

3. When the greatest-integer value of *n* is greater than *k,* the system automatically defaults to the program line following the ON . . . GOTO statement.

6-2 Scrambled Numbers from RND(n)

A number of years ago, computer technologists began realizing the importance of having access to a table of random numbers. Nowadays, virtually all BASIC schemes include a random-number-generating function designated RND(n), where n is some user-specified number that determines the range of random numbers.

Technically speaking, RND(n) is not a true random-number generator. Rather, it is a function that generates a long sequence of quasi-random numbers; and it turns out that the sequence is repeated after a time. Nevertheless, RND(n) is adequate for most applications of small computers, and for most practical applications, it is a true random generator.

Now there is another problem with the RND(n) function that is far more significant: Manufacturers of BASIC-oriented personal computers cannot seem to get together on what to do with the function when n is a number equal to 1 or less.

There is universal agreement about n values greater than 1. Whenever n is an integer greater than 1, RND(n) yields up a random number between 1 and n. So if you specify a statement such as Y=RND(1Ø), Y will be set to some integer value between 1 and 10; and that value will most likely change each time the statement is executed.

Principle. A RND(n) statement generates a randomly selected number between 1 and n inclusively every time it is encountered in a program—provided n is greater than 1.

Here is a simple program for demonstrating the operation of the RND(n) statement:

EXAMPLE 6–3

```
10 CLS
20 FOR N=0 TO 55
30 PRINT RND(10),
40 NEXT
50 END
```

The program in this case fills the screen with four columns of random numbers between 1 and 10. If you want to extend the range of random values to 100, simply change line 30 to read PRINT RND(1ØØ).

Getting a set of random numbers beginning with a number other than 1 is a simple matter of doing a bit of arithmetic. Suppose that you want to generate random numbers in the range 0 to 9. There are still 10 integers involved here, so RND(1∅) is still appropriate; and all that has to be done to adjust the upper and lower limits is to subtract 1 from the result: RND(1∅)-1. Substitute that expression into line 30 in Example 6–3 and you will fill the screen with columns of random numbers between 0 and 9.

In fact, the result of any RND(n) statement can be modified by combining it with some other mathematical expression.

But the matter becomes less specific when dealing with n values of 1 or less. On Radio Shack's TRS–80, RND(1) always turns up a value of 1, while RND(∅) produces random numbers between 0 and 1 exclusively.

Note. Check the BASIC manual for your own system to see how it handles RND(n) when n is equal to 1 or less.

Before going into some fun and instructive applications of the RND(n) statement, it is important to return to the notion that the numbers are actually quasi-random, not truly random. The numbers are generated according to a program, or *algorithm,* built within the BASIC structure. This algorithm relies upon picking up a single random number and using it as the basis for generating all the others.

Whenever the computer system is turned on and whenever a program is first run, the system automatically selects that first "seed" number. It will then use that same seed throughout the program, generating a long sequence of quasi-random numbers from it.

To lend a bit more randomness to the RND(n) function, it is a good idea to change that seed number occasionally; and that can be done every time the system encounters a RANDOM statement in the program.

Principle. A RANDOM statement generates a new, randomly selected "seed" number for the BASIC random-number-generating algorithm.

RANDOM does not have to be used at all for very simple programs. Where RND(n) is used a large number of times within a more complex program, however, the RANDOM statement ought to be included at a few selected points.

Just where a programmer ought to insert a RANDOM statement is mostly a matter of taste, habit, and style. Bear in mind that it does nothing more than "reseed" the little automatic program for generating random numbers for RND(*n*). Of course, using RANDOM in a program that does not include any RND(*n*) statements is a waste of program memory.

Here is a short program that demonstrates some of the entertaining features of the RND(*n*) function:

EXAMPLE 6-4

```
10 CLS
20 PRINT TAB(RND(63))"."
30 GOTO 20
```

This program prints a single period on a line, and at a horizontal position determined by the TAB value. The TAB value in this case is a randomly generated number between 1 and 63—so the period appears on the line at any one of the 63 available spaces [excluding TAB($\emptyset$)].

After printing the period somewhere on a line, line 30 in the program instructs the computer to return to line 20. The system then prints another period on the next line and at some point that is again randomly determined.

Overall, the result is a screen full of randomly tabbed periods that begin moving up the screen as the scrolling effect takes place. The viewer gets the impression of moving amid stars in outer space.

Since this program is built around a continuous GOTO loop, the only way to get out of it is by striking the BREAK key.

Of course, any decent spacecraft ought to have a speed control on it. So polish the program by inserting the following statements:

```
15 INPUT "SET SPEED (1 TO 100)"; S
25 FOR T=0 TO 100-S: NEXT
```

Now the program looks like this:

```
10 CLS
15 INPUT "SET SPEED (1 TO 100)";S
20 PRINT TAB(RND(63))"."
25 FOR T=0 TO 100-S: NEXT
30 GOTO 20
```

Now the program begins by asking for a number between 1 and 100 that represents how fast you want to move through the "stars." After entering that value, you will see the first "star" printed somewhere along the next line as the system executes the instruction in line 20. After that, there will be a short time delay before the next star appears. That time delay is fixed by line 25, using a FOR . . . TO, NEXT combination that counts between 0 and 100–S.

Incidentally, the whole idea behind using 100–S instead of just S is to make the "speed" appear proportional to the size of the number entered at line 15. You ought to be thinking about such little details by now. It is impractical to teach little tricks of this type because there are so many of them, but it so happens that having a command of such "tricks" often makes the difference between an ordinary programmer and a highly successful one. The only practical way to gather the right kind of insight is by thinking things through, using your imagination and, above all, trying your ideas on a firsthand basis.

6-3   Developing a Dice Game Program

An ordinary die—the kind used for countless games in the world today—is a fine example of a random-number generator. The little thing tends to generate random integers between 1 and 6.

Simulating the action of a single die is a rather straightforward programming operation.

EXAMPLE 6-5

```
10 CLS
20 INPUT R$
30 D=RND(6)
40 CLS
50 PRINT D
60 GOTO 20
```

Basically, this program generates a randomly selected number between 1 and 6 each time the operator strikes the ENTER key. The numeral appears in the upper left-hand corner of the screen, because the screen is cleared by line 40 before the numeral is printed. Figure 6-1 is a flowchart for this sort of program.

Now if you want to give the program a bit more class, try inserting the following lines:

```
42 PRINT "DICE-1"
44 FOR N=0 TO 5: PRINT: NEXT
50 PRINT TAB(30)D
```

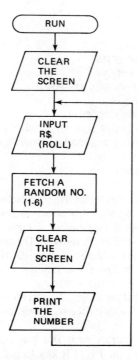

Figure 6-1 Flowchart for a simple dice-roll program (Example 6-5).

With this slight modification at work, the expression DICE-1 appears in the upper left-hand corner of the screen, while the randomly selected number (the die value) is near the center of the screen.

Inserting line 44 into the program effectively causes six carriage-return operations to appear in sequence, thus moving the next line of printed information seven lines below that of the expression DICE-1. Rewriting line 50 to include a TAB(3∅) then causes the numeral to appear about halfway across the screen.

The die is still "rolled" each time the user strikes the ENTER key, and the result always appears near the center of a neat-looking screen.

A good many dice games call for using two dice at the same time, as the following example illustrates.

EXAMPLE 6-6

```
10 CLS
20 INPUT R$
30 RANDOM
40 D1=RND(6):D2=RND(6)
50 CLS
60 PRINT "DICE-2"
70 FOR L=0 TO 5:PRINT:NEXT
80 PRINT TAB(20)D1;:PRINT TAB(40)D2
90 GOTO 20
100 END
```

With this program, the user effectively rolls two dice each time he strikes the ENTER key (entering the null string in response to the INPUT statement in line 20). Line 40 is responsible for generating random numbers between 1 and 6 for the two dice, designated D1 and D2.

After the two values are selected in line 40, the CLS statement in line 50 clears the screen and then line 60 causes the message DICE-2 to appear in the upper left-hand corner of the screen.

Line 70 carries the system down the screen six additional lines, and line 80 causes the values of the two dice to appear side by side, but separated by 20 tab spaces.

A question mark and cursor near the lower left-hand side of the screen reminds the user to strike the ENTER key to roll the dice again.

The RANDOM statement in line 30 isn't absolutely necessary for this simple RND(n) program, but it is included here for purposes of illustration. In this case, the random-number generator is "reseeded" each time the user rolls the dice.

If you think you understand these dice programs and, hopefully, have had a chance to try them on a machine, it is time to go on to something even more sophisticated.

A few dice games require a single die, and many games require two of them. But there are some families of games that require any number of dice, up to five of them. The following program lets the user select the number of dice to be used in a game. What is more important, however, is the introduction of a different sort of way to use the ON . . . GOTO statement. See if you can figure out how and why the program works the way it does.

EXAMPLE 6-7

```
10 CLS
20 INPUT "NUMBER OF DICE USED (1 TO 5)";N
```

```
30 IF N>5 THEN 70
40 D1=RND(6):D2=RND(6):D3=RND(6):D4=RND(6):D5=RND(6)
50 FOR L=0 TO 5:PRINT:NEXT
60 ON 6-N GOTO 80, 90, 100, 110, 120
70 PRINT "BAD NUMBER OF DICE. DO AGAIN.":GOTO 20
80 PRINT TAB(10)D5;
90 PRINT TAB(20)D4;
100 PRINT TAB(30)D3;
110 PRINT TAB(40)D2;
120 PRINT TAB(50)D1;
130 FOR L=0 TO 5:PRINT:NEXT
140 INPUT "ENTER TO ROLL AGAIN";R$
150 RANDOM:CLS:GOTO 40
```

Lines 10, 20, and 30 merely get things started, allowing the user to select the number of dice to be used in the game. Line 30 takes care of the case where the user might enter a number larger than 5, which would, of course blow up the whole program. If the user does respond to the INPUT statement in line 20 with an N value larger than 5, line 30 picks up the fact and sends control down to line 70.

Whenever line 70 is executed, the user sees the message BAD NUMBER OF DICE. DO AGAIN; and control is automatically returned to line 20, where things start all over again.

This goof-proofing feature makes it impossible to start the game until the user enters a value for N is 5 or less. What about values that are less than 1? Well, that situation will be covered later in a different fashion.

After the user enters the proper number of dice, the five RND(6) statements in line 40 generates a random number, between 1 and 6 inclusively, for each of the five dice. All five pick up a random value on this line, no matter how many are actually used in the game. The die values, you might note, are designated D1, D2, D3, D4, and D5.

After picking up a random value for each of the dice, line 50 causes the system to skip down six lines on the screen before printing anything. Then comes the ON . . . GOTO statement in line 60.

Notice the use of ON 6-N GOTO *line numbers*. Why is the math expression 6-N used here instead of the usual sort of N expression? You'll see why in a moment.

What is more important now is to see how the program is protected from entering "number of dice" less than 1. Recall from Chapter 5 that an ON *n* GOTO *line numbers* statement defaults and goes to the next program line if the least-integer value of *n* is greater than the number of designated *line numbers*. In this particular program, the system will default to line 70 if 6-N is greater than 5 (there are five line numbers specified in the statement).

Now that means 6-N must not be greater than 5, and that is the same as saying N must not be less than 1. So if the user happens to respond to the INPUT statement in line 20 with a number less than 1, the program will begin normal execution until it defaults at line 60. At that time, control goes to line 70, which prints out the error message and causes the whole program to start again from line 20. The user then has a chance to correct the mistake.

The program is thus fully protected against invalid entries as far as the number of dice to be used is concerned. Line 30 takes care of the instances where the user might try to specify too many dice, and the default feature of the ON . . . GOTO statement takes care of cases where the user might try to enter a number of dice that is too small. The conditional statement in line 30 represents a very direct approach to the matter, while the trick in lines 60 and 70 represent a somewhat more subtle approach. But using the ON . . . GOTO feature to cover the case where N is less than 1 saves at least one program line.

Certainly, one could insert a line 35 that might read IF N<1 GOTO 70; or better yet, amend line 30 to include a logical OR clause of the kind described later in this book. But it is always better to take advantage of existing features, doubling up functions wherever possible—making the sequence of operations in lines 60 and 70 cover the case where N is less than 1, for example.

A programmer doesn't do this sort of thing just to show off. It is more a matter of using some of the less obvious features of existing program statements to keep the wits sharpened and pick up additional experience. At some time and in some way, such sharp-witted experience will pay off, giving the programmer a chance to do some things far more efficiently and effectively than most others in the business can. Some wise philosopher of practical life once stated that 10 percent additional effort reaps 100 percent superior results. That's the case in point here. And if you can buy the idea, you can start putting it to work right now.

Lines 80 through 120 are responsible for printing the dice values along a single line near the middle of the screen. Looking at the various TAB values, you can see that the value of D5 die is always printed near the left-hand side of the screen, the value of D4 is printed a bit farther to the right (10 additional tab values, to be precise), and the value of dice D3 is printed near the middle of the screen.

In short, the values for D5 through D1 are printed from left to right across the screen. D1 is printed near the right-hand edge and D5 near the left-hand edge.

To see why the dicd values are printed in this reverse order (and why line 60 uses a 6–N expression), consider a particular example. Suppose the user decides to use two dice. That being the case, line 60 selects the GOTO line number on the basis of 6 minus 2, or 4. The fourth GOTO line in line 60 is 110. So calling for two dice means the dice-value printing operation begins at line 110.

Now line 110 calls for printing the value of D2 at TAB 40, followed by line 120, which calls for printing the value of D1 at TAB 50. After that, the system runs out of printing statements and goes on to other things.

Suppose, however, the user specifies five dice. That being the case, line 60 does its GOTO operation on the basis of 6 minus 5, or the first designated GOTO line, line 80 in this case. Going to line 80 means doing all five printing and tabbing operations specified in lines 80 through 120. The values for all five dice thus appear lined up across the middle of the screen.

Again, there are more straightforward ways to specify the number of dice values to be printed—ways more obvious than using a 6-N expression in line 60 and printing the dice values in reverse order. Given the statements described through the first six chapters of this book, however, there is good reason to doubt that any alternative method could produce a simpler program than the one in this example.

Lines 130 through 150 are responsible for properly recycling the program for another roll of the dice. Line 130 injects another set of six blank lines, and line 140 prints the message ENTER TO ROLL AGAIN and give the user a chance to "roll the dice" by striking the ENTER key—entering the null string value for R$.

Upon seeing that the user has hit the ENTER key, the program reseeds the random-number generator, clears the screen, and returns program control back to line 40. Line 40 sets new random values for all the dice, and the whole thing is under way again.

Note that program control does not return back to the very beginning. There is no need to specify the number of dice each time they are rolled. The only way to select a different number of dice is by getting out of the program with a BREAK and entering RUN to start from the beginning.

Example 6-8 is a modified version of the dice game just described. This revised version adds a total dice score and a message indicating how many dice are in play.

EXAMPLE 6-8

```
10 CLS
20 INPUT "NUMBER OF DICE TO BE USED (1 TO 5)";N
30 IF N 5 THEN 70
40 D1=RND(6):D2=RND(6):D3=RND(6):D4=RND(6):D5=RND(6)
50 FOR L=0 TO 5:PRINT:NEXT
55 T=0
60 ON N-6 GOTO 80, 90, 100, 110, 120
70 PRINT "BAD NUMBER OF DICE. DO AGAIN":GOTO 20
80 PRINT TAB(10)D5;: T=T+D5
90 PRINT TAB(20)D4;: T=T+D4
100 PRINT TAB(30)D3;: T=T+D3
110 PRINT TAB(40)D2;: T=T+D2
120 PRINT TAB(50)D1;: T=T+D1
130 FOR L=0 TO 5: PRINT:NEXT:PRINT TAB(40)"TOTAL="T
140 INPUT "ENTER TO ROLL AGAIN";R$
150 RANDOM:CLS:PRINT N"-DIE GAME":GOTO 40
```

The basic operation of this program is identical to the one described in Example 6–7. Lines 80 through 120, however, each include a summing statement that totals the values shown on the dice. The value of T is set to zero whenever the program is run (line 55); and after the system does a GOTO to one of the dice-value printing lines, the value of T is totaled up from that point on. The last program statement in line 140 is responsible for printing out the dice-value total, T.

The additional message statement in line 150 causes N–DIE GAME to appear in the upper left-hand corner of the screen. N, of course, is the number of dice selected by the user in response to the INPUT statement in line 20.

A challenging variation of either of these two dice programs would be one that shows images of the actual dice rather than numerical equivalents of the values. The job could be done with some TAB graphics, and the programming task is left to the student who happens to possess an extraordinary level of positive motivation.

6–4   A Sentence-Generating Program

One of the most fruitful areas of computer research these days is in the area of machine or artificial intelligence. This sort of work quite often takes the form of having a machine generate understandable words and sentences that relay some meaningful information about the world as the machine perceives it.

The program in Example 6–9 is a sentence-generating program that serves as another illustration of how RND(n) and ON . . . GOTO statements can be applied. If you feel intellectually prepared to deal with matters bordering on the vanguard of modern computer technology, you will enjoy this one. And if you happen to have ready access to a computer system, you ought to enter and run this program before studying its more subtle details. You will be a better person for it.

EXAMPLE 6–9

```
10 CLS: FOR L=0 TO 6: PRINT: NEXT
20 PRINT "THIS IS A COMMUNICATIONS PROJECT."
25 PRINT "YOUR COMPUTER WILL BE ATTEMPTING TO COMMUNICATE"
30 PRINT "MEANINGFUL AND HIGH-CLASS INFORMATION TO YOU."
35 PRINT "STRIKE THE 'ENTER' KEY WHEN YOU ARE INTELLECTUALLY"
40 PRINT "PREPARED TO ASSIMILATE MORE KNOWLEDGE."
45 INPUT S$
```

```
50 CLS:A=RND(5):B=RND(5):C=RND(5)
60 ON A GOTO 100, 105, 110, 115, 120
70 ON B GOTO 125, 130, 135, 140, 145
80 ON C GOTO 150, 155, 160, 165, 170
90 PRINT "THE "A$" "B$" THE "C$
95 PRINT: PRINT: GOTO 35
100 A$="DOG": GOTO 70
105 A$="CAT": GOTO 70
110 A$="MOUSE": GOTO 70
115 A$="ELEPHANT": GOTO 70
120 A$="TURTLE": GOTO 70
125 B$="ATE": GOTO 80
130 B$="JUMPED OVER": GOTO 80
135 B$="CHASED": GOTO 80
140 B$="SLIPPED AND SQUASHED": GOTO 80
145 B$="SAT ON": GOTO 80
150 C$="CHICKEN": GOTO 90
155 C$="GARDEN HOSE": GOTO 90
160 C$="LAKE AND ALL ITS CONTENTS": GOTO 90
165 C$="HOUSE": GOTO 90
170 C$="ELEPHANT": GOTO 90
```

This program embodies practically every principle discussed in the first chapters of this book. It's a real showpiece of intellectual endeavor; and if you are a student, you might want to demonstrate this program to your parents or spouse, showing them that the time and money invested in a higher education is worth the sacrifice.

There are some principles illustrated in this example that go beyond the actual performance of the program. Note, for instance, the extensive heading statement. Most computers will accept PRINT lines having up to 255 characters. Most personal computers do not use "intelligent terminals," though, and it's quite likely that a long heading statement will be broken and picked up on the next line right in the middle of a word—at an awkward place that isn't marked by a hyphen and syllable break. So the usual procedure is to use multiple-line PRINT statements that break the sentence or paragraph exactly where you want it broken.

Line 50 is simply another application of a multiple-statement RND($\underline{n}$) operation, specifically generating three numbers between 1 and 5. A RANDOM statement could be inserted at the beginning of line 50 to reseed the random-number generator each time it is used.

Operations bounce around a great deal between lines 60 through 80 and 100 through 170. You can see how this set of three ON . . . GOTO statements work together by assigning some arbitrary values to variables, A, B, and C. Of course, those values have to be integers between 1 and 5 inclusively.

Note that there are no goof-proofing statements surrounding the ON (*numerical variable*) GOTO *line numbers* statements. There is no need for them. The values of A, B, and C are selected by the computer itself; and as everyone knows, computers never make mistakes.

Of course, you can assign any values you desire to the A$, B$, and C$ string variables in lines 100 through 170. In this particular application A$ variables represent the subject of a sentence, B$ is the verb, and C$ is the direct object.

EXERCISES

6-1   What is the greatest-integer value for the following numbers:
  (a)   2.4
  (b)   5.55
  (c)   67.8
  (d)   67.01

6-2   Which of the following numbers will *not* be generated by the function RND(2∅)?
  (a)   1
  (b)   ∅
  (c)   1.2
  (d)   19
  (e)   2∅
  (f)   21

6-3   What is the purpose of the RANDOM statement when used in conjunction with RND(n) statements elsewhere in a program?

6-4   Write a single-statement line for generating random integers between –5 and +5.

6-5   Under what condition does a ON . . . GOTO statement default to the program line that follows it?

6-6   What is the purpose of line 50 in Example 6-7?

6-7   Under what two conditions does the computer execute line 70 in Example 6-7?

6-8   What is the reason for placing semicolons at the end of lines 80 through 120 in Example 6-7?

6-9   The PRINT TAB statements in Example 6-7 are all written on separate program lines. Why is this done, as opposed to collecting them on one or two lines, separating each with a colon? For example:

    80 PRINT TAB(1∅)D5;: PRINT TAB(2∅)D4;:   and so on

6-10 Write a two-dice program that will clearly indicate a WIN!! whenever the sum of the dice values is 7 or 11.

6-11 Referring to Example 6-9, suppose line 50 yields A=1, B=4, and C=3.

- (a) How will the system respond to the ON A GOTO . . . statement in line 60?
- (b) How will the system respond upon going to line 70?
- (c) How will the system respond upon going to line 80?
- (d) What message appears on the screen after executing line 90?

CHAPTER 7

Integrating Smaller Programs
with
GOSUB and RETURN

Statements introduced in this chapter:

GOSUB   RETURN   REM

The programming examples cited so far in this book have been instructive and, hopefully, somewhat entertaining as well. These haven't been your run-of-the-mill programs, however. In the context of modern BASIC programming, they have been exceedingly simple programs.

To be sure, the programs appearing in the first few chapters have done their intended task, but the fact of the matter is that little was expected of them in the first place.

Maybe you are now thinking that a person has to be some sort of genius to assemble more useful and complex BASIC programs. Unfortunately for the ego, that isn't the case. BASIC includes a scheme which, among other things, greatly simplifies the task of building complex programs.

With this particular scheme at hand, a programmer can write, enter, test, and debug bite-sized portions of a program. And after getting all those little building blocks working, the programmer can write just one more program that ties them together into an integrated unit.

These "bite-sized portions" or "building blocks" are actually what are known as *subroutines*—relatively small programs that generally stand on their own.

> *Definition.* A *subroutine* is a relatively small program that performs a single function or class of functions. It is quite often capable of being run as a separate program in its own right.

So, when it comes to building rather complex BASIC programs, the programmer generally divides the job into smaller subroutines. Each subroutine can be treated individually at first and then integrated with all the others by means of a main controlling subroutine.

7-1 A First Look at Subroutines

Suppose you devise a TAB graphics program that causes the figure of an arrow to travel from left to right across the top of the screen. The program might look something like this:

EXAMPLE 7-1a

```
100 FOR H=4 TO 58
110 CLS
120 PRINT TAB(H)"———->"
130 NEXT
140 END
```

Every time you enter RUN 100, the arrow moves across the screen, startin the upper left-hand corner and moving to the upper right-hand corner. Everything comes to a stop after that, because the END statement in line 140 returns the system to its command mode.

This is just another one of those instructive, but hardly sophisticated, demonstration programs. Note, however, that the line numbers begin at 100. There is a good reason for using larger-than-normal line numbers—the program is going to be a subroutine within a larger program.

At any rate, the program in Example 7-1a works so well that you decide to write another program to make the arrow turn around and move from left to right. That program might look this this:

EXAMPLE 7-1b

```
200 FOR H=58 TO 4 STEP -1
210 CLS
```

```
220 PRINT TAB(H)"<————"
230 NEXT
240 END
```

Entering RUN 200, you will see the arrow pointing to the left and moving across the top of the screen from right to left.

Now you should have these two small programs in the computer's memory. You can select either one by entering RUN 100 or RUN 200. But now you want to combine the two programs, creating the impression of an arrow moving continuously back and forth across the screen.

You ought to be able to figure out some ways to combine the two programs by altering a couple of statements and using some new GOTO statements. But that's defeating the point of the demonstration.

The idea is to combine the two programs, treating them as subroutines and devising a third program for integrating into a single unit.

Subroutines are *called* by means of a GOSUB *line number* statement, where *line number* is the first line number in the subroutine being called. In this sense, GOSUB *line number* works just like the unconditional GOTO *line number* statement.

So think about this:

EXAMPLE 7-1c

```
10 CLS
20 GOSUB 100
30 GOSUB 200
40 GOTO 20
50 END
```

This little program first clears the screen and then calls the subroutine beginning at line 100—the little program specified in Example 7-1. Upon executing line 20, the system finds itself running the program that starts at line 100. It still looks like a GOTO 100 statement, right?

What is important now, however, is what happens after the system is finished executing subroutine 100. As it stands, line 140 in that subroutine will return the system to the command mode, and it's all over.

Of course, you don't want the program to conclude that way, so you must do something to subroutine 100—amend line 140 to show a RETURN statement, rather than END.

Subroutine 100 is called by line 20 in the controlling program. The

RETURN statement at the end of subroutine 100 tells the system to go back to the calling program, picking up where it left off. A RETURN statement in subroutine 100, in other words, sends the computer back to line 30—the line following the GOSUB 100 statement.

So now the system is at line 30, which is another GOSUB statement. In this case it calls subroutine 200—the one specified in Example 7-1b. Now if that subroutine is also revised so that it concludes with a RETURN statement at line 240, control goes back to line 50 of the calling program when subroutine 200 has done its job.

The GOTO 20 statement is responsible for recycling the sequence, sending the system back to line 20, which, in turn, calls subroutine 100.

The overall effect on the screen is the figure of an arrow that moves continuously back and forth across the top of the screen, with its point aimed in the direction of travel.

> *Principle.* A GOSUB *line number* statement *calls* a subroutine that begins with the designated line number.
>
> Every subroutine must include a RETURN statement that returns operation to the line following the one that called the subroutine in the first place.

Doing a LIST command, the overall program has this general appearance:

EXAMPLE 7-1d

```
10 CLS
20 GOSUB 100
30 GOSUB 200
40 GOTO 20
50 END
100 FOR H=4 TO 58
110 CLS
120 PRINT TAB(H)"---->"
130 NEXT
140 RETURN
200 FOR H=58 TO 4 STEP -1
210 CLS
220 PRINT TAB(H)"<----"
230 NEXT
240 RETURN
```

Admittedly, this does not make a very compelling case for using subroutines; the job could be done easier with other programming tools already at your disposal. The point, however, is to demonstrate the operation of the GOSUB *line number* statement and its inseparable counterpart, RETURN.

The general programming procedure was to build the individual subroutines separately, checking each one individually to make certain it performed its intended job. Each was assigned a block of memory so that it could coexist without interfering with another.

Finally, the calling program was written and the subroutines were modified slightly to accommodate the need for RETURN statements.

7-2 Designing Moderately Complex Programs with Subroutines

In this section you are going to take a tour through a complete programming job for a moderately complicated task. While studying this material, you should be conscious of the following principles:

1. The importance of carefully defining the task at hand and specifying how the results are to be presented.

2. The usefulness of subroutines as a means for breaking down a complex task into manageable pieces.

3. The power of subroutines as a means of reducing the number of often-repeated operations.

In addition to these main ideas, you will find a host of little tricks and procedures that characterize routine work with subroutines. These will be spelled out and discussed as the occasion arises.

The main idea of this project is to test the quality of the random-number generator in your own computer. As mentioned in Chapter 6, home computers normally generate a quasi-random sequence of numbers that does tend to repeat itself. The program described here will show just how "quasi" quasi-random is.

The general procedure will be to simulate a coin-toss situation— one where 50–50 odds is the ideal result. The program will "toss a coin" a designated number of times and then compile a figure representing the number of "heads" divided by the total number of tosses. The result will be a number between 0 and 1, with 0.5 being the theoretical best result.

And while you're at it, you might as well compare the results of tossing the coin with and without the RANDOM seeding operation. If there is something to the notion that one can get better random numbers by seeding the number generator at certain intervals, the score ought to be closer to 0.5 when using RANDOM than when it is not used.

It's a nice little scientific study that can be about as meaningful as you want it to be.

So the main objective of the program is now defined in at least some general terms: Toss a coin (generate numbers 1 and 2 in a random fashion) some designated number of times and compile the statistical result. Do it first without the benefit of the RANDOM statement, and then with the RANDOM statement inserted into the works.

It now appears there are three aspects to this program. The first is to designate the number of tosses, go through the tossing operations and display the results. Being able to designate the number of tosses is important because it has a significant bearing on the statistical quality of the results—the more times the coin is tossed, the greater the statistical reliability of the final figures.

The tossing operation, itself, is divided into two phases: one without using the RANDOM statement and another that uses the RANDOM statement.

Of course, the results must be displayed on the screen in some meaningful fashion.

Figure 7-1 outlines the general procedure in the form of a preliminary flowchart. When the operator enters RUN, the system should request the number of times the coin is to be tossed (N). After that, the system begins tossing the coin without the RANDOM statement; and this phase continues until the coin is tossed N times. The results of this first phase are then compiled and displayed on the screen.

After that, phase 2 goes into effect, tossing the coin N times with the RANDOM statement inserted into the program. And after N tosses, the results are compiled and displayed on the screen.

You must have a complete understanding of this preliminary flowchart to get any real appreciation of how the program itself will be assembled and executed. One of the most common causes of problems with modern computer programming arises from the fact that the program designer failed to get a complete grasp of the situation before starting to write statements.

Where do you go from here? The answer to that question is another one of those things that depend on the programmer's own style. Some would begin by sketching some program lines at the very beginning, making some notes about the problems encountered and fixing up some of the problems as things develop.

Other programmers would take the preliminary flowchart and

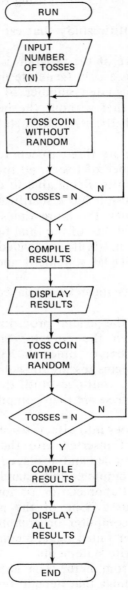

Figure 7-1 A preliminary flowchart for the coin-toss experiment.

begin sketching in more details, not even thinking about getting close to the computer for awhile.

Still others would start dividing the job into specific subroutines, entering some program lines into the machine and modifying things as they go along.

Who's to say there is a *best* way to approach the situation from this point? But to get this discussion moving along, the approach used here will be to design the main subroutines first and then weave them together later.

The key operation in the program is presenting the information on the screen. The importance of this operation lies in the fact that it requires a definition for just about every variable used in the program. So by starting with the display format, you will have a pretty good idea about what has to be done elsewhere.

Borrowing an idea from the disciplines of psychology and human engineering, there ought to be some way to assure the operator that something is actually taking place every step along the way. It is going to take some significant amount of time to do all those coin tosses, and an operator would be justifiably concerned about watching a blank screen—wondering if anything at all is actually taking place.

Weaving this notion into the program, it seems important, or at least highly desirable, to generate a screen display every time a coin is tossed. The fact that all that information might be virtually worthless is beside the point.

Bearing these things in mind, it can be seen that there should be three distinctly different phases in the display process: one kind of display when tossing the coin without the RANDOM statement, another display when tossing the coin with RANDOM, and finally, a display that shows the overall results.

Figure 7–2a through c shows some sketches of the screen as it ought to appear during the three main display phases.

Aside from serving as general guides for formatting the three different kinds of displays, the sketches in Fig. 7–2 help define most of the variables to be used in the program. Here's what the programmer had in mind with regard to the variables:

N = number of times the coin is to be tossed in each phase of the program. This will be specified by the operator at the beginning of a test session.

AH = number of times "heads" appears while running without the RANDOM statement.

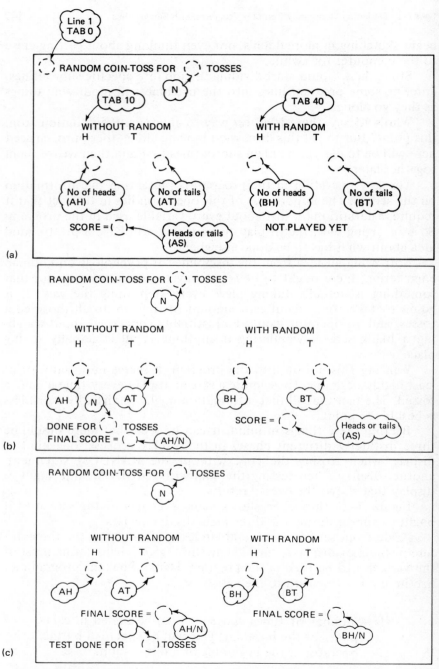

Figure 7-2 Display formatting plans for the coin-toss experiment. (a) Phase-1 format. (b) Phase-2 format. (c) Phase-3 format.

AT = number of times "tails" appears while running without the RANDOM statement.

A$ = result of a current toss—HEADS or TAILS.

AH/N = final score for running without the RANDOM statement, expressed as the ratio of number of heads to the total number of tosses.

BH = number of times "heads" appears while running with the RANDOM statement.

BT = number of times "tails" appears while running with the RANDOM statement.

BH/N = final score for running with the RANDOM statement, expressed as the ratio of number of heads to the total number of tosses.

Now there is enough information available to begin composing a subroutine called ** DISPLAY **.

```
100 REM ** DISPLAY **
110 CLS:PRINT "RANDOM COIN-TOSS FOR "N"TOSSES"
120 FOR L=0 TO 4:PRINT:NEXT
130 PRINT TAB(10)"WITHOUT RANDOM";:PRINT TAB(40)"WITH RANDOM"
140 PRINT TAB(10)"H          T";:PRINT TAB(40)"H          T"
150 PRINT:PRINT TAB(9)AH;:PRINT TAB(18)AT;
152 PRINT TAB(39)BH;:PRINT TAB(48)BT
```

That takes care of the text that is common to all three phases of the display. You have not yet encountered the REM statement in line 100, so that calls for some explanation.

REM is one program statement that causes absolutely no operation to take place. It is simply a way of indicating some note for the programmer's convenience. You can follow a REM statement with any combination of characters you choose, as long as they all appear on the same line.

In this particular case, REM is used to assign something of a title to the subroutine. The title is DISPLAY, and the asterisks are included merely to make the REMark stand out from the rest of the text in the program.

When the programming for this job is completed, you will be able to find the DISPLAY subroutine rather easily amid many other lines and subroutines.

> *Principle.* The REM statement signals a line of text that is printed in the memory for the programmer's own convenience—usually for the purpose of labeling a subroutine or explaining important program steps. The computer takes no action when encountering a REM line (other than ignoring it and going to the next line).

So the DISPLAY subroutine begins at line 100 with a REM statement, immediately followed by a line that first clears the screen and then prints the message RANDOM COIN-TOSS FOR *n* TOSSES, where *n* is the value of N. Presumably, the main program will give the operator an opportunity to enter the value of N before the system ever begins executing this subroutine.

Line 120 causes the system to skip down five lines on the screen, and then line 130 prints the headings WITHOUT RANDOM and WITH RANDOM. The semicolon in line 130 suppresses the carriage return so that the two headings appear on the same line.

Line 140 merely prints the headings H and T for the two phases of the coin-toss test. The T's are separated from their H's by about eight spaces.

Line 150 might contain something of a surprise. The numerical values of AH and AT are tabbed in a strange-looking place. As shown in the diagrams in Fig. 7–2, the numerical values of AH and AT ought to appear directly under their respective H and T headings, and not tabbed one space to the left as designated in line 150. But when you run the program, you will find them lining up perfectly. Why is that?

Recall from an earlier lesson that the computer automatically leaves a space for a minus sign whenever it encounters a PRINT *numerical variable* type of statement. Since there will never be any negative values for AH and AT in this program, the figures have to be tabbed one space to the left so that they will line up with their headings. It is the imaginary minus sign that appears at TAB 9 and 18—the numbers, themselves, appear right where they ought to be, TAB 10 and 19.

Line 152 works the same way, printing the numerical values of BH and BT under their respective headings.

The program can be run just as it is now, giving you a chance to doublecheck the formatting. Most systems will initialize the values of the numerical variables to zero, so you will see a zero wherever a numerical variable occurs in the program. Other than that, you can get a very good idea of what you have done so far; and if there are problems with the program or formatting, this is the time to take care of them. Always solve your problems as you go along. Even the little problems, left unresolved, can return later to haunt you. And maybe by then they will turn out to be big problems.

Continuing with this DISPLAY subroutine:

```
160 PRINT: ON P GOTO 170, 180, 190
170 PRINT TAB(10)"SCORE="A$;:PRINT TAB(40)"NOT PLAYED YET"
175 RETURN
180 PRINT TAB(10)"DONE FOR "N"TOSSES";
182 PRINT TAB(40)"SCORE="A$
185 PRINT TAB(10)"FINAL SCORE="AH/N: RETURN
190 PRINT TAB(10)"FINAL SCORE="AH/N;
192 PRINT TAB(40)"FINAL SCORE="BH/N:PRINT:PRINT
195 PRINT"TEST DONE FOR "N"TOSSES": RETURN
197 END
```

This completes the DISPLAY subroutine—one that will be run whenever the system does a GOSUB 1∅∅.

A new variable, P, is introduced in line 160. There are three different display modes already sketched out in Fig. 7-2. Variable P is a phase designator. In the main program, you will be setting P equal to 1, 2, or 3, indicating which display phase should be executed.

So when the system gets down to line 160, it clears the screen and then does an ON . . . GOTO operation based on the value of P. If the system is running, the first display phase (as in Fig. 7–2a), the ON . . . GOTO statement sends operations to line 170, and that particular line calls for printing out the information indicating a HEADS or TAILS score for the WITHOUT RANDOM phase, and showing a NOT PLAYED YET message for the WITH RANDOM column.

After working through the PRINT operations in line 170, the system is told to do a RETURN in line 175. Now you haven't written the program that calls the DISPLAY subroutine yet, so there is nowhere for the system to return. That will be worked out later.

But now suppose the system is working in display phase 2 and P=2 when this subroutine is executed. That being the case, line 160 sends operations down to line 180 to print out the messages described for Fig. 7–2b. The RETURN statement, concluding line 185, signals the end of the display phase 2 operation and sends control back to the calling program.

Finally, when the system is wrapping up the test and going into phase 3 of the display routine, line 160 sends operations down to line 190; and that line initiates a series of PRINT statements that generate the text unique to Fig. 7–2c.

The system returns to the main program when it gets to the RETURN statement in line 195.

So lines 160 through 197, in combination with lines 100 through 152, make up the complete DISPLAY subroutine. The entire subroutine can be tested now, but only by doing some temporary surgery on it. For one thing, the subroutine cannot run properly without having a value for P. Then, too, you are going to get an error condition from lines 185, 190, or 192 if N is equal to zero.

To test the DISPLAY subroutine at this point, it is necessary to insert a line that initializes the values of P and N. Try this:

1Ø5 P=1:N=1

Upon entering RUN 1ØØ, you should see a display quite similar to that in Fig. 7-2a. The numerical values will probably be zeros, but that's alright.

To check the phase 2 picture, insert 1Ø5 P=2:N=1 and then RUN 1ØØ. Compare the result with Fig. 7-2b. And to check out the final phase of the display scheme, insert 1Ø5 P=3:N=1 and, again, do a RUN 1ØØ. Be sure to delete line 105 when you are finished with these tests.

So much for designing, programming, testing, and, maybe, debugging the DISPLAY subroutine. In itself, it isn't very complicated.

What is needed next is another subroutine for tossing the coin, TOSS. Here is the beginning of it:

```
200 REM ** TOSS **
210 ON P GOTO 230, 260
220 STOP
230 DØ=RND(2)
240 ON DØ GOTO 250, 255
250 A$="HEADS":AH=AH+1: RETURN
255 A$="TAILS":AT=AT+1: RETURN
```

Line 200 merely prints the name ** TOSS ** so that the subroutine can be easily found in the overall program listing. The real work begins in line 210.

Line 210 uses the same phase variable, P, that the DISPLAY subroutine does. Whenever P=1, the system is running its WITHOUT RANDOM phase; and that being the case, line 210 tells the system to pick up operations from line 230.

The "coin tossing" is done at line 230, generating a 1 or 2 each time it's encountered. The sequence of 1's and 2's from this line ought to be fairly random, and that is precisely what this whole program is supposed to show. The fact that it is all put into a coin-tossing format is simply window dressing.

After line 230 picks a 1 or 2 at random, line 240 sends operations to one of two other lines. If DØ happens to be a 1, line 240 sends things to line 250, where the string variable, A$, is set as HEADS. In other words, the play is HEADS whenever DØ turns up 1.

But when DØ turns out to be 2, line 240 sends operations down to line 255, where A$ is set to TAILS. DØ=2 really means TAILS.

Going to line 250 from the ON . . . GOTO statement in line 240 also increments the value of AH—a numerical variable representing the number of times "heads" appears during phase 1 of the project. Line 250 then concludes with a RETURN statement that carries operations out of the TOSS subroutine and back to the main calling routine.

The same sort of thing happens if DØ turns up a 2. By line 255, A$ is fixed at TAILS, the AT "tails counter" is incremented by 1, and control returns to the main program.

All of this if P=1. What if P=2? You need more program to answer that question.

```
260 RANDOM:DØ=RND(2)
270 ON DØ GOTO 280, 285
280 A$="HEADS":BH=BH+1:  RETURN
285 A$="TAILS":BT=BT+1:  RETURN
290 END
```

If P=2 back in line 210, the ON . . . GOTO statement in that line sends the system to line 260; and line 260 is the one that does a RANDOM seeding operation before the RND(n) step. After that, the operation of this part of the TOSS subroutine is identical to the phase 1 portion in lines 240 through 255. A$ is set to HEADS or TAILS, the phase 2 heads and tails counters are incremented by 1, and operations are returned to the main calling program (which, if you haven't noticed yet, still isn't written).

Incidentally, the STOP statement in line 220 is one of those programmer's tricks that reflect a cautious style. The TOSS subroutine should never be called while the system is in its phase 3 mode—the one that merely prints out the overall results of the project. If TOSS should be called during phase 3 (because the programmer goofed), P would be equal to 3, and the ON . . . GOTO statement in line 210 would force a default to line 220.

Recall that a STOP statement is a programmable version of the

BREAK key command; and if you ever see a BREAK AT LINE 22Ø or some similar sort of error message, you'll certainly know what went wrong: TOSS was called while P is equal to 3.

It is more difficult to check out the TOSS subroutine than the DISPLAY portion of the scheme. The main problem is that TOSS doesn't include any PRINT statements that spell out what is happening. If your system includes a well-defined set of error messages, as most current systems do, you can use them to your advantage here.

TOSS, you see, has four exit points that are clearly marked with RETURN statements. If you have been following these programming procedures according to plan, none of these RETURN statements have anywhere to go—and that means error messages when you run the subroutine.

Try inserting 2Ø5 P=1, then do a RUN 2ØØ. If DØ happens to pick up a value of 1, you will find an error message on the screen that indicates an attempt to RETURN nowhere from line 250. The only time the system will attempt to get out of the subroutine from line 250 is when DØ=1, so you know that part of the scheme is working.

What's more, machine-generated error messages are generally accompanied by an immediate return to the command mode of operation. That means you can check the values of A$ and AH in this case by entering PRINT A$ and then PRINT AH. If things are working according to plan, doing a PRINT A$ should cause the HEADS expression to appear. And doing a PRINT AH under these same circumstances should cause the system to print a 1 (assuming, of course, that the value of AH was initialized to zero when you did the RUN 2ØØ).

The point of this part of the discussion is to show that machine-generated error messages aren't always blows to the programmer's ego. They can be used as test and troubleshooting tools.

Inserting P=2 at line 205 should cause an error message from either line 280 or 285, depending on whether the DØ in line 260 picked up a value of 1 or 2.

Think it through a little bit and you should be able to see how this TOSS subroutine can be tested by using error messages. Don't forget to delete line 205 before going to the next and final step in this program.

What next? Pull the two subroutines together with a master program. Figure 7–3 is an updated version of the program's flowchart, and that will be the basis for writing the master program in this particular case. After studying this flowchart, you shouldn't have much trouble seeing how the master program should be structured.

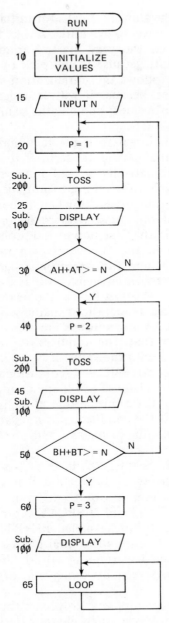

Figure 7–3 Final flow-chart for the coin-toss experiment.

The first step in the flowchart calls for initializing some variables. Not all the variables have to be initialized at this point—just those that must be set from the very start. Variable N should not be initialized at this point, because it will pick up an assigned value in the INPUT step that follows the initialization step. DØ doesn't have to be initialized, either, because it will be assigned a value of 1 or 2 during the TOSS subroutines; and by the same token, there is no need to initialize A$.

What this all boils down to is the fact that the "counters" AH, AT, BH, and BT should be set to zero. If it so happens that your system does not automatically set all numerical variables to zero when a program is first run, failing to initialize these counters will produce some very strange results when it comes to counting the number of heads and tails tosses. So to be on the safe side, they should be set to zero in the first step of the program.

The second step in the flowchart is a rather straightforward INPUT N operation where the operator designates the number of times the coin is to be tossed in each of the two tossing phases.

The phase counter, P, is set to 1 in the next step, forcing the system to carry out phase 1 operations, namely TOSS and DISPLAY. The TOSS and DISPLAY subroutines are run in the next two steps; and immediately after that, the numbers of "heads" and "tails" are summed and compared with the value of N.

According to the AH+AT>=N conditional block, operations move on to the second phase (P=2) if the condition is satisfied; that is, the total number of tosses in the first phase is equal to the desired number of tosses, N. If the conditional is not satisfied, however, control returns to the beginning of phase 1, and the TOSS and DISPLAY sequence is repeated.

From all appearances, phase 2 in Fig. 7-3 appears identical to phase 1, the only difference being that P has different values. In reality, the two operations are quite different, but the differences are hidden within the TOSS and DISPLAY subroutines.

Once the conditional block labeled BH+BT>=N is satisfied, P is set to 3 and the system enters the final phase. The final results are displayed on the screen (by running DISPLAY with P=3), and the display is held on the screen by doing one of those GOTO "yourself" statements.

So now you have a complete flowchart for the entire program. This is the time to look over such charts carefully, doublechecking your thinking and, in fact, the principle of the whole thing. If it seems to make sense, it is time to use it as a guide for writing the main program. Here it is:

```
10 CLS:AH=0:AT=0:BH=0:BT=0
15 INPUT "SPECIFY NUMBER OF TOSSES PER PHASE";N
20 P=1:GOSUB 200
25 GOSUB 100
30 IF AT+AT =N THEN 40
35 GOTO 20
40 P=2:GOSUB 200
45 GOSUB 100
50 IF BH+BT=N THEN 60
55 GOTO 40
60 P=3:GOSUB 100
65 GOTO 65
70 END
```

And that's it. That is the program that pulls together the two subroutines and makes things work. Assuming TOSS and DISPLAY are still residing at lines 200 and 100 in the program memory, you are ready to check out the whole thing.

You have already tested the subroutines; so if the program doesn't work properly, the trouble is most likely in the main program. In any event, you should now run through the main program in an "on-paper" fashion, justifying each statement and comparing it with the flowchart.

By now you are in a good position to appreciate the real power of subroutines and their associated GOSUB and RETURN statements. Imagine what this program would be like if you hadn't designed the tossing and displaying operations as subroutines! The TOSS subroutine, for instance, is called with GOSUB 200 on two entirely different occasions, and the DISPLAY subroutine is called by GOSUB 100 on three different occasions. Without using them as subroutines, most of their lines would have to be repeated through a long and ghastly complicated program.

Note. Subroutines should be used whenever a program requires a certain class of operations to be executed more than one time.

And don't forget that using subroutines simplifies the process of writing the program as well as the program itself. By building the subroutines first, you are able to set aside most of the detailed operations involved in them. In the flowchart in Fig. 7–3, for example, the two subroutines are specified as single operational blocks—there is no need for flowcharting each of them in great detail. This allows you to devote your mental energy to the overall structure of the main program.

There is yet another advantage to writing subroutine-oriented programs: It is relatively easy to modify the program's overall structure.

While running the program as it stands right now, you might find the messages and numbers flying by too quickly. Whatever the reason might be, you decide it would be nice to slow things down a bit, giving the experimenter a chance to view the operations at a slower pace. Maybe you even decide that the tossing operation ought to be a purely manual one, doing something such as tossing the coin one time by striking the ENTER key.

For the sake of making a point of all this, assume you think it is necessary to give the user three options: normal automatic tossing, automatic tossing with a time delay between each toss, and fully manual tossing. Rather than rewriting the entire program to include these options or, worse yet, writing a complete program for each option, write up another subroutine.

```
300 REM ** TOSS MODE SELECT **
310 PRINT"SELECT TOSS MODE: 1=AUTO, 2=AUTO WITH DELAY, 3=MANUAL"
320 INPUT M
330 IF M<1 THEN 350
340 ON M GOTO 360, 370, 380
350 PRINT:PRINT"INVALID SELECT NUMBER. TRY AGAIN.":GOTO 310
360 RETURN
370 FOR TD=0 TO 500:NEXT:RETURN
380 INPUT X$: RETURN
390 END
```

Whenever this TOSS MODE SELECT subroutine is run, the operator is asked to enter an integer: 1, 2, or 3. Presumably, entering a 1 causes the coin-toss experiment to run in its normal mode, entering a 2 lets the program run automatically, but with a time delay between successive coin tosses, and entering a 3 lets the operator do each coin toss manually.

So the operator inputs this mode value, M, at line 320. Line 330 protects the program from erroneous M values that are less than 1. If, indeed, the operator enters a number less than 1, line 330 sends operations down to line 350; and line 350 does two things: it prints the INVALID SELECT NUMBER message and returns operations to line 310 again.

If line 330 is not satisfied (M is greater than 1), the program goes to line 340—an ON . . . GOTO statement that uses the value of M as a basis for specifying where operations are to go. Before seeing what happens if M is a valid entry, look at what happens if M happens to be greater than 3.

If M is greater than 3 (or, to be more accurate, 4 or greater), the ON . . . GOTO statement defaults to line 350; and as already described, this is an error line that returns operations to line 310, giving the operator a chance to enter a valid value for M.

Now suppose the operator enters a 1 in response to the INPUT statement in line 320. According to line 340, M=1 carries operations down to line 360, and that line is made up of the statement, RETURN. In other words, if M=1, operations simply leave this subroutine and go back to the program that called it in the first place. Nothing changes—the main program will be run as if this particular discussion never existed.

But if the operator enters a 2, line 340 sends operations down to line 370. That line is made up of a sequence of statements that create a time delay before doing a RETURN to the calling operation. That represents the AUTO WITH DELAY option.

Finally, entering a 3 in response to the INPUT M statement ultimately carries the computer to line 380. Line 380 is one of those statements that halts all operations until the null string is entered or, in other words, the operator strikes the ENTER key. After the operator strikes the ENTER key, the RETURN statement at the end of line 380 returns operations back to the calling program.

The TOSS MODE SELECT program can be tested by itself upon doing a RUN 3ØØ and responding to the SELECT TOSS MODE message with a 1, 2, or 3. The subroutine will conclude at one of three RETURN statements, depending on the value of M you enter.

Since you have not yet written any GOSUB 3ØØ statements, running this subroutine will result in an error message that ought to include the line number containing the RETURN. The error message generated by the computer ought to specify an error in line 360 if you have entered a 1 at line 320. It should specify an error at line 370 if you have entered a 2, and it should show an error at line 380 if you have entered a 3.

Also enter a 0 and a 4 to check the goof-proofing statements.

All that remains to be done is to fit this new subroutine into the main program. There are a number of ways to go about it, but the following sequence of insertions gets the job done in a very effective and efficient fashion:

```
12 GOSUB 3ØØ
27 GOSUB 34Ø
47 GOSUB 34Ø
```

Now that was relatively painless, wasn't it? GOSUB 3ØØ is placed at line 12, between the lines that initialize the counting variables (line 10) and the one that asks for a value of N (line 15). The operator thus has a chance to initialize the value of M each time the program is started.

But what is subroutine 340 called in lines 27 and 47? Well, lines 27 and 47 follow the DISPLAY subroutine in phases 1 and 2 of the overall program. You don't want to set the value of M after every display subroutine, just at the first part of the program. So by doing a GOSUB 34Ø, the M-setting part of the TOSS MODE SELECT subroutine is omitted, going directly to the part that actually determines the mode of operation.

So if the operator initially sets the value of M at 1 (in response to the INPUT statement called by line 12 and, subsequently, line 320), M will hold that value of 1, no matter how many times the program calls line 340.

> *Note.* As long as an appropriate RETURN concludes the sequence, it is possible to call any part of an existing subroutine.

The entire subroutine 300 is thus called only as part of the program's initializing process. After that, line 340 is called, and the system responds with normal automatic coin tossing, delayed automatic coin tossing or purely manual coin tossing—depending, of course, upon the numerical value of M.

Now you know what subroutines are for:

1. They allow the programmer to build relatively complex programs in a piecemeal fashion, and then weave things together with a master program.

2. They can simplify the program itself by replacing repeated sequences of operations with one subroutine that can be called any number of times.

3. They make it possible to modify and extend programs without having to do extensive surgery on the existing work.

EXERCISES

7-1 What is the purpose of a REM statement? How does the computer respond upon encountering a REM statement in a program?

7-2 Which of the following do you think are valid subroutine-calling statements?

   (a) 1Ø GOSUB 4ØØ

   (b) 1Ø IF A>5Ø THEN GOSUB 4ØØ

   (c) 1Ø ON A GOSUB 4ØØ, 5ØØ, 6ØØ, 7ØØ,
        where A is an integer between 1 and 4 inclusively.

7-3 How would you go about testing the following subroutines before they are written into a master program?

   (a) 2ØØ REM ** COUNT **
        21Ø A=A+1:CLS:PRINT A
        22Ø IF A>=1Ø RETURN
        23Ø GOTO 21Ø
        24Ø END

   (b) 2ØØ A1=2:A3=3:A4=25:A6=A5/A1:RETURN

   (c) 2ØØ REM "DECIDE"
        21Ø ON Q GOTO 23Ø, 24Ø
        22Ø RETURN
        23Ø A=B*C:CLS:PRINT A:RETURN
        24Ø A=B/C:CLS:PRINT A:RETURN

7-4 What do you think is the meaning of the expression *nested subroutines*? What are the implications of the idea? See if you can make up a program that uses some nested subroutines.

7-5 Name at least three distinctly different advantages of using subroutine-oriented programs, then write an illustrative example of each.

7-6 Carefully define the differences between a GOTO *line number* and a GOSUB *line number* statement. Study the ways these two statements are used in the examples in this chapter and see if you can arrive at some guidelines for using one or the other under a given set of circumstances.

CHAPTER 8

More about Composing Programs with Subroutines

The ability to "think programming" is just as important as becoming thoroughly acquainted with the family of BASIC statements and how to use them. However, many students of BASIC become so involved with learning the language itself that the thought processes required for composing good programs is almost completely ignored.

Composing a good computer program is very much like composing a song. Everyone has access to the fundamental tools and can learn to write notes and other symbols on a sheet of paper. But it takes a special quality of creative thinking to assemble the notes into something truly meaningful.

Most people aren't accustomed to having such a high degree of freedom when it comes to doing something. Most of us are far more accustomed to doing things in a proper step-by-step fashion, with each step having a well-defined standard of being right or wrong. The implication is that doing each step in a proper fashion guarantees a single, well-defined, and "correct" result. This rather conventional and comfortable way of doing things is often called a "cookbook" or "checklist" process. It is a comfortable way of doing things because its mastery requires little beyond some basic training and rote memorization. Toss in a dash of talent and a cup of experience and you might end up doing some useful work of passable quality.

Certainly, it is possible to apply cookbook/checklist thinking to BASIC computer programming. In fact, an element of this sort of thing is necessary for getting started in the first place. A good programmer, however, has to outgrow this narrow view of things and eventually move out into a less comfortable, but far more challenging and rewarding, world.

In the world of truly creative computer programming, the strict notions of right and wrong ways of doing things begin losing their significance. Assuming, of course, the programmer is using program statements and commands properly, it becomes difficult to judge the quality of a new program.

The first test of a good computer program is quite naturally one of finding out whether or not it works as intended. That should go without saying. But beyond that, the matter becomes one of subjective judgment.

Mathematicians use the term "elegant" to describe an especially high-quality proof of some mathematical idea. It might be possible to prove the same idea in a dozen different ways, but only a few will have the special quality of elegance—and it is the elegant one that will endure.

It is taken for granted that the mathematical proof "works" and holds together in a self-consistent fashion. But the elegant proof is one that gets straight to the point, makes its case, stands alone on its own merits, and sets the standard for further work.

The same idea holds true for computer programming. Persons armed with an understanding of the fundamental programming statements can sledgehammer their way through most programming tasks—and get it all to work. It takes a special quality of creativity and insight to do the same job with finesse and elegance.

But what difference does it make as long as the program works? It is possible to cite a number of reasons from human psychology, philosophy, and the work ethic; but the most far-reaching reason is this: A continuous exercise of creative programming gradually prepares one to deal with that certain kind of problem that baffles lesser talents. A persistent pursuit of elegance and excellence opens doors to new ideas that are otherwise locked tightly closed.

As long as someone will someday open such doors to newer and better things, why not work yourself into the position of being that one individual who will do the job first? The choice is yours, and you ought to be making it as soon as possible.

The primary purpose of this chapter is to illustrate the thinking involved in creating BASIC computer programs. Hopefully, it will not come across to you as a "method" or cookbook listing of how programs are supposed to be written. Although it is necessary to present the ideas one step at a time, it is not at all a linear process—a checklist sort of process that implies each step is whole and adequate before the next step is begun. You will find yourself going around and around several times, changing and extending earlier ideas on the basis of what you discover later.

None of the steps in the programming process is complete—not even the first one—until you enter RUN and find things working exactly as you planned. Even then, you might wonder if there are a few rough edges that might be smoothed.

While working your way through this chapter, you are going to find that subroutines and flowcharts are invaluable tools. Of course, all the programming statements and principles described so far in this book are important, too; but they take on almost trivial significance compared to the overall perspectives engendered by using subroutines and flowcharts.

8-1 A Dynamic Programming Process

The general, creative programming process is a dynamic one that calls for an almost continuous input of new information, reorganization of older information, and redefinition of what is going on. A thread of rationale must run through the whole process, however, holding things together long enough to make it all work in the long run.

Here are some general procedures. Again, these are not to be considered step-by-step procedures, but rather a list of ordered priorities. When you sit down to start the job, the first item is of top priority; and after getting the material together, the second item takes top priority, and so on.

You will return to some of the steps a number of times, each time making a bit more progress toward the end of the job. Think of it as a spiraled process—one where you go around and around, but making some headway all along.

1. Define the task at hand.
2. Outline a plan of approach.
3. Define some subroutines.
4. Reexamine the plan and subroutines in the light of the task.
5. Write, enter, and test the key subroutines.
6. See if the main flowchart can be more clearly drawn.
7. Reexamine the main flowchart and existing subroutines in the light of the main task at hand.
8. Write the main program according to the flowchart.

9. Test and debug the program.

10. Add any necessary or desirable programming features.

11. Document the entire program.

The first priority is to define the task at hand. Unless you know exactly what you are trying to do, you don't stand much chance of doing it. Maybe that sounds too obvious for serious consideration, but you will find programmers who ignore the idea and waste a lot of time and effort writing programs that go nowhere. It is a frustrating experience that can be avoided by taking some time and care at the outset.

It is hard to say what is necessary for defining the task, because the necessary ingredients depend so heavily on the nature of the task. Basically, you have to know what the final results should be, what input parameters are available, and anything important that goes on from beginning to end.

After getting some confidence in this matter of knowing what has to be done, the next priority is roughing out a general approach. Sometimes the nature of the task itself dictates the approach to programming it. That's nice—it makes the second priority a rather easy thing to handle.

But there are times when the approach will appear to be anyone's guess. It will be a wide open field, and it's up to your own experience, knowledge, and intuition to devise a workable plan of approach.

In either case, the plan ought to take the form of a rough flowchart. Don't get bogged down in too much detail at this time. Relax and try viewing the situation from an overall perspective. Label the blocks in the flowchart with very general expressions such as COUNT TO 100, DISPLAY THE RESULTS, DO A TIME DELAY, and INPUT THE CURRENT VALUE OF MONEY SPENT. If the program is an extensive one, you will find it helpful to avoid specific BASIC statements at this stage of the game—you'll be running the risk of getting sidetracked or lost in detail that really isn't important at this time. *You must have a way to retain an overall perspective on the task,* and this preliminary, rough plan should serve that purpose.

Once you are satisfied with the general plan of approach and you have a decent functional flowchart, it is time to jot down some ideas for subroutines. Quite often, you will find yourself writing a subroutine for just about every block on the preliminary flowchart. It won't always work out that nicely, however; and you shouldn't spend too much time trying to fit one subroutine to each block on the flowchart.

As you work on the subroutines, you will find yourself wondering whether or not they will really work. This is especially true when working on a job you have never done before. If at all possible, test some of the ideas on the machine. You will then know whether or not you are on the right track.

By the time you have worked your way through the third priority, you are going to have a very good idea of how simple or difficult the task is going to be. If things seem simple, you are in fine shape for moving on. But if things seem to be getting overly complicated and perhaps a bit out of hand, the real problem might rest with your approach.

The world is basically a simple place that is made to appear complicated only by one's perspective; and it is this bit of homely philosophy that makes the fourth priority an important one: reexamine the plan and subroutines in the light of the main task.

It is at this fourth priority level that your own skill, talent, creativity, and fortitude come into play. In the extreme cases, you might even find it necessary to work out another approach or maybe redefine the task. Throwing away all the work you have done to this point can mean one of two things: either you have completely lost patience with the job, or you've been blessed with a bit of hard-won insight that promises to smooth out the work.

In the first instance, you're just postponing the inevitable; and in the second, you've just conquered it. In either case, you eventually wind up at the fifth level of priority.

You should write, enter, and test the subroutines only after you know exactly what you are trying to do. Writing one subroutine often calls for having previously established the values of some variables; and since those values might be established by yet another subroutine, you aren't going to write very good ones until everything fits together.

When the key subroutines appear to mesh together properly, rework the flowchart. This time the flowchart can be labeled with more specific details—more specific PRINT statements, names of the subroutines, and so on. The subroutines themselves do not have to be flowcharted in great detail, but the revised chart should more clearly indicate how you are handling the task.

Now you are down to the eighth priority level. It's the proper time to write the main program that calls the subroutines at the proper times and does all the little tasks that are too simple to occupy subroutine space. This program ought to be a reflection of your revised flowchart. Ideally, it will follow the main flowchart in every detail; but in practice you might find yourself modifying the flowchart a little bit to suit your evolving program. That isn't a case of cheating but one of applying some practical wisdom.

Then run the whole program, looking first for gross errors and then for finer annoyances. Make any relevant modifications in the flowchart as you go along.

A programmer rarely anticipates every detail of the system from the outset, and the need for altering the existing program or adding some extra features shows up quite clearly when running the whole thing. So the tenth priority level is to add any of those necessary or newly discovered possibilities that make the program a bit more useful or attractive to the user.

Every program must be thoroughly documented. As wise old Murphy (the Murphy of Murphy's Law) says: "If it can go wrong, it will." That applies to electronically stored computer programs. Imagine weeks of hard work going down the drain in a few micro-seconds when something goes wrong—a power outage garbles the computer memory, someone carries your cassette tape too close to an alternating magnetic field, and all those other nasty things that make up the nightmares of developmental programmers.

Write down your program as you go along. If you have access to a line printer, keep a running log of program listings.

8-2 A Feasibility Study for Buying a New Home

Can we afford to buy the dream home we have just found? What kind of home *can* we afford? If we can afford a new home, what will the monthly payments be and should we buy—with a VA, FHA, or conventional loan?

These are questions prospective home buyers must ask them-selves, and the purpose of this section is to compose a BASIC pro-gram that will help answer those questions. The example illustrates the general procedures for designing subroutine-oriented programs, and it introduces a couple of new ideas along the way.

The first part of the job is to carefully define the task at hand. This can be a time-consuming and tedious task at times, but it is generally a manageable task as long as you don't try to do too much at one time.

After giving the matter some careful consideration, you might de-cide the job ought to be divided into three categories of operations:

Option A—Given the price of a new home, calculate the monthly payments and recommend a loan plan.

Option B—Given the amount of money available for making

monthly payments, calculate the maximum price of a new home.

Option C—Given the buyer's gross annual income, calculate the maximum price that should be paid for a new home and its monthly payments.

This plan gives the user a choice of three different ways to approach the situation. Most will probably use only one of the three options, but the others should be readily accessible if needed.

Now it is possible to go to great lengths gathering the relevant information, but for the sake of making some important points about BASIC programming, it is necessary to use some rather crude calculations—calculations that will never put you into good standing with the local real estate board. Settling for rough estimates does not affect the validity of the programming procedures, however.

Here is the list of relevant variables, definitions, and equations:

CN = price of the new home

CO = selling price of the old home

OM = balance remaining on the old mortgage

OS = balance remaining on any second mortgage

ME = cost of moving and improvements to be subtracted from the equity in the old home

DP = down payment available for the new home (assuming that it all comes from equity in the old home)

MP = actual monthly payments on the new home

FR = personal funds available for making monthly payments

AI = buyer's gross annual income

$$DP = CO - OM - OS - ME \tag{1}$$

$$MP = \frac{8.2(CN - DP)}{1000} \tag{2a}$$

$$CN = \frac{1000MP}{8.2 + DP} \tag{2b}$$

$$FR = \frac{0.2AI}{12} \tag{3}$$

According to Equation (1), the amount of available down payment is simply the selling price of the old house, less the amount due on mortgages and moving expenses. This is a rather reasonable and conventional approach to figuring the down payment available. Some buyers will, of course, add some cash from savings to this figure, but that feature isn't included in this particular scheme. Add it in yourself if you wish.

The monthly payment suggested in Equation (2a) is based on the rough notion that payments are close to 8.2 dollars per thousand owed on the new home. Subtract the amount of down payment from the cost of the new home, and you wind up with the balance due. Dividing by 1000 yields the number of thousands in the figure, and all that remains is to multiply it all by that ballpark figure, 8.2.

Equation (2b) is simply a reorganized version of Equation (2a). In this case, the equation solves for the cost of a new home, given the desired monthly payments and the amount of down payment that is available.

Equation (3) uses the rule of thumb that says one should not involve more than 20 percent of one's gross annual income in mortgage payments. If you don't happen to agree with the 20 percent figure, simply adjust the 0.2 coefficient in Equation (3) accordingly.

Figure 8-1 shows the overall plan of the program. Upon entering RUN, it should first list the options that are available and give the user an opportunity to select one of them. The options are printed in the PRINT OPTIONS block, and the user's reply is accepted at the INPUT OPTION block.

If the user happens to select option A, the OPTION A conditional is satisfied and control moves over to DO OPTION A. If, on the other hand, the user selects option B or C, the OPTION A conditional is not satisfied and the system searches the two remaining conditionals, OPTION B and OPTION C, for one that is satisfied.

If none of the three option-selecting conditionals is satisfied, the user has entered an invalid choice. In that case, PRINT ERROR MESSAGE informs the user of the mistake and carries operations all the way back to the beginning. Presumably, the user will eventually get out of that error loop by entering a valid selection at INPUT OPTION. In any event, the system is protected from invalid selections that could cause a great deal of confusion.

As the computer completes its work on one of the three options, control is passed to a conditional that is labeled AGAIN. This conditional will be satisfied by merely striking the ENTER key to input the null string. The idea is to return to the beginning of the operation for the sake of selecting another option.

Incidentally, AGAIN loops back to itself as long as it is not satisfied. This provides a convenient means for holding the results of the selected option on the screen until the user is ready to do something else.

The discussion to this point covers the first two priorities in the programming process: defining the task at hand and roughing out a plan of approach.

The next general step is to define some subroutines that fit into the overall plan. It would certainly appear from the flowchart in Fig. 8-1 that DO OPTION A, DO OPTION B, and DO OPTION C should each be treated as a subroutine. PRINT OPTIONS and INPUT OPTION are going to be somewhat involved in terms of formatting information on the screen, so they should also be treated as a separate subroutine.

So it appears that the flowchart in Fig. 8-1 lends itself to three separate subroutines. The mainder of the work can be done in the main program.

Figure 8-2a is a flowchart for the option A subroutine. It first requests some standard information concerning the selling price of the old home, mortgage balances, and moving expenses. After that, it requests the selling price of the new home under consideration.

Recall that the purpose of option A is to calculate the monthly payments for a new home, based on the amount of down payment that is available. So there is a need to calculate the value of MP from Equation (2a) and print it out on the screen. CALCULATE MP and PRINT MP take care of that job.

After that, the user inputs the gross annual income, calculates the recommended maximum monthly payments from Equation (3), and prints the result. See blocks INPUT AI and PRINT FR.

Finally, the system makes a couple of wise recommendations based on the figures that are available. If the actual monthly payment is equal to less than the recommended budget level (FR), the system recommends buying the new home, and says so at PRINT RECOMMEND MESSAGE.

Then the question is whether the buyer ought to get a conventional loan (where the available down payment is at least 15 percent of the purchase price of the new home) or apply for a VA or FHA loan (where the down payment is less than 15 percent or, indeed, nothing at all). The conditional labeled DP$>$=.15*CN takes care of this decision-making task.

That all assumes the user has the personal income necessary for making the monthly payments—the conditional labeled MP$<$=FR is satisfied. If that particular conditional is not satisfied, the implica-

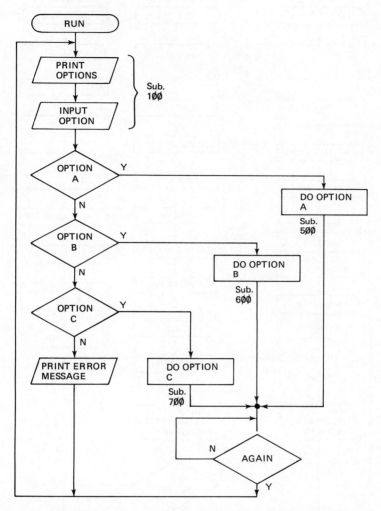

Figure 8-1 Flowchart of the main program sequence. Subroutine numbers were added after the appropriate subroutines were prepared and tested.

tion is that the buyer cannot afford to make the mortgage payments, and the NOT RECOMMENDED MESSAGE tells him so.

In any event, control returns to the main calling program after making these recommendations.

The option A flowchart in Fig. 8-2a appears to be a nice little program in itself. And it turns out that it includes some operations that could also be written as subroutines.

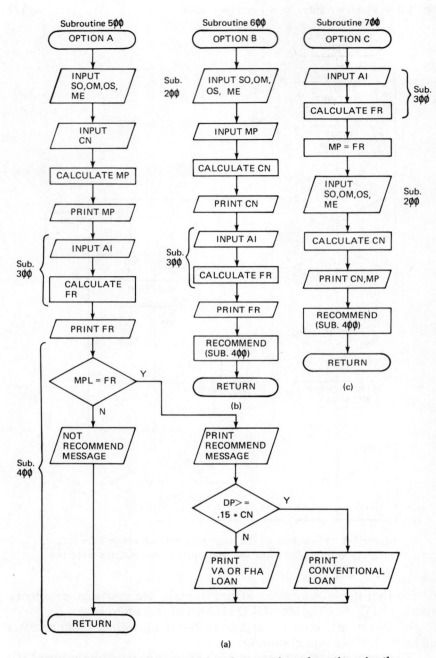

Figure 8-2 Flowcharts of the three main subroutines in the home-buying feasibility program. (a) The OPTION A subroutine. (b) The OPTION B subroutine. (c) The OPTION C subroutine.

So now you have the notion of writing subroutines within sub-routines. This is altogether possible with home computers, and it can be a valuable tool for getting things pulled together in an effective fashion.

Definition.   A *nested subroutine* is simply a subroutine within a subroutine.

Note.   There is always some limit to how deeply subroutines can be nested—a limit on how many times you can put a subroutine within a subroutine, within a subroutine, and so on. Check the manual for your own computer system to find out deep the subroutine nesting can go.

Figure 8-2b is the flowchart for a subroutine that carries out operations for option B. It is almost identical to the flowchart for option A. It looks simpler only because it takes for granted that all the closing recommendations will be handled in a separate subroutine. The only real difference between the two is that the flowchart for option A calculates the value of MP, based on the INPUT value of CN, while option B figures the value of CN on the basis of an INPUT value of MP.

The flowchart for the option C subroutine, Fig. 8-2c, is quite different from the other two. This one begins by accepting the AI figure and calculating FR. After that, it sets MP=FR, accepts the basic information about the present home, calculates CN, and then prints CN and MP. It concludes by making recommendations—the same set of recommendations used by options A and B.

The feature that guides the plan of these three major subroutines is one that makes a great deal of common sense: Values of variables must be available before they are printed or used in other equations. Other than that, the whole process is quite flexible, and the flow-charts shown in Fig. 8-2 aren't necessarily the "right" ones or, to be absolutely honest, the "best" ones.

Now it is time to start writing some subroutines, entering them into the computer, and checking them out. It is possible to start at a number of different places, but the wisest choice is generally the point where most variables are involved. In this case, it means start-ing with the subroutine that lets the user enter information about the present home.

The subroutine could be started at any line number, but it's a good idea to leave lower-numbered lines for the main controlling program. In this case the first subroutine starts at line 200.

```
200 REM $$ INPUTS $$
210 INPUT "SALE PRICE OF OLD HOME $";SO
220 INPUT "BALANCE ON OLD MORTGAGE $";OM
230 INPUT "BALANCE ON SECOND MORTGAGE $";OS
240 INPUT "EXPENSES FOR MOVING AND IMPROVEMENTS $";ME
250 DP=SO-OM-OS-ME
260 PRINT: PRINT "DOWN PAYMENT AVAILABLE $"DP
270 RETURN
```

By the time you have studied the basic definitions, equations, and flowcharts, you should have no trouble understanding the operation of this little subroutine. The only thing that is new as far as these lessons is concerned is the use of dollar signs within the quoted messages. The idea is to insert dollar signs ahead of all the dollar figures in the program.

A good way to test the INPUTS subroutine is by entering this little program:

```
10 CLS: GOSUB 200
20 PRINT SO,OM,OS,ME,DP
30 PRINT "OK": INPUT X$: GOTO 10
```

This test program clears the screen and calls subroutine 200—the one just entered. While executing subroutine 200, the system will request values for SO, OM, OS, and ME; calculate the value of DP; and print the value of DP after writing DOWN PAYMENT AVAILABLE $.

You know the subroutine is put together properly when you see the values repeated on the screen (line 20 of the test program), followed by an OK. You can repeat the test any number of times by striking the ENTER key after seeing OK and a question mark (line 30).

Another useful subroutine can be one that accepts the value of AI from the keyboard and uses it to figure the value of FR. This is an exceedingly simple routine; but since it is used in all three options, you might as well designate it as a subroutine. The choice is yours.

```
300 REM  $$ INCOME $$
310 INPUT "GROSS ANNUAL INCOME $";AI
320 FR=AI*.2/12
330 RETURN
```

Assuming that you decide to build the INCOME subroutine, specify it as subroutine 300.

Subroutine 400 can be the one that makes the recommendations about whether or not the purchase is a wise one and, if so, the type of loan the user should look for. This one is outlined in detail in the flowchart in Fig. 8–2a, and it is represented by a single, subroutine block in Fig. 8–2b and c.

```
400 REM  $$ RECOMMEND $$
410 IF MP<=FR THEN 430
420 PRINT "PURCHASE NOT RECOMMENDED"
425 PRINT "($"MP-FR" SHORT ON MONTHLY PAYMENTS)":RETURN
430 PRINT "PURCHASE RECOMMENDED"
440 IF DP>=.15*CN THEN 460
450 PRINT TAB(5)"BY VA OR FHA LOAN":RETURN
460 PRINT TAB(5)"BY CONVENTIONAL LOAN":RETURN
```

A routine suitable for checking out RECOMMEND is one that looks something like this:

```
10 CLS: INPUT "MP, FR, DP"; MP,FR,DP:GOSUB 400
20 PRINT MP,FR,DP
30 PRINT "OK": INPUT X$; GOTO 10
```

Upon running this test program, it first calls for some values of MP, FR, and DP; then it runs subroutine 400. The test program ought to be run several times, plugging in values that cause PURCHASE NOT RECOMMENDED, PURCHASE RECOMMENDED BY VA OR FHA LOAN, and PURCHASE RECOMMENDED BY CONVENTIONAL LOAN. If you have never been much of a mathematician before, this is your chance to build some confidence.

These three subroutines—INPUTS, INCOME, and RECOMMEND—contain just about all the variables used anywhere in the overall program. So now it's time to string them together with three other subroutines: OPTION A, OPTION B, and OPTION C.

Subroutine 500, OPTION A, is written almost exclusively from the flowchart in Fig. 8–2a. Here it is:

```
500 REM $$ OPTION A $$
510 CLS: GOSUB 200
515 INPUT "PRICE OF NEW HOME $";CN
520 MP=8.2*(CN-DP)/1000
530 PRINT "MONTHLY PAYMENT IS $"MP
540 PRINT: GOSUB 300
```

```
550 PRINT "FUNDS AVAILABLE FOR MONTHLY PAYMENTS $"FR
560 PRINT: GOSUB 400
570 RETURN
```

Subroutine 500 can be related to the option A flowchart in Fig. 8–2a by the following rationale:

Line 510	INPUT SO, OM, OS, ME
Line 515	INPUT CN
Line 520	CALCULATE MP
Line 530	PRINT MP
Line 540	INPUT AI, CALCULATE FR
Line 550	PRINT FR
Line 560	ALL RECOMMEND operations
Line 570	RETURN

The best way to check out the operation of subroutine 500 is by entering a RUN 5ØØ. All of the relevant nested subroutines will be called and executed, asking for relevant information that is needed for all the PRINT operations and calculations.

Writing the BASIC statements for OPTION B follows much the same sequence:

```
600 REM $$ OPTION B $$
610 CLS: GOSUB 200
615 INPUT "DESIRED MONTHLY PAYMENTS $";MP
620 CN=1000/8.2*MP+DP
630 PRINT: PRINT "MAXIMUM COST OF NEW HOME $"CN
640 GOSUB 300
650 PRINT "FUNDS AVAILABLE FOR MONTHLY PAYMENTS $"FR
660 PRINT: GOSUB 400
670 RETURN
```

This OPTION B subroutine follows the flowchart in Fig. 8–2b. The rationale and testing methods are left to the reader.

As mentioned earlier in this section, the OPTION C subroutine is a bit different from the other two. Nevertheless, it follows the flow-chart in Fig. 8–2c in a step-by-step fashion.

```
700 REM $$ OPTION C $$
710 CLS: GOSUB 300
```

```
720 MP=FR: PRINT: GOSUB 200
730 CN=1000/8.2*MP+DP
740 PRINT "MAXIMUM COST OF NEW HOME $"CN
750 PRINT: GOSUB 400
760 RETURN
```

Again, the rationale and method for testing this subroutine are left to the reader. Being fully acquainted with the definitions, equations, and intended task ought to make the analysis a rather straightforward affair.

Thus far, the procedure is down to the sixth priority level in the general programming process—seeing if the main flowchart could be more clearly drawn. In this case some of the labels for the blocks in Fig. 8-1 could be reworked to reflect subroutine numbers and actual BASIC statements that are relevant at key points. In a general sense, the main flowchart in Fig. 8-1 is in pretty good shape.

The eighth priority level is the next one calling for some clear-cut action: Write the main program according to the main flowchart. Thus far, all that has been done is to develop the subroutines and, incidentally, some subroutines within the subroutines. The final step in the actual programming process is to write the main program according to the flowchart in Fig. 8-1.

But hold on a minute! The very first step in the main flowchart calls for a rather extensive printout of the available options. You decided earlier in the job that this PRINT OPTIONS operation ought to be delegated to a separate subroutine. So there is yet one more subroutine to write.

Before showing a version of this OPTIONS subroutine, note how a programming job that is carefully and completely spelled out from the beginning is almost foolproof. We almost forgot an important part of the work—something that is easy to do when working through an extensive program. The fact that the whole plan was set up in advance, however, makes it possible to walk away from the whole thing for a day or two at a time without losing track of what has happened and what must be done.

Here is the subroutine for PRINT OPTIONS:

```
100 REM $$ CHOICES $$
110 PRINT "OPTION A -- GIVEN COST OF NEW HOME,"
120 PRINT TAB(12)"CALCULATE MONTHLY PAYMENTS."
125 PRINT TAB(20)"OR"
130 PRINT "OPTION B -- GIVEN DESIRED MONTHLY PAYMENTS,"
140 PRINT TAB(12)"CALCULATE MAXIMUM PRICE OF NEW HOME."
145 PRINT TAB(20)"OR"
```

```
150 PRINT "OPTION C -- GIVEN INCOME, CALCULATE"
160 PRINT TAB(12)"THE MAXIMUM COST OF A NEW HOME AND"
170 PRINT TAB(12)"THE MONTHLY PAYMENTS."
180 PRINT:PRINT:INPUT"ENTER OPTION 'A','B' OR 'C'"A$
190 RETURN
```

Studying this particular subroutine, you should find that it encompasses the PRINT OPTIONS and INPUT OPTIONS blocks on the main flowchart in Fig. 8–1.

The simplest and most reliable way to test subroutine 100 is by simply entering RUN 1ØØ. You should see something like this on the screen.

```
>RUN 100
OPTION A -- GIVEN COST OF NEW HOME,
              CALCULATE THE MONTHLY PAYMENTS.
                        OR
OPTION B -- GIVEN DESIRED MONTHLY PAYMENTS,
              CALCULATE MAXIMUM PRICE OF NEW HOME.
                        OR
OPTION C -- GIVEN INCOME, CALCULATE
              THE MAXIMUM COST OF A NEW HOME AND
              THE MONTHLY PAYMENTS.

ENTER OPTION 'A','B' OR 'C'?_
```

With that job out of the way, the main calling program comes next.

```
10 CLS
20 GOSUB 100
30 IF A$="A" THEN 50
35 IF A$="B" THEN 70
40 IF A$="C" THEN 90
45 PRINT "ERROR. TRY AGAIN":GOTO 20
50 CLS: GOSUB 500
60 GOTO 95
70 CLS: GOSUB 600
80 GOTO 95
90 CLS: GOSUB 700
95 INPUT X$: GOTO 10
97 END
```

This is the master program that pulls together all the work done so far. All that remains of the programming process is to run it thoroughly, trying all the options.

But there are still two steps remaining in the general program composing procedures; and one of those is to make any necessary or desirable modifications. In this case the program has been fairly well debugged. What about *desirable* modifications?

You recall that the BASIC language accepts large numbers without the benefit of commas. Ten thousand, for example, *must* be entered as 1ØØØØ, not as 1Ø,ØØØ. The system would be confused by the comma, either generating erroneous results or an automatic error message. Your user might not know that, though; so the program ought to include a notation to the effect that commas must not be used in large numbers.

There are a number of ways to handle this particular modification, but here is a very straightforward one:

```
51Ø CLS:PRINT "DO NOT INCLUDE COMMAS IN ENTRIES"
515 PRINT: GOSUB 2ØØ
61Ø CLS:PRINT "DO NOT INCLUDE COMMAS IN ENTRIES"
615 PRINT: GOSUB 2ØØ
71Ø CLS:PRINT "DO NOT INCLUDE COMMAS IN ENTRIES"
715 PRINT: GOSUB 3ØØ
```

This is a matter of modifying the first instruction line in each of the three OPTION subroutines and then adding one more line in each case. Note how these modifications alter the programs for OPTION A, OPTION B, and OPTION C.

The feasibility program is complete and ready to go. If you had composed this program on your own, it would be absolutely essential to write down the entire program listing, either by hand or by means of an automatic line printer. In either case, the program must be documented for future reference. Otherwise, you run a needless risk of losing the benefit of many hours of hard work.

If you have been entering this program as the discussion progressed, enter the LIST command. You will be justifiably impressed with the complexity of the program as it slips by on the screen. Indeed, it is a program of respectable proportions; but if you have considered each element of it separately, you might not have been aware of the actual extent of the work.

Bear in mind that this has not been a lesson in programming real estate problems. The real point has been to illustrate the kind of thinking and work that goes into composing a moderately complex program for any sort of application. So if your acquaintances in the real estate business object to the ballpark approach to their profession, it doesn't matter. If you have gained a better, almost intuitive, appreciation of composing good programs, you have passed the lesson.

EXERCISES

8-1 Describe the meaning of the expression *nested subroutines*.

8-2 The following program contains nested subroutines. Make up a complete list of program line numbers in the order in which they are actually executed. Sketch out the printed text as it appears on the screen when the program is completely executed.

```
10 CLS:GOSUB 70
20 GOSUB 90
30 GOSUB 50
40 GOTO 40
50 PRINT "SUBROUTINES"
60 RETURN
70 PRINT "THESE ARE";
80 RETURN
90 PRINT "NESTED"
100 RETURN
110 END
```

8-3 Repeat the work requested in Exercise 8-2 for the following program:

```
10 CLS: PRINT "START AT 10"
20 GOSUB 100
30 PRINT "AT THE START AND ENDING"
40 PRINT "DONE"
50 END
100 PRINT "AT SUB 100": GOSUB 200
110 PRINT "AT SUB 100 AND RETURNING":RETURN
200 PRINT "AT SUB 200": GOSUB 300
210 PRINT "AT SUB 200 AND RETURNING":RETURN
300 PRINT "AT SUB 300": GOSUB 400
310 PRINT "AT SUB 300 AND RETURNING":RETURN
400 PRINT "AT SUB 400": GOSUB 500
410 PRINT "AT SUB 400 AND RETURNING":RETURN
500 PRINT "AT SUB 500 AND RETURNING":RETURN
```

8-4 Subroutines 600 and 700 in Section 8-2 both contain the sequence CALCULATE CN followed by PRINT CN. Devise a subroutine for this sequence, beginning at line 800 and having any literal name you choose. Rewrite the programs for OPTION B and OPTION C to include your new subroutine (and, of course, eliminate the original references to CAL-

CULATE CN and PRINT CN). Do your modifications have any effect on the main program that is based on the flowchart in Fig. 8-1?

8-5 Sketch the text that appears on the screen after running the program in section 8-2, assuming that you selected option A. "Input" the requested values of your choice. Repeat this work for options B and C.

8-6 See if you can devise a complete subroutine-oriented program based on a single die-rolling routine. The idea is to roll a die by striking the ENTER key, pick up a random number between 1 and 6 inclusively, and display the result as a set of asterisks that take on the typical die pattern. (*Hint:* Use tabular graphics and consider the possible application of a statement such as ON N GOSUB *line numbers.*) Flowchart your process and document it clearly and thoroughly.

CHAPTER 9

More about BASIC
Math and Numbers

Although you have already had ample opportunity to work with some BASIC math expressions and numbers, the examples cited in the lessons have carefully sidestepped a few important issues and, alas, some special difficulties as well.

Perhaps you have been devising some math programs of your own and, in the process, stumbled across one or two of these issues and difficulties. In any event, a closer and more detailed look at BASIC math and numbers is in order.

9-1 Order of Math Operations

Think in terms of ordinary arithmetic and evaluate the following expression:

$$2 \times 4 + 3 = \underline{\quad}$$

That's "two times four plus three." What is it equal to? 11 or 14? Do you multiply 2 times 4 and then add 3? Or should you add 4 plus 3 and then multiply by 2?

Without being aware of a certain convention concerning the order in which arithmetic operations are performed, the problem is an ambiguous one.

One way to resolve the ambiguity is by inserting parentheses into the expression:

$$(2 \times 4) + 3 = \underline{\quad}$$

or

$$2 \times (4 + 3) = \underline{\quad}$$

Since expressions within parentheses are solved first, the solution in the first instance is $8 + 3 = 11$; and in the second instance, $2 \times 7 = 14$. The positioning of the parentheses dictates the order of operation.

Using parentheses can indeed go a long way toward resolving any ambiguity concerning the order of operation. However, there is a conventional procedure for ordering operations that makes the use of parentheses unnecessary.

The convention states that *multiplication and division operations are to be executed before operations involving addition and subtraction.* That being the case, the proper solution to the original problem is 11. In other words,

$$2 \times 4 + 3 = (2 \times 4) + 3 = 11$$

BASIC math uses the same convention.

In BASIC math, the highest priority of execution is given to expressions enclosed in parentheses. And if the expression contains nested parentheses, the system always works its way from the innermost to the outermost set. Example 9-1 illustrates how BASIC deals with sets of nested parentheses.

EXAMPLE 9-1

Original problem	2*((4*3)+((9-1)/4)+1)
First step	2*((4*3)+(8/4)+1)
Second step	2*(12 + 2 +1)

Third step   2*15

Final step   30

Of course, the bulk of this activity takes place behind the scenes; and as far as the user and programmer are concerned, the only apparent parts of the job are the original problem and the final step.

The second priority of execution is given to the exponential operation—the one signaled by an up arrow symbol (↑). A mathematical statement such as x^3, for instance, is expressed in BASIC as x↑3.

Example 9–2 brings together an expression in parentheses and an exponential operation. Note the order of execution.

EXAMPLE 9–2

Original problem   4*(1+3)↑2

First step   4*4↑2

Second step   4*16

Final step   64

BASIC takes care of the expression in parentheses first and then does the exponentiation.

The third level of priority is assigned equally to multiplication and division operations. Having two different operators with the same level of priority can cause some ambiguity, however, if an additional convention isn't tacked on. Namely, multiplication and division operations are always carried out in a left-to-right fashion. Consider this example:

EXAMPLE 9–3

Original problem   2*4/1∅

First step   8/1∅

Final step   .8

Going from left to right, BASIC multiplied 2 times 4 and then divided the result by 10.

This is merely an illustrative example, however, and it doesn't make a really convincing case for having to run the multiplication and division operations from left to right. In this case you'll get the same answer if you happen to work from left to right: $2*4 = .8$.

The need for working equal-priority math functions from left to right becomes more apparent when they are mixed with operations of the fourth level—addition and subtraction.

Like multiplication and division, addition and subtraction operators carry equal weight and are always executed from left to right.

EXAMPLE 9-4

Original problem	$2*4-1+8/2$
First step	$8-1+8/2$
Second step	$8-1+4$
Third step	$7+4$
Final step	11

BASIC first multiplied 2 times 4 and then divided 8 by 2. That took care of the left-ro-right execution of the higher-order multiplication and division operations. After that, in the third step, BASIC subtracted 1 from 8 and then added 4 to the result to come up with the final answer.

The original problem in Example 9–4 is terribly ambiguous if you don't follow the rules of priority and left-to-right execution. Without following the rules, you can view the original problem in quite a number of different ways, and come up with just about as many different solutions to it. BASIC looks at the thing just one way—the way dictated by the rules.

Principle. BASIC always solves mathematical equations in the following sequence:

1. Expressions enclosed within parentheses, beginning with the innermost set and working outward.
2. Exponentiated expressions; from left to right if more than one such expression is present.
3. Multiplication and division, from left to right.
4. Addition and subtraction, from left to right.

Example 9–5 incorporates all the principles of priority described to this point.

EXAMPLE 9-5

Original problem	2*(1+(12/6*3+2)↑2-6)
First step	2*(1+(2*3+2)↑2-6)
Second step	2*(1+(6+2)↑2-6)
Third step	2*(1+8↑2-6)
Fourth step	2*(1+64-6)
Fifth step	2*(65-6)
Sixth step	2*59
Final step	118

The first objective in solving this example is to clear out the inner set of parentheses. But to do that, BASIC must apply the rule that multiplication and division take precedence over addition, first working with multiplication and division from left to right. See the first and second steps.

The inner set of parentheses is eliminated only after doing the addition indicated in the second step. Even after that, another set of parentheses remains to be worked out; so BASIC does the exponentiation (fourth step), followed by a left-ro-right execution of the addition and subtraction (fifth and sixth steps).

The parentheses are finally gone by the sixth step, and all that remains is a single multiplication.

Knowing exactly how a computer will handle a mathematical equation is quite important. But unless you happen to be checking out someone else's program or doublechecking your own, you normally approach the situation from a different angle—writing BASIC equations from scratch rather than analyzing existing BASIC equations.

9-2   Writing Ordinary Equations in BASIC

The priorities BASIC assigns to the execution of operations in an equation are absolutely inflexible, which means that the programmer must follow the rules to the finest detail when writing the equations. Being "close" doesn't count, and the computer has no way of telling the difference between what you meant to say and what you actually said. Every mathematical equation written into a BASIC format must be exactly right; otherwise, you will end up with some crazy results or an error signal.

First take a look at some rather straightforward examples, and then consider some examples that have some hidden pitfalls.

EXAMPLE 9-6 Given the values of A, B, and x, write a program that solves the equation $Ax^2 + Bx = C$ and prints the value of C.
 In BASIC, the equation ought to take this form

$$C=A*X\uparrow2+B*X$$

The program might look like this:

```
10 CLS:INPUT "VALUES OF A, B AND X";A,B,X
20 PRINT"C="A*X↑2+B*X ; END
```

Assuming that you enter values $A = 2$, $B = 3$, and $X = 4$, the computer handles the equation as follows:

Original problem	2*4↑2+3*4
First step	2*16+3*4
Second step	32+12
Final step	44

What you will see on the screen is

```
VALUES OF A, B AND X? 2,3,4
C= 44
READY
>_
```

It works just fine.

EXAMPLE 9-7 The distance covered by a freely falling body is given by the general equation, $S = \frac{1}{2}gt^2 + v_0 t$, where g is the prevailing gravitational constant, v_0 the initial velocity of the body, and t the time that has passed.
 The BASIC version of this equation can take the form

$$S=1/2*G*T\uparrow2+V\emptyset*T$$

For the sake of checking the operation of the BASIC version, let G=32, T=2, and V∅=1∅. Applying these values to the original equation, S=84. Now walk through the BASIC version:

Original problem	1/2*32*2↑2+1∅*2
First step	1/2*32*4+1∅*2

Second step	.5*32*4+1Ø*2
Third step	16*4+1Ø*2
Fourth step	64+1Ø*2
Fifth step	64+2Ø
Final step	84

So it works. Such a problem causes some programmers a bit of difficulty, however—especially programmers who have extensive experience with ordinary math equations. An unwary programmer might try this:

$$S=1/2GT\uparrow2+VØT$$

What is wrong with this version? People accustomed to working with mathematical equations have a habit of omitting the multiplication operator. The lack of an operator between variables *implies* a multiplication operation. Unfortunately for such people, no part of a computer program can be written by implication.

EXAMPLE 9–8 Write a BASIC statement for solving the equation $\sqrt[3]{a+b}$, or the cube root of the sum of *a* and *b*. Now the only provision for working with radicals in BASIC involves the mathematical principle $\sqrt[n]{x} = x^{1/n}$. The radical is expressed as a fractional exponent. Mathematically speaking, $\sqrt[3]{a+b}$ can be represented as $(a+b)^{1/3}$; in BASIC, it should look like this:

$$(A+B)\uparrow(1/3)$$

You can test the idea by substituting some convenient values for variables A and B—such as 2 and 6, respectively. That should yield the cube root of 8, or 2. See if the BASIC equation works:

Original problem	(2+6)↑(1/3)
First step	8↑(1/3)
Second step	8↑.333333
Final step	2

It works. Plug it into a program and run the equation for a number of different values for A and B. It will work every time.

In retrospect, however, is it necessary to enclose the fractional exponent in parentheses? Couldn't the BASIC form of the equation be written

$$(A+B)\uparrow1/3?$$

Substitute the same values for A and B, and walk through the BASIC rules for working equations.

Original problem	(2+6)↑1/3
First step	8↑1/3
Second step	8/3
Final step	2.66667

That is hardly the correct solution to the problem as it is supposed to be solved. Without the parentheses enclosing the exponential fraction, the 1/3 division operation takes a lower priority than the exponentiation does, so the exponent is taken to be the numeral 1 in the fraction's numerator.

Study these two versions of the equation originally cited in this example. The second version is quite representative of the kinds of programming errors you will be making.

One of the best ways to master the technique for writing mathematical equations in BASIC is to transcribe equations found in technical books. If you are not especially good at solving the problems yourself, there is nothing lost by using examples already worked out in the book. Simply rewrite the equations in a BASIC format and run them on the computer. Any mistakes you make in the programming ought to show up quite clearly. In that case, it is up to you to figure out what you did wrong.

EXAMPLE 9-9 Solve the equation $Ax^2 + Bx + C = 0$ for the two possible values of x, given the values of A, B, and C.

The simplest way to approach the situation is by applying the *quadratic equation*:

$$x = \frac{-B \pm \sqrt{B^2 - 4AC}}{2A}$$

The ± operator in the numerator of the quadratic equation implies there are two answers to the problem—that there are two possible values for x. One value comes about when $-B$ is added to the radical expression; the second comes about when the radical expression is subtracted from $-B$. It is altogether possible that the product $4AC$ can be larger than B^2. Whenever that is the case, the equation calls for taking the square root of a negative number, and the result is a set of *imaginary solutions*. Home computers cannot deal with imaginary solutions without some help from the programmer; so to keep this task down to manageable proportions, the program ought to give up whenever the solutions are imaginary. Set up the program to print out *real solutions* only.

```
10 CLS:INPUT "INPUT A, B, C";A,B,C
20 R0=B↑2-4*A*C
```

```
30 IF R0<0 THEN 90
40 R=R0↑.5
50 X1=(-B+R)/(2*A)
60 X2=(-B-R)/(2*A)
70 PRINT "X1="X1,"X2="X2
80 GOTO 100
90 PRINT "IMAGINARY ROOTS"
100 INPUT X$; GOTO 10
```

The values of A, B, and C are entered from the keyboard in line 10. Line 20 then solves the expressions inside the radical: $B^2-4*A*C$. The result is assigned to variable R0.

If R0 is negative, the roots are imaginary and the system ought to pass on the problem, printing simply IMAGINARY ROOTS. This is what happens if the conditional statement in line 30 is satisfied.

Line 40 takes the square root of the expression under the radical and assigns it to variable R. In this case, using an exponent of 0.5 gets around the fractional-exponent difficulty described in Example 9-8. Alternative procedures would be to use R=R0 (1/2) or, better yet, R=SQR(R0). Recall from Table 1-1 that SQR(n) extracts the square root of n.

Line 50 completes the solution of the quadratic equation for the case where -B is added to the radical term. Line 60 picks up the second solution where the radical term is subtracted from -B. The solutions are assigned to X1 and X2, respectively. See if you can work out the equations in those two lines of the program without having to install two sets of parentheses.

Note. When in doubt about how a BASIC math equation is going to work out, use parentheses to force things to work your way. That might be considered an "underground" statement in some sophisticated circles of BASIC programmers, but it can get you off the hook and save a lot of trouble sometimes. The idea is based on the fact that operations in parentheses always take precedence over all others.

The remainder of the program—lines 70 through 100—is fairly straightforward. These lines merely present the results on the screen and give the operator a chance to do another problem by striking the ENTER key.

9-3 A Roundup of Other BASIC Functions

Table 9-1 summarizes all the math functions that are available on most BASIC-oriented home computer systems. You have seen some

Table 9-1   A Summary of BASIC Math Functions

Basic Syntax	Meaning	Function
T(n)	greatest-integer value of n	integer$<=n$
ABS(n)	absolute value of n	$\sqrt{n^2}$
SQR(n)	square root of n	$\sqrt{n}$, where $n>=0$
LOG(n)	natural log of n	$\log_e n$ or $\ln n$
EXP(n)	natural exponent of n	n^e
SIN(n)	sine of n	$\sin(n)$, where n is in radians
COS(n)	cosine of n	$\cos(n)$, where n is in radians
TAN(n)	tangent of n	$\tan(n)$, where n is in radians
ATN(n)	arctangent of n or inverse tangent of n	$\text{Arctan}(n)$ or $\text{Tan}^{-1}(n)$

of them already, but they are repeated here for the sake of convenience and completeness.

This is not the place to launch a lengthy and detailed dissertation on the mathematics involved in these BASIC functions. A good college textbook on intermediate mathematics treats such subjects in all their glory. The task at hand is one of BASIC computer programming; so other than a few remarks and some examples, it is up to the reader to dig out the mathematics of the affair in another source.

The INT(n) function is worthy of special note because several other BASIC statements apply the function automatically. Take, for example, the ON (n) GOTO *line numbers.* Recall from Chapter 6 that n can be a math expression that generates numbers that are not necessarily integers. It is logically necessary, however, to count line numbers with whole numbers, or integers. As described in Chapter 6, a value of n that is something like 2.554 going into an ON(n) GOTO *line numbers* statement will first be "rounded" to 2—the greatest-integer value of 2.554. In short, BASIC does an automatic INT(n) before executing an ON(n) GOTO *line numbers* statement.

As long as the n in an INT(n) expression is zero or more (positive), you can think of the function doing no more than simply dropping off all the decimal values. So a number such as 1.1 becomes 1, and 89.999 becomes 89. But that isn't quite the case for numbers less than zero (negative). For instance, the greatest-integer value of –2.1 is –3, and the greatest-integer value of –2.9 is –3.

Technically speaking, INT(n) picks up the next integer that is less than or equal to n. And since a number such as –4 is considered less than –3, it figures that –2.1 and –2.9 would both have greatest-integer values of –3. By the same line of reasoning, 2.1 and 2.9 would both have greatest-integer values of 2.

You can get a good feeling for INT(n) by putting the system into the command mode and entering a lot of PRINT INT(n) statements, where you select the n values yourself. In the command mode, the system will respond immediately by printing the greatest-integer value.

The ABS(n) function returns the absolute value of any number n. To put it simply, ABS(n) drops the minus sign from any negative number but leaves any positive number unchanged. For instance, ABS(–2.4) = 2.4, and ABS (2.4) = 2.4.

There are two features of the LOG(n) function that require some special attention. First, the function returns the natural, base e, logarithm of n. This is the base most commonly used in engineering and scientific applications, and it is *not* the base 10 system most often used in elementary math courses. In much engineering and scientific literature, the natural logarithm is expressed as $\ln(n)$, while the *common* (base 10) logarithm is expressed as $\log(n)$.

A second important feature of the LOG(n) function is that it is not defined for n when n is zero or negative. In fact, the only valid range for *any* log function is $n > 0$.

There are times, however, when you will want to program common logs; and unless you write the program very carefully, there is always a chance of coming up with a value for n that is zero or negative. Here is how to deal with both of these situations.

The basic formula for converting from natural to common logarithms is $\log_{10}(n) = 0.4343 \log_e(n)$. In the BASIC syntax, this can be written as

$$CL = .4343*LOG(n)$$

where n is any number larger than zero and CL is your own variable designation for common, base 10 log.

You can try this conversion with the system in the command mode by entering PRINT .4343*LOG(1∅). The system immediately returns 1.00001—a number very close to the base 10 log of 10 (which is 1.00000).

> *Note.* To get the common, base 10 log of a number, *n*, use the function .4343*LOG(*n*).
>   To get the natural, base *e* log of a number, *n*, use the function LOG(*n*).

A program that uses the LOG(*n*) function ought to be goof-proofed against the possibility of attempting to take the log of a number equal to or less than zero. An error sequence such as the following one will take care of the problem nicely:

EXAMPLE 9-10

.
.
.

```
100 INPUT N
110 IF N<=0 THEN 130
120 Y=LOG(N): GOTO 140
130 PRINT "N MUST BE GREATER THAN ZERO. TRY AGAIN":GOTO 100
140 PRINT Y
```

.
.
.

The function EXP(*n*) simply raises any number *n* to the *e*th power, where *e* is a constant value very close to 2.71828. The same sort of function can be carried out by means of the BASIC formula *n*↑2.71828. But, of course, EXP(*n*) is far easier to use and it runs much faster on the computer. Again, this is one of those functions normally reserved for engineering and scientific applications.

The three trigonometric functions SIN(*n*), COS(*n*), and TAN(*n*) call for some explanation. In BASIC, *n* must be specified in radians rather than degrees; and in the case of TAN(*n*), values of *n* that are integer multiples of $\pi/2$ are invalid. There are no such restrictions on the values of *n* for SIN(*n*) and COS(*n*).

Having to work in radians instead of degrees can pose some problems at times. It turns out, however, that a simple conversion process can solve the difficulty whenever it arises:

$$N=.017453*ND$$

where ND is the angle in degrees and N is the angle in radians—the *n* value required for BASIC SIN(*n*), COS(*n*), and TAN(*n*).

So if you want the system to do something such as printing the sine of an angle expressed in degrees, try this:

```
10 INPUT N
20 PRINT SIN(.017453*N)
30 END
```

This is a nifty little trick, because the conversion from degrees to radians takes place within the trig statement itself. The same conversion sequence works for COS(*n*) and TAN(*n*), but only as long as N is not some integer multiple of 90 for the TAN(*n*) function.

Next is a short program that shows how to avoid invalid values of *n* when using the TAN(*n*) function in degrees. The program also illustrates a common and powerful application of INT(*n*).

EXAMPLE 9-11

```
10 CLS
20 INPUT "ENTER ANGLE IN DEGREES";N
30 IF INT(N/90)=N/90 THEN 60
40 PRINT "N=",N,"TAN(N)=",TAN(.17453*N)
50 INPUT X$: GOTO 10
60 PRINT "INVALID N (MULTIPLE OF 90 DEGREES). TRY AGAIN"
70 GOTO 20
80 END
```

The user actually enters some angle N in degrees at the INPUT statement in line 20. Line 30 uses an INT(*n*) function to see whether or not N is an integer multiple of 90. If that is the case, INT(N/90) is equal to N/90 and the condition is satisfied, and control is sent down to the error message in line 60.

If, however, the conditional statement in line 30 is *not* satisfied—N is not an integer multiple of 90—the system prints the value of N, followed by the tangent of the angle.

Line 50 merely gives the user a chance to run the program again by striking the ENTER key.

> *Note.* It is possible to work with BASIC trig functions using degrees instead of radians by using the following expressions:
>
> $$SIN(.017453*N)$$
>
> $$COS(.017453*N)$$
>
> $$TAN(.017453*N)$$
>
> where N is the angle variable in degrees.

Some engineering and scientific applications call for three other trig functions; secant, cosecant, and cotangent. These expressions are merely inverted versions of the cosine, sine, and tangent functions respectively. So

$1/COS(n)$ returns the secant of n

$1/SIN(n)$ returns the cosecant of n

$1/TAN(n)$ returns the cotangent of n

The ATN(n) function returns the inverse-tangent value. Given any number n, the system returns the angle, in radians, whose tangent is equal to n. The angle, incidentally, will be the *principal angle,* as described in trigonometry textbooks.

It is sometimes necessary to determine the inverse-sine and inverse-cosine for $-1<=n<=1$. It is possible to work with these functions in BASIC by applying the standard ATN(n) and SQR(n) functions.

Note.

To get $Sin^{-1}(N)$, use ATN(N/SQR(-N*N+1))

To get $Cos^{-1}(N)$, use -ATN(N/SQR(-N*N+1))+1.5708
where $-1<=N<=1$.

9-4   User-Defined Math Functions with DEF FN

As shown in Table 9-1, BASIC includes a generous number of commonly used mathematical functions. But as described in Section 9-3, those standard functions must be modified at times to suit special conditions—entering an angle in degrees instead of radians, for instance.

Many BASIC systems include a statement that allows you, the programmer, to define your own special math functions; and once the functions are thus defined in the program, you can call them much the same way the standard functions are called.

Suppose, for example, that you have a program calling for finding the sine of some angles a number of different times. The catch is that the user is inputting angles in degrees. Taking care of the situation is a matter of altering the SIN(n) function to accommodate angles in degrees, and as shown earlier, it's done with the expression SIN(.017453*N).

Now that isn't bad if you have to do it only once or twice in a given program; but what if the situation calls for doing the conversion a relatively large number of times? The job can get pretty tedious. That is where the DEF FN statement comes to the rescue.

Somewhere in the early part of the program, you can write a line that looks something like this:

DEF FNS(N) = SIN(.017453∗N)

And then when you want to work out the sine of N later, all you have to do is refer to function S(N). Maybe you want to input a value of N and then print the sine of it:

INPUT N
PRINT FNS(N)

That will do it.

In a formal sense, the DEFN FN statement can be written as

DEF FN*name* (*numerical variable* or *math*) = *desired function.*

In this case *name* can be any single-letter character between A and Z. The term or expression enclosed in parentheses can be a numerical variable, a numerical value, or a math expression. The *desired function* is the math function you want to define.

So a statement such as DEF FNS (N) = SIN(.017453∗N) breaks down this way: DEF FN is the standard syntax that tells the computer that a user-defined function is at hand. The S is the function name selected by the user, and N is a numerical variable that is somehow assigned a numerical value before the function is called. In our example here, it is some angle to be expressed in degrees. The *desired function* actually defines the function, and it must be composed of characters and expressions the standard BASIC uses.

> **Principle.**   DEF FNX(n) = *function* lets the user define a custom mathematical function, X(n), that can be then applied as a function belonging to usual family of BASIC functions.
>
> X identifies the function and can be any letter A through Z. The n term is the variable to be worked on, and *function* is the definition of the function being created.

Unfortunately, not all BASIC home computer systems include

the DEF FN statement. Consult your manual to see if you have this advantage available to you.

9-5   Some Notes about Numbers and Scientific Notation in BASIC

Computers are often portrayed as exceedingly accurate and precise machines. It is said they make absolutely no mistakes, and whatever appears as a mistake is actually due to poor programming.

Well, I hate to be the bearer of bad news, but you are going to find your little computer isn't all that accurate and precise. Specifically, it has trouble handling certain kinds of numbers; and the only saving feature is that the shortcomings are predictable. The bottom line is that you, the programmer, ought to be aware of the system's quirks and make provisions for dealing with them.

If you want to get a firsthand look at how errors can creep into the works, run this program:

EXAMPLE 9-12

```
10 N=0
20 N=N+.1
30 PRINT N
40 GOTO 20
```

Now you could reasonably suppose that this program would print out an endless list of numbers, from zero to infinity in steps of .1. As long as the program is running, you would expect to see only one digit to the right of the decimal point, right?

Try it, and watch what happens. Somewhere along the line, the program seems to undergo spasms where more than one number appears to the right of the decimal point—the accuracy goes to pieces temporarily.

Exactly where and how often the problem arises, and how long it lasts, depends a lot on the electronics in the system you are using. On the Radio Shack TRS–80, the inaccuracies first creep in as this program counts past 7.7. The glitch looks like this:

```
        .
        .
        .
7.7
7.79999
```

```
7.89999
7.99999
8.Ø9999
8.2
 .
 .
 .
```

Everything goes along fine until it is time to count and print 7.8. Instead, the system produces 7.79999; and the little error persists until it gets down to 8.2.

The program in Example 9–12 is just one way of detecting groups of these little inaccuracies; and they occur rather frequently, and tend to last longer, as the program runs.

There isn't much to be gained by going into a lengthy technical discussion about the reasons that this sort of thing happens. In a nutshell, the problem is caused by the fact that computers do their calculations on the basis of binary numbers rather than decimal numbers. BASIC works with decimal numbers for the convenience of the user and programmer. And that means decimal numbers from BASIC have to be converted into binary numbers before they can be handled by the electronics. After that, the electronic results have to be translated from binary into decimal form again.

"Something is always lost in the translation," as the old saying goes; and this is just one example of how accuracy can get "lost" on a computer.

This is a grossly oversimplified explanation, but it should suffice for most programmers.

The inaccuracies of this sort creep into math operations other than the counting one specified in Example 8–12. They can crop up just about anywhere.

Now, of course, this means that some results of calculations are going to have some small errors in them. Most people can live with that sort of thing. 7.79999 is close enough to 7.8 for most practical purposes.

However, there is a far more serious situation involved here. Consider the following modification of Example 9–12:

EXAMPLE 9–13

```
1Ø N=Ø
2Ø N=N+.1
3Ø PRINT N
35 IF N=7.8 END
4Ø GOTO 2Ø
```

Presumably, the program will run until it prints 7.8, and then it comes to a stop. But it won't do that—it just keeps running along, passing 7.8 as though it never existed. Why? Because the exact value, 7.8, *never did* exist. Numbers such as 7.79999 and 7.89999 were there, but they bracket the 7.8 value.

Nasty little feature, isn't it! What's worse is writing a program that looks perfect on paper but doesn't work on the machine because of such a problem.

Take heart—there is an easy way around all this. In this particular case, modify line 35 in Example 9-13 to read

```
35 IF N>=7.8 END
```

Now the program will do its intended task.

Note. Make a habit of using "greater than or equal to" or "less than or equal to" expressions in all conditional statements. Use absolute equality expressions with great wisdom and care.

Develop the habit of using >= and <= in place of =, and you will rarely run into the problems caused by rounded and translated numbers. The computer still makes its "mistakes," but now you know how to cover for it.

While on the subject of roundoff errors and such, you have probably noticed that your system never prints numbers having any more than six digits in them. That's the case, anyway, if you are using the usual *single-precision* accuracy.

Not all the numbers have all six digits specified, however. Doing an operation such as PRINT 1/2 causes the machine to return .5— a single-digit number that effectively has five zeros following it. The system automatically suppresses, or truncates, trailing zeros in a decimal expression (as most people do). In fact, getting a number having less than six digits implies that the number is quite accurate.

Try PRINT 1/3 and you will get .333333 printed on the screen. Try PRINT 2/3 and you get .666667 for an answer. Irrational fractions result in unending decimals; but in the real world, one has to draw the line somewhere and round off the result. Your computer system, using single-precision accuracy, rounds off the answer at the sixth digit.

Now here is an important question: How does a system limited to six digits handle very large and very small numbers? The answer is rather straightforward: BASIC is set up to handle power-of-ten, *scientific notation.*

As an example, a small number such as .000123 can be expressed as 1.23×10^{-4}. The computer cannot handle superscripts and fancy notation like that, so it formats the same thing as 1.23E–Ø4.

> *Note.* An E character appearing within a BASIC number indicates that the number is expressed in scientific notation.

Just as BASIC can print out numbers in scientific notation, it can accept them from the keyboard. The computer will know exactly what you mean if you type in a number such as 6.28E–23. That's a whale of a small number, but BASIC can deal with it. On the other hand, the memory could not handle the same number expressed as 628 preceded by a decimal point and 22 zeros.

Different computer systems treat the formatting of numbers in scientific notion according to different conventions. The ideas are fundamentally the same and unambiguous.

On the TRS–80 system, for example, you can enter a PRINT 123E–3 and get back 1.23E–1. The system automatically adjusts the position of the decimal point and exponent so that one digit appears to the left of the decimal point. Other systems might behave differently under the same circumstances.

As another example, entering PRINT 1ØØØØØØØØØ causes the system to return 1ØØØØØØØØØ. A different computer might respond with 1E+9 instead.

The program in Example 9–14 lets you figure out the notational peculiarities of your own system:

EXAMPLE 9-14

```
10 CLS
20 INPUT "VALUES OF A, B"; A,B
30 PRINT A, B, A/B
40 INPUT X$: GOTO 20
```

With this program, you can enter all sorts of numbers in scientific notation, and then see how the system interprets the pairs of numbers and works out their ratio. Running this program on Radio Shack's TRS-80, the activity on the screen looks like this:

```
VALUES OF A, B? .ØØØ123, 123ØØØ
 1.23E-Ø4        123ØØØ          1E-Ø9
?
```

It interpreted the value of A(.ØØØ123) as 1.23E–Ø4, B as 123ØØØ (no automatic conversion to scientific notation), and recorded the ratio of A/B as 1E–Ø9.

Get the program in Example 9–14 plugged into your own machine and play around until you recognize the peculiarities.

The important thing is that BASIC is indeed equipped to deal with scientific notation.

9-6   Dropping Decimals with FIX

If most of the material in this chapter has seemed to be terribly technical and esoteric, you can take a breather with the FIX(n) function.

All FIX(n) does is drop any and all numbers to the right of a decimal point. PRINT FIX(1.23456), for example, results in 1; and PRINT FIX(–123.45) gives –123. That is all there is to it.

If that seems too simple to be of any importance, you can look at it this way:

$$\text{For } n >= \emptyset \qquad \text{FIX}(n) = \text{INT}(n)$$

$$\text{For } n < \emptyset \qquad \text{FIX}(n) = \text{INT}(n)+1$$

EXERCISES

9-1 Apply the rules of BASIC to solve the following equations:
  (a) 2*4/2*4
  (b) (2*4)/2*4
  (c) 2*4/(2*4)
  (d) (2*4)/(2*4)
  (e) 2+4/2–4
  (f) (2+4)/2–4
  (g) 2+4/2*2↑2
  (h) 2*3*((3–6*2) –6/3)+1/–2

9-2 Transform the following standard equations into the BASIC syntax. Assume that the values of the variables are available.
  (a) $A = \frac{1}{2}BH$
  (b) $V = E^3$
  (c) $S = \frac{1}{2}GT^2 + V_0T + S_0$

(d) $V_c = V_0 + C \ln(VT - 1)$

(e) $H = \sqrt{A^2 + B^2}$

(f) $D = \sqrt{(V_1 - V_0)^2 + (W_1 - W_0)^2}$

9-3   Evaluate the following functions written in BASIC:

(a)   INT(23.1)

(b)   INT(23.9)

(c)   INT(23.5)

(d)   INT(-23.1)

(e)   INT(-23.9)

(f)   INT(1.23*.01)

(g)   FIX(23.1)

(h)   FIX(-23.1)

9-4   State the order of priorities for execution of BASIC math operations.

9-5   What values of n are invalid for the BASIC function TAN(n)?

9-6   Suppose that you wrote the following statement into a program. Assuming that the value of P is available, how would you specify an operation that would print the result of the function?

DEF FNU(P)=(P+2)↑(1/3)

9-7   Express the following numbers in BASIC scientific notation:

(a) 1.23×10^{12}

(b) 1.234×10^{-6}

(c) 123×10^{-12}

9-8   Express the following BASIC numbers in standard scientific notation:

(a)   5.65E+2

(b)   3.33333E-02

(c)   1.89E+10

CHAPTER
10

An Introduction
to
Logical Operations

Statements introduced in this chapter:

AND   OR   NOT   ELSE   LEN *(string)*

In a manner of speaking, computers are essentially high-speed count-ing machines. Much of the work you can now do with BASIC ulti-mately rests on the machine's ability to count and do arithmetic very rapidly and accurately.

But, of course, computers can do much more than count and do arithmetic. Unlike most electronic calculators (which also count and do arithmetic accurately and relatively quickly), a computer can exhibit a wide range of logic and control operations. Perhaps with-out realizing it, you have been doing some elementary sorts of logical and control operations already. Getting your computer to print a desired text format on the screen is one fine example of a computer-controlled operation. Some counting and arithmetic is going on be-hind the scenes, but the text-formatting example is essentially a control function.

The primary purpose of the work in this chapter is to demon-strate logical and control functions in a very clear fashion. You ought to be fully conscious of the fact you are doing something other than arithmetic, and in the process, you will be getting a bit of insight into a whole realm of computer applications that have little, if any, direct bearing on matters of calculation and arithmetic.

10-1   Logical Operators for IF . . . THEN Statements

Although it is probably safe to assume that most people now being exposed to a post–high school technical education are getting some training in Boolean logic, there's no harm in summarizing the fundamental ideas before applying them to personal-computer BASIC.

The logical operators most often included in BASIC-oriented home computers are AND, OR, NOT, and ELSE. As shown later in this chapter, it is possible to synthesize some of the other common Boolean expressions, such as NAND and NOR, from the four primary ones.

Consider this rather simple and ordinary statement: "If Sue *and* Bill visit us tonight, we will go to the movies." It is a rather straightforward conditional, IF . . . THEN sort of statement—IF Sue *and* Bill visit us tonight, THEN we will go to the movies.

What is of immediate significance, however, is the *and* conjunction. It implies that we will go to the movies only if *both* Sue AND Bill show up. If either one or both fail to show up, the statement implies that we will not be going to the movies (maybe Sue AND Bill have our share of the ticket money).

In an AND-type logical statement, *all* conditions linked by the AND operator must be true before the statement itself is satisfied. If any one of the conditions is not satisfied, the entire statement is not satisfied.

Try this short BASIC program:

EXAMPLE 10-1

```
10 CLS: INPUT A,B
20 IF A=1 AND B=2 THEN 40
30 GOTO 10
40 PRINT "THAT'S RIGHT":INPUT X$
50 GOTO 10
```

The AND logical operator is applied in line 20 of this program. If A is equal to 1 (and nothing else) AND B is equal to 2 (and nothing else), then the system prints the message in line 40: THAT'S RIGHT. If either of these variables have values other than those specified in line 20, the system defaults to line 30 and that causes the whole process to start over again.

The only way you can get the computer to print THAT'S RIGHT is by setting A=1 AND B=2. Any other combination of values merely restarts the program.

Principle. An AND conditional statement is satisfied only when all the conditions are exactly met.

To get some idea of how an AND conditional statement can simplify computer programs, consider how you might carry out the operations in Example 10–1 without the benefit of the AND operator:

EXAMPLE 10-2

```
10 CLS: INPUT A,B
20 IF A=1 THEN 40
30 GOTO 10
40 IF B=2 THEN 60
50 GOTO 10
60 PRINT "THAT'S RIGHT":INPUT X$
70 GOTO 10
```

In this example each of the input conditions must be tested separately, each having its own IF . . . THEN conditional statement. Using the AND operator, however, makes it possible to do the same job with a single IF . . . THEN statement.

Any number of conditions can be linked by the AND operator, and the conditions themselves can be math operations, math functions, string expressions, and, for that matter, any valid BASIC relational expression. Here are a few more examples:

```
IF (A+B=4.5) AND (A+C/2=12) THEN . . .
IF (A>=B) AND (C=1) AND (A/4<C) THEN . . .
IF A$="MOST" AND B$="MORE" THEN . . .
```

In all instances, the conditions linked by the AND operator must be satisfied before the statement, as a whole, is satisfied.

An OR statement is something quite different. Suppose you say: "If Sue *or* Bill visits us tonight, we will go to the movies." This is still a conditional IF . . . THEN statement, but the implication is that we will go to the movies if *either* Sue *or* Bill *or* both show up.

The requirements for satisfying an OR conditional statement are a bit looser than for an AND statement. Only one of the conditions must be met in order to satisfy the overall statement.

Principle. An OR conditional statement is satisfied whenever any one or more than one of its conditions are met.

Compare these two programs. They do exactly the same thing.

EXAMPLE 10–3a

```
10 CLS: INPUT A,B
20 IF A=1 OR B=2 THEN 40
30 GOTO 10
40 PRINT "THAT'S RIGHT":INPUT X$
50 GOTO 10
```

EXAMPLE 10–3b

```
10 CLS: INPUT A,B
20 IF A=1 THEN 50
30 IF B=1 THEN 50
40 GOTO 10
50 PRINT "THAT'S RIGHT":INPUTX$
60 GOTO 10
```

Running either of these programs, responding to the INPUT statement in line 10 by entering A=1 is sufficient to get the THAT'S RIGHT statement. It makes no difference at all what you do with the B variable.

By the same token, you can get the THAT'S RIGHT message by inputting B=2, no matter what you do with the A value. And finally, you can also get the THAT'S RIGHT message by inputting A=1, B=2. Satisfying either or both of the requirements is sufficient.

The two examples do the same job, but the one in Example 10–3a uses the OR operator to simplify the programming job and, in fact, make the whole program run a bit faster.

Any number of conditions can be connected by OR operators; and as in the case of the AND statements, the conditions can be simple equality statements, math expressions, statements of inequality, math functions, and string expressions.

The fun really starts, however, when you combine AND and OR operators within the same IF . . . THEN clause. Consider, for example, the relative complexity of this seemingly innocent statement: "If

Sue *and* Bill *or* Jack visits us tonight, we will go to the movies." Here are the requirements spelled out in this statement:

1. We will go to the movies if both Sue and Bill visit. Jack does not have to come.
2. We will go to the movies if Jack visits. Sue and Bill do not have to show up.
3. We will go to the movies if Sue, Bill, and Jack visit.

Looking at the same situation from a negative point of view:

1. We won't go to the movies if just Sue visits.
2. We won't go to the movies if just Bill visits.
3. We won't go to the movies if none of the three show up.

One of the most useful and, in fact, vital applications of AND and OR operators is that of setting upper and lower boundaries on variable quantities. The standard BASIC inequalities are adequate for setting upper or lower boundaries, but not both at the same time. Upper boundaries, for example, can be set by means of expressions such as A<1∅ and A<5∅. By the same token, lower boundaries can be set by using expressions such as A>∅ and A>=1∅. But home-computer BASIC generally cannot handle both at the same time— ∅<A<=1∅ won't work, even though it represents a common sort of mathematical expression.

In a literal sense, the expression 0<A<=10 means the value of A is greater than zero but less than or equal to 10. The BASIC version of the same idea must be expressed this way: A>∅ and A<=1∅. That does it. It is saying that A has to be greater than zero AND, at the same time, less than or equal to 10.

Try this experiment:

EXAMPLE 10-4

```
1∅ CLS: LET A=∅
2∅ IF A>∅ AND A<=1∅ PRINT A
3∅ LET A=A+1: GOTO 2∅
```

This is basically an unending counting program, but it prints only those integer values of A between 1 and 10 inclusively.

Although the value of A is initialized at zero in line 10, it is not printed on the screen because it is excluded by the A ∅ part of the logical condition in line 20. Line 20 allows values 1 through 10 to be printed, however. After that, line 20 excludes additional values of A, and the counting proceeds indefinitely without affecting the printout at all.

So what you see is a simple listing of numbers 1 through 10. You can prove to yourself that the system is still counting by doing a BREAK, followed by entering PRINT A in the command mode. The result will be some relatively large number—one representing the progress of the counter.

Whenever a BASIC expression includes more than one logical operator, they are treated with equal priority and read from left to right. To see how this works, consider a computer-instruction program that displays this question and possible answers:

```
Q: WHO IS BURIED IN GRANT'S TOMB
   1  LINCOLN
   2  GRANT
   3  EISENHOWER
   4  NONE OF THE ABOVE

   ?_
```

Presumably, the operator is going to enter an integer between 1 and 4 inclusively, and some portion of the program evaluates the answer and makes some appropriate comments. The important point here, however, is to goof-proof the process by actively prohibiting any answer except 1, 2, 3, or 4.

Suppose the operator's answer is INPUT as a numerical value for variable A. The answering process can be goof-proofed by means of this sort of statement:

IF A<>INT (A) OR A<1 OR A>4 THEN *line number.*

where *line number* is a statement that signals an invalid answer to the question. The answer to the question would be invalid if A<>INT(A) because that means the operator entered a number having some decimal or fractional part—the question calls for integer answers. The answer would also be invalid if A<1, because that means the operator replied with a number less than 1, including 0 and all negative numbers. And finally, A>4 would be invalid because such an answer would be some number greater than 4.

Now the goof-proofing statement just described eliminates invalid answers to the question. The same thing could be accomplished in a different fashion:

If A=INT(A) AND A>0 AND A<5 THEN *line number.*

where *line number,* in this instance, carries the program to a valid sequence of operations. The answer is *valid* if it meets the AND qualifications. In the first example, the answer is *invalid* if it meets the OR qualifications.

Both statements accomplish the same goof-proofing, and the programmer's choice is a matter of taste or convenience.

A NOT expression completely turns around any logic expression following it. Referring to some examples cited earlier in this section, suppose that you are in this situation: "We will go to the movies only if both Sue AND Bill do NOT show up."

That is basically an AND-type situation—one that is satisfied only if Sue AND Bill are together. But here we are negating the AND clause. We will NOT go to the movies if Sue AND Bill show up. In other words, we will go to the movies if just Sue or just Bill or neither of them comes. But if they both come, we will not go. Apparently, Sue and Bill, together, provide some sort of entertainment that makes it unnecessary to go to the movies.

Maybe that sounds very much like an OR conditional to you— if Bill OR Sue shows up, we will go to the movies. There is a difference, however. With this OR conditional, we still go to the movies if they both show up. With the NOT-AND statement, we do not go if they both show up.

Compare these two examples:

EXAMPLE 10-1

```
10 CLS: INPUT A,B
20 IF A=1 AND B=2 THEN 40
30 GOTO 10
40 PRINT "THAT'S RIGHT": INPUT X$
50 GOTO 10
```

EXAMPLE 10-5

```
10 CLS: INPUT A,B
20 IF NOT(A=1 AND B=2) THEN 10
30 PRINT "THAT'S RIGHT": INPUT X$
40 GOTO 10
```

Both programs do exactly the same job. They print the message THAT'S RIGHT only if the operator enters the sequence 1, 2 in response to line 10 in both instances. Entering any other sequence of numbers merely restarts the program.

The use of a NOT/AND conditional in Example 10-5 shortens the program by one line, however. Instead of printing THAT'S RIGHT whenever

A=1 AND B=2 (as in Example 10-1), the message is *not* printed if the combination A=1 AND B=2 is NOT satisfied.

The programs accomplish the same task, but the programmer's thinking is just a bit different. And although it might seem confusing to use negated AND statements at this time, the fact that such statements can simplify programs makes it worth your effort to get negated logic straightened out in your mind.

Note the parentheses enclosing the AND conditionals in line 20 of Example 10-5. The parentheses are essential in this instance because, you might recall, all logical operators carry the same level of priority and are executed strictly from left to right. Using the parentheses forces the system to consider the A=1 AND B=2 statement *before* it negates the result with the preceding NOT expression. Logic statements, like math expressions, give priority to expressions within parentheses. If the parentheses in this example were to be omitted, the NOT expression would apply only to the A=1 portion of the AND statement, and the overall result would be quite different.

Principle. A NOT expression within a conditional statement completely reverses the conditions necessary for satisfying the statement.

Of course, NOT expressions can be used in conjunction with OR operators as illustrated in the following examples:

EXAMPLE 10-3a

```
10 CLS: INPUT A,B
20 IF A=1 OR B=2 THEN 40
30 GOTO 10
40 PRINT "THAT'S RIGHT": INPUT X$
50 GOTO 10
```

EXAMPLE 10-6

```
10 CLS: INPUT A,B
20 IF NOT(A=1 OR B=2) THEN 10
30 PRINT "THAT'S RIGHT": INPUT X$
40 GOTO 10
```

As you might suspect by now, these two programs do exactly the same task. The analysis of the situation, however, is left to you.

10-2 Tightening Up Conditional Statements with ELSE

Whenever any conditional statement is not satisfied, program control normally goes to the next line in the program listing. You have been taking advantage of this fact through all of the conditional statements cited thus far in this book. The principle applies to mathematical conditionals as well as logical conditionals.

But now the principle has to be modified somewhat. Instead of saying program control *always* goes to the next program line whenever a conditional statement is not satisfied, we ought to qualify the principle by adding *unless told to do otherwise*. The "otherwise" is made possible by the ELSE expression.

Compare the following program with that in Example 10-1:

EXAMPLE 10-7

```
10 CLS: INPUT A,B
20 IF A=1 AND B=2 THEN 30 ELSE 10
30 PRINT "THAT'S RIGHT": INPUT X$
40 GOTO 10
```

Literally speaking, line 20 says: If A=1 AND B=2 at the same time, THEN go to 40; ELSE (otherwise) go to 10. Using the ELSE expression eliminates the need for a separate GOTO 10 statement line.

Principle. An ELSE expression included in a conditional statement directs program control in the event the conditions specified in the statement are not satisfied.

A great many conditional statements cited in earlier examples can be simplified by using ELSE expressions within them.

Here is a short program for listing integers between 0 and 9:

EXAMPLE 10-8

```
10 CLS: A=1
20 IF A<10 THEN 30 ELSE END
30 PRINT A: A=A+1: GOTO 20
```

As long as A is less than 10, the conditional statement in line 20 is satisfied and line 30 is called to print the value of A, increment it, and then test its value. Whenever the conditional in line 20 is no longer satisfied (the value of A is equal or greater than 10), the ELSE expression comes into the picture and the program is ended.

10-3   A "High-Low" Game Using Logical Operators

Here is a tricky little game that illustrates the use of all the logical operators described in Section 10-1. As usual, you can expect to find some new ideas of other kinds tucked into the program.

The game requires two players. One player selects a combination of numbers and letters, and it is up to the other player to find the exact combination. Clues provided through the course of the game give especially sharp players a better chance of finding the combination in a short time.

The combinations, for the sake of simplicity, are limited to a number between 1 and 9, followed by a letter between A and D. No other combination works—and you can be sure the program will let you know that.

So the first player, called the selector, enters a number between 1 and 9 and a letter between A and D. That player then clears the screen and lets the guesser go to work. The program keeps a running tally of the number of invalid or incorrect guesses. After entering a valid guess, the guesser is told whether either of the two characters is higher or lower than the one hidden away in the system's memory. The catch is that the machine doesn't tell the player which one of the two characters is too low or too high.

The game goes along until the guesser finally hits upon the right combination. The final tally is that player's score. The player's then change around their roles, and the whole thing is run again. The player ending up with the lowest tally is the winner.

Figure 10-1 is the flowchart for this high–low guessing game. When it is started, the player selecting the "secret" combination sees the screen filled with instructions. It looks something like this:

SELECTOR:

       ENTER:
               1. A NUMBER BETWEEN 1 AND 9
               2. A COMMA
               3. A LETTER BETWEEN A AND D

               EXAMPLE - - 1,C

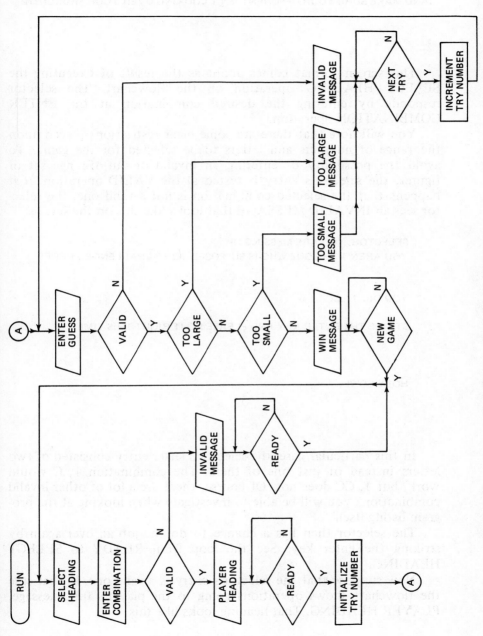

Figure 10-1 Flowchart for High-Low.

213

(AND MAKE SURE YOUR OPPONENT ISN'T LOOKING OVER YOUR SHOULDER)

?_

This screen format comes about as the result of executing the SELECT HEADING operation on the flowchart. The selector responds by entering the desired combination at the ENTER COMBINATION operation.

You will note that there are some clear restrictions placed upon the range of numbers and letters to be selected for the game. To avoid the possibility of entering an invalid or out-of-range set of figures, the selector's entry is tested at the VALID operation. If it happens that the selected combination is not a valid one, the selector sees an INVALID MESSAGE that looks like this on the screen:

SELECTOR, YOU ARE MESSING UP.
YOU AREN'T THE ONE WHO IS SUPPOSED TO BE CHALLENGED HERE!

YOU DID 1 ,CC

STRIKE THE ENTER KEY AND PLEASE DO IT RIGHT THIS TIME.

HOLY COW!

?_

In this particular case, the selector's letter entry consisted of two letters instead of just one of them. The combination 1, C would work, but 1, CC does not. Of course, there are a lot of other invalid combinations you will be able to investigate when looking at the program listing itself.

The selector then has a chance to do the job all over again by striking the enter key. See the loop from READY to SELECT HEADING.

Now suppose that the selector's entry is a valid one. In that case the flowchart shows operations going to the player's first message, PLAYER HEADING. That heading looks like this:

PLAYER:
TIME FOR YOU TO GO TO WORK.

FIGURE OUT THE RIGHT COMBINATION OF
A NUMBER BETWEEN 1 AND 9 AND A LETTER BETWEEN A AND D.

EXPRESS YOUR REPLIES AS NUMBER–COMMA–LETTER

EXAMPLE – – 1,C

STRIKE THE ENTER KEY WHEN YOU ARE READY TO START.

?_

When the player is ready to go, he strikes the ENTER key to satisfy the READY conditional. As a result, the system sets the counter—one that counts the number of unsuccessful guesses—to one. That is the INITIALIZE TRY NUMBER operation appearing on the flowchart.

The player then enters the first guess at ENTER GUESS. The guess is then evaluated according to three sets of criteria. It is checked at VALID to see whether or not the number–letter entry is valid (much the same sort of test applied to the selector's entry earlier in the program). If the player's guess consists of one or more invalid terms, the system returns an INVALID MESSAGE that says, YOU MESSED UP THE ENTRY. THAT WILL COST YOU A TRY.

If the entry is a valid combination of number and letter, the next conditional operation determines whether one or both of the characters are larger than those entered by the selector. If indeed that is the case, the system responds with a TOO LARGE MESSAGE.

But if neither term is too large, the system then compares the characters to see if either or both are too small. An appropriate TOO SMALL MESSAGE appears on the screen if that is the case. Otherwise, the implication is that the guessed terms are right on the money—if they aren't too large or too small, and they are valid characters, that is a very safe assumption.

Whenever the player hits upon the right combination of characters, a flashing WIN MESSAGE appears on the screen, and then the whole thing can be restarted by satisfying the NEW GAME condition. The latter operation will be nothing more than entering the null string by striking the ENTER KEY.

Every time the player misses a guess, he gets another chance by satisfying the NEXT TRY conditional. That, again, is a simple matter of striking the ENTER key; and as a result INCREMENT TRY NUMBER advances the number of tries and control returns back the ENTER GUESS. Incidentally, ENTER GUESS also shows the number of tries the player has made.

Once you see what the game is supposed to do and how the flow-chart displays the operations, you shouldn't have too much trouble following the program itself. With that in mind, there is little more to the analysis of the program than pointing out the new or critical features.

Lines 5 through 55 in the program in Example 10-9 comprise the SELECT HEADING and ENTER COMBINATION blocks on the flowchart. There is nothing new among those program lines.

Lines 60, however, includes several points of special interest. First note that it represents the first VALID conditional on the flowchart. The job of this line is to determine whether or not the selector has entered a valid combination of terms.

In line 60, the expression N<>INT(N) is a technique that tests number N to see whether or not it is an integer. This particular expression is satisfied if N is not an integer.

Then there is the expression N<1, followed shortly thereafter by N>9. The first checks for N values less than 1, while the second checks for N values greater than 9. What we are doing here is checking for N values that are invalid because they fall outside the range 1 through 10.

EXAMPLE 10-9

```
5 REM ** SELECT HEADING **
10 CLS:PRINT"SELECTOR:"
20 PRINT:PRINT
30 PRINT TAB(10)"ENTER"
32 PRINT TAB(15)"1. A NUMBER BETWEEN 1 AND 9"
34 PRINT TAB(15)"2. A COMMA"
36 PRINT TAB(15)"3. A LETTER BETWEEN A AND D"
40 PRINT:PRINT TAB(25)"EXAMPLE -- 1,C"
50 PRINT:PRINT"(AND MAKE SURE YOUR OPPONENT ISN'T LOOKING OVER
   YOUR SHOULDER)"
55 PRINT:PRINT:INPUT N,N$
60 IF NOT(N<>INT(N) OR N<1 OR N>9 OR LEN(N$)>1 OR N$>"D") THEN 1
00
70 CLS:PRINT"SELECTOR, YOU ARE MESSING UP."
75 PRINT"YOU AREN'T THE ONE WHO IS SUPPOSED TO BE CHALLENGED
   HERE!"
80 PRINT:PRINT:PRINT"YOU DID"N", "N$:PRINT:PRINT"STRIKE THE ENTER
   KEY AND PLEASE DO IT RIGHT THIS TIME."
85 FOR L=0 TO 3:PRINT:NEXT:PRINT"HOLY COW!"
90 PRINT:PRINT:INPUT X$:GOTO 10
95 REM ** END OF SELECT PHASE **
```

```
100 CLS:PRINT"PLAYER:"
110 PRINT"TIME FOR YOU TO GO TO WORK."
115 PRINT"FIGURE OUT THE RIGHT COMBINATION OF"
120 PRINT"A NUMBER BETWEEN 1 AND 9 AND A LETTER BETWEEN A AND D.
"
125 PRINT:PRINT:PRINT"EXPRESS YOUR REPLIES AS NUMBER-COMMA-
LETTER."
130 PRINT:PRINT TAB(10)"EXAMPLE - - 1,C"
135 PRINT:PRINT:PRINT"STRIKE THE ENTER KEY WHEN YOU ARE READY TO
START."
140 PRINT:INPUT X$
150 L=1
160 CLS:PRINT"THIS IS TRY"L
165 PRINT:PRINT:PRINT
170 INPUT"WHAT IS YOUR GUESS";M,M$

200 REM ** TRY TESTING PHASE **
210 IF M<>INT(M) OR M<1 OR M>9 OR LEN(M$)>1 OR M$>"D" THEN 300
220 IF M>N OR M$>N$ THEN 310
225 IF M<N OR M$<N$ THEN 320

240 FOR F=0 TO 10:CLS:FOR LN=0 TO 8:PRINT:NEXT
250 FOR T=0 TO 100:NEXT:CLS:FOR T=0 TO 100:NEXT:NEXT
255 PRINT "YOU DID IT IN"L"TRIES"
260 INPUT"ENTER TO PLAY ANOTHER GAME";X$
265 GOTO 10

300 PRINT"YOU MESSED UP THE ENTRY. THAT WILL COST YOU A TRY":GOT
O 350
310 PRINT"SORRY, SOMETHING IS TOO LARGE":GOTO 350
320 PRINT"SORRY, SOMETHING IS TOO SMALL":GOTO 350
350 PRINT:PRINT:INPUT"HIT THE ENTER KEY TO TRY AGAIN";X$
360 L=L+1: GOTO 160
```

After testing the value of N on three points of validity, line 60 takes up the problem of testing the alphabetical character. That character has been assigned to string variable N$ in line 55, and its first test for validity is by a string function that has not yet been discussed—LEN(*string expression*). ALL LEN(N$) does is count the number of characters in the string expression. In this game, the string expression is supposed to have only one character—thus the inequality, LEN(N$) 1. The entry is invalid if there is more than one character in the N$ expression.

Note. The LEN(*string expression*) statement returns an integer equal to the number of characters in the specified *string expression*.

And finally, line 60 checks the value of N$ "D". Recall that inequalities used with string expressions indicate the relative position of the expressions in the alphabet. So if N$ "is greater than" D, it means it comes after D in the alphabet.

Line 60 thus checks the validity of the selector's letter entry by making certain it is only one letter and it is a letter between A and D.

Now all of these inequality functions are tied together by OR operators. In other words, the entire statement is true if any one of the individual inequalities is true. All of the inequalities, however, test for negative conditions—all the relevant invalid conditions. For that reason, the whole set of conditions is negated by the NOT expression preceding them.

Putting it all together, line 60 is satisfied if not a single one of the terms in the expression is true. If N is less than 1, for example, the line is NOT true. If N$ has more than one character in it, the line is NOT true, and so on.

If line 60, as a whole, is true, THEN control goes down to line 100. Otherwise, operations pick up at line 70.

Assume for the time being that line 60 is not satisfied. The selector's entry, in other words, has something wrong with it. That being the case, lines 70 through 95 take care of the necessary INVALID MESSAGE and READY operations, ultimately returning control back to line 10. At line 10, the selector has a chance to try entering a valid set of characters.

Lines 100 through 150 take care of the PLAYER HEADING, its corresponding READY conditional, and the INITIALIZE TRY NUMBER blocks on the flowchart.

Lines 160 through 170 print the player's try number (line 160) and prompt the player to enter the guess (line 170). The guess combination is assigned numerical variable M and string M$.

Line 210 checks the guessed entry for validity, using the same criteria applied to the selector's entry. Note, however, that the OR expressions in line 210 are not negated by a NOT operator as is done in line 60. Line 210 actually checks for the bad entries and, if satisfied, calls line 300 to print out the INVALID MESSAGE.

Lines 220 and 225 check to see whether either of the guessed characters is greater or less than the selected values. In line 220, for instance, something is wrong (a bad guess) if M>N, M$>N$, or both.

The remainder of the program includes no new ideas. You should be able to analyze it for yourself, using the flowchart as a general guide.

EXERCISES

10-1   Account for all conditions for variables A and B that satisfy (make true) the following statements:

(a)   IF A=∅ AND B=1 THEN . . .

(b) IF A=∅ OR B=1 THEN . . .

(c) IF NOT(A=∅ AND B=1)THEN . . .

(d) IF NOT(A=∅ OR B=1) THEN . . .

(e) IF A=∅ AND B=1 OR B=∅ THEN . . .

(f) IF A=∅ and (B=1 OR B=∅) THEN . . .

(g) IF A=∅ AND NOT(B=1 OR B=∅) THEN . . .

10–2 Why is the statement IF B=∅ AND B=1 THEN . . . nonsense?

10–3 Write BASIC IF . . . THEN conditional statements for the following inequalities:

(a) $0 \leqslant A \leqslant 10$

(b) $0 < A \leqslant 10$

(c) $0 \leqslant A < 10$

(d) $0 < A < 10$

10–4 Describe in literal terms the meaning of the following BASIC statements:

(a) IF N=INT(N) AND N>∅ THEN . . .

(b) IF N=INT(N) OR N>∅ THEN . . .

(c) IF SIN(N)>∅ THEN . . .

CHAPTER
11

A First Look
at
Data Processing

Statements introduced in this chapter:

DATA   READ   RESTORE   PRINT USING

Computers have often been called data processing machines. The applications of personal computers, as described thus far in this book, have not dealt with the entire field of data processing. In fact, the applications cited through the first ten chapters have belonged to special areas that might be called control and calculation applications.

The control applications have dealt with situations such as formatting the presentation of information on the CRT monitor and, of course, controlling the execution of programs. In a broader sense, control applications of computers make up a large share of all computer work being done today, including the control of automated processes, machinery, and, in fact, entire factories.

The calculation applications are those aimed at solving mathematical equations. You've already had a chance to do a lot of calculation work in the preceding chapters. But if all you ever want to do is calculation work, it is simpler and less expensive to use an electronic calculator. Using a computer system as a calculating machine (and nothing more) sells short its real potential.

But to this point, little has been done with data processing as such. You have seen very little in the way of processing information taking the form of names, dates, serial numbers, and any other meaningful descriptive expressions that are not limited to numerical quantities or simple string expressions.

Much of the work remaining in this book deals with processing lists of information—information of all kinds. The procedures might appear to be cumbersome and restrictive in the early going here, but you will find things smoothing out as you go along.

11-1   Reading Lists of Numerical Data

Your introduction to processing lists of data is going to involve lists of numbers. This might not be the most compelling sort of application, but it is the most straightforward. Bear in mind that the procedures outlined in this section apply equally well to lists of nonnumerical data.

Working with lists of data, as described in this chapter, calls for using two different statements: DATA and READ. The two must be used in conjunction. One without the other is meaningless.

The DATA statement signals the presence of a line of data. Since DATA and its associated list of information make up a program statement, it must be preceded by a valid line number. As an example:

100 DATA 2,4,8,16,32,64

That is a complete DATA line. It has a valid line number (100), the DATA statement, and a list of data following it. There are six items in the data list here. There can be any number of items in the list, just as long as each item is separated from the preceding one by a comma. (Some personal computer systems have a limit on the number of items in a single DATA line. Check your owner's manual for details.)

Principle. DATA *item list* is a BASIC program statement that contains a number of items separated by commas. The statement must carry a valid program line number.

Now the unusual thing about the DATA *item list* statement is that the computer does nothing whenever it encounters the statement in a program. It is treated much as a REM statement. And what is even more unusual is the fact that it makes no difference where the DATA *item list* is located in the program—at the beginning, at the end, or anywhere in between.

So what in the world does the DATA statement do? Well, it serves no real purpose until the computer encounters a READ *variable name* statement. The READ statement tells the computer to *read* the data associated with the DATA statement. Indeed, DATA and READ must be used in conjunction with one another.

Before going into more detail, try a program that uses the DATA and READ statements:

EXAMPLE 11-1a

```
10 DATA 2,4,8,16,32,64
20 CLS
30 FOR N=1 TO 6
40 READ D
50 PRINT D
60 NEXT
70 END
```

This is a rather simple program. When you RUN it, you will see the list of numbers in the DATA line printed vertically on the screen:

```
        2
        4
        8
       16
       32
       64
     READY
     >_
```

Note the presence of DATA *item list* in line 10, and its associated READ *variable name* in line 40. Since the *item list* is composed entirely of numerical values, the *variable name* for the READ statement must be a numerical variable—D in this case.

Now notice that the FOR . . . NEXT combination of statements between lines 30 and 60 cause the READ statement to be executed exactly six times. The DATA list, in other words, is read six times—one time for each item in the list.

Furthermore, each time the item list is read in line 40, the corresponding value of D is printed by the statement in line 50. The FOR . . . NEXT loop thus causes the program to READ and PRINT six items in the DATA listing—no more, and no less.

Looking at the situation in a more general way, the first time the FOR . . . NEXT loop is executed, the READ statement picks up the first item in the DATA list. The second time the READ statement is executed, it picks up the second item in the DATA list. The third time READ is executed, it picks up the third item; and so on to the end of the process.

Principle.   Items in a DATA *item list* are always read from left to right, one at a time, each time the corresponding READ statement is executed.

This principle leads to an important programming note: The number of times a READ statement is executed must be less than or equal to the number of items in the associated DATA list. In Example 11-1a, the FOR . . . NEXT loop causes the READ statement to be executed exactly six times—a number of times equal to the number of items in the DATA list.

You don't have to read all the items, however. For example, you can change line 30 to read: FOR N=1 TO 4. In that case, the READ statement will be executed just four times, and the program will end up printing just the first four items.

Any attempt to execute the READ command a number of times that exceeds the number of items in the DATA list causes the computer to generate an out-of-data error message.

To illustrate the fact that the DATA *item list* command can appear anywhere in the program, rewrite the program in Example 11-1a to look like this:

EXAMPLE 11-1b

```
20 CLS
30 FOR N=1 TO 6
40 READ D
50 PRINT D
60 NEXT
70 END
80 DATA 2,4,8,16,32,64
```

Run this program, and you will find that the results are exactly the same as running Example 11-1a—even though the DATA *item list* statement follows an END statement!

Or try this:

EXAMPLE 11-1c

```
20 CLS
30 FOR N=1 TO 6
40 READ D
45 DATA 2,4,8,16,32,64
50 PRINT D
60 NEXT
70 END
```

The DATA *item list* can go anywhere, even in the middle of a FOR . . . NEXT loop.

While the DATA *item list* statement can be placed absolutely anywhere in the program, most programmers select a more obvious and convenient place, either at the very beginning or at the end. That's more a matter of personal taste and habit than anything else.

It is possible, and quite desirable in some circumstances, to place more than one DATA *item list* statement within a program. As far as reading multiple DATA lines is concerned, however, they are all treated as though they are a single DATA line.

EXAMPLE 11-1d

```
10 DATA 2,4,8
15 DATA 16,32,64
20 CLS
30 FOR N=1 TO 6
40 READ D
50 PRINT D
60 NEXT
70 END
```

In this example, the item list from previous examples is split between two separate DATA statements. The overall result is the same, however. Reading begins with the first item in the DATA line carrying the lower line number and works, one item at a time, through the final item in the higher-numbered DATA line.

Principle. Multiple DATA *item list* commands are treated as a single DATA *item list* command. The items in the lowest-numbered DATA line will be read first, and the items in the highest-numbered DATA line will be read last.

Perhaps it is a purely academic point at this time, but it is a fact that multiple DATA lines can be scattered anywhere throughout the program.

EXAMPLE 11-1e

```
10 DATA 2,4,8
20 CLS
30 FOR N=1 TO 6
40 READ D
50 PRINT D
60 NEXT
70 END
80 DATA 16,32,64
```

The results of running this example are no different from any of the other examples cited so far.

Bear in mind one overriding principle, however: The number of times the READ statement is executed must not exceed the total number of items contained in DATA lines. You can scatter the DATA lines all over the place if you want, and the scheme works as long as you do not violate this one main principle.

All of the programs cited so far in this chapter use a single READ *variable name* statement. Specifically, every item in the DATA lines is assigned the same variable name, D. It is often necessary, however, to assign different variable names to different items in a DATA listing, and that means using more than one READ statement in the program.

A case in point would be a simple record-keeping program for stock inventory. In keeping with the fact that we are working only with numerical items, each item in the inventory carries a stock number (as opposed to a descriptive name). And associated with each stock number is a current quantity and cost.

The basic idea is to enter the stock number, quantity, and cost as DATA items, and at some convenient time run a complete listing of all that information. Here's a program for doing the job:

EXAMPLE 11-2

```
10 CLS
20 PRINT "STOCK NO.","QTY IN STOCK","COST"
30 FOR N=1 TO 5
40 READ S: READ Q: READ C
```

```
50 PRINT S,Q,C
60 NEXT
70 END
100 REM ** DATA **
110 DATA 100,20,2.55
111 DATA 101,220,3.95
112 DATA 103,0,1.85
113 DATA 104,11000,1.35
114 DATA 110,23,6.95
```

This program is divided into two distinctly different sections: the main programming section in lines 10 through 70, and the data section in lines 100 through 114. Upon running the program, you should see something like this on the screen:

STOCK NO.	QTY IN STOCK	COST
100	20	2.55
101	220	3.95
103	0	1.85
104	11000	1.35
110	23	6.95
READY		
>_		

The program contains five separate DATA lines, each containing three items. The job could be done with a single DATA line containing 15 items, but there is a method to the madness. Note that each DATA line contains a stock number, quantity in stock, and corresponding cost—in that order. Whenever the stock listing changes for one item, you have to alter only one DATA line. If the information were all contained in a single DATA line, you would have to edit the line or rewrite the whole thing.

Even though the data are broken up into five different lines, the items are still read in sequence, beginning with the first item in line 110 and ending with the last item in line 114. So how are the stock numbers, quantities, and costs kept separate and properly lined up on the screen?

To shed some light on the answer to that question, notice that line 40 is made up of three separate READ statements, each assigning a different variable name to the items they read. Each time the FOR . . . NEXT loop is executed, then, line 40 reads three different DATA items in succession.

The first time the FOR . . . NEXT loop is executed, for example, READ S picks up the first item in DATA line 110, READ Q picks up the second item in that DATA line, and READ C picks up the third item. So there they are— just like 1-2-3. On that first pass through the FOR . . . NEXT loop, S=100, Q=20, and C=2.55

Line 50 merely calls for a printing of the three values picked up by line 40.

On the second pass through the FOR . . . NEXT loop, line 40 picks up values for the next three items in the DATA listing—the items from DATA line 111. And on the third pass through the loop, line 40 picks up the three items, in sequence, from DATA line 112.

This operation continues, reading the DATA listing three items at a time, until the FOR . . . NEXT loop has cycled five times, and the program is ended.

The loop is executed five times, and there are three READ statements included in each execution. That figures out to a total of 15 READ operations. That figure lines up exactly with the total number of items in the DATA listing.

If you are following this discussion, you might be seeing a bit ahead toward some of the exciting possibilities inherent in DATA/READ statements. And you might be formulating a few questions concerning ways to alter the DATA listings as well. Before pushing the discussion further, however, take a moment to consider something else that can be done with this program.

Suppose that you revise line 20 to read

    20 PRINT "STOCK NO.","QTY IN STOCK","COST","VALUE"

and then change line 50 to read

    50 PRINT S,Q,C,Q*C

These revisions create a fourth column of information that represents the total value of the stock item. It is simply the product of quantity and cost per item.

Can you think of a way to make the program end by printing the total value of the stock?

> *Note.* It is possible to perform mathematical operations on DATA items as they are READ.

11-2 Reading Lists of String Data

The general principles for structuring and applying DATA and READ commands to numerical items carry over to string items. The most important difference—a rather logical one, however—is that the *variable name* associated with the read statement must be a string variable.

Getting down to cases right away, here is a computerized "date book."

EXAMPLE 11-3

```
10 CLS
20 PRINT"NAME","ADDRESS";:PRINT TAB(40)"PHONE"
25 PRINT
30 FOR N=1 TO 4
40 READ N$,A$,T$
50 PRINT N$,AS;:PRINT TAB(40)T$
60 NEXT
70 END
100 DATA ALICE,123 CLEARVIEW,221-4567
110 DATA BETTY,16 E. MAIN,221-8990
120 DATA CARLA*,452 CENTRAL APT.7,556-7734
130 DATA DORIS,1556 STATE,433-8876
```

The program works in a way quite similar to the stock-listing program in Example 11-2. In this case, however, the data consist of string items. The FOR . . . NEXT loop cycles four times, with three READ operations taking place each time. That's a total of 12 DATA items, and that figure matches the number of items available in lines 100 through 130.

Running this program, you see something like this on the screen:

NAME	ADDRESS	PHONE
ALICE	123 CLEARVIEW	221-4567
BETTY	16 E. MAIN	221-8990
CARLA*	452 CENTRAL APT.7	556-7734
DORIS	1556 STATE	433-8876
READY		

>_

See if you can see how the formatting statements in the program are responsible for setting up this particular arrangement of data on the screen. That exercise will be a nice review of some material not used since Chapter 5.

Incidentally, take note of the difference between the READ statements in line 40 of Examples 11-2 and 11-3. Both do the same job, but the latter is more efficient and easier to use—it's an example of a multiple READ statement.

The string expressions used in Example 11-3 are rather simple, and they were selected to avoid some problems inherent in DATA listings of string expressions. Notice, for example, that the street number and apartment number in DATA line 120 are not separated by a comma. What do you suppose would happen to the system if you inserted a comma at that point?

The machine in that case would have no way of knowing whether it was supposed to print the comma or interpret it as a comma separating items in the DATA listing. Actually, the machine would automatically view it as a comma dividing items in the list. The list, as far as the machine is concerned, would then contain a total of 13 items, instead of 12. Everything would get scrambled up from that point on. Carla's phone number, for example, would then be APT.7, the next name on the list would be 556–7734 (instead of DORIS), and so on.

There is a way around this sort of problem, however, and it is spelled out in the following note.

Note. String items in a DATA listing must be enclosed in quotation marks if the item includes:

1. Any commas.
2. Any semicolons.
3. A leading space, or blank, at the beginning.

So you could have the system print 452 CENTRAL, APT.7 if DATA line 120 is revised to read

```
120 DATA CARLA*,"452 CENTRAL,APT. 7",556-7734
```

Using lists of string DATA can save a lot of translation work in some cases. Consider a simple poker-dealing program. This program selects five "cards" at random from a DATA list of 13 items.

EXAMPLE 11–4

```
10 DATA 2,3,4,5,6,7,8,9,10,J,Q,K,A
20 CLS
30 FOR NC=1 TO 5
40 FOR N=1 TO RND(13):READ P$:NEXT
50 PRINT TAB(25)P$;" ";
60 RESTORE:NEXT
70 FOR L=1 TO 15:PRINT:NEXT
80 INPUT X$:GOTO 20
```

The DATA line, line 10, is the source of string items representing the available cards. The DATA line is read five times in succession as indicated by the FOR . . . NEXT loop running between lines 30 and the end of line

60. Of course, all the statements appearing between those two points are executed five times for each complete deal of the cards.

Line 40 is the one responsible for selecting the card and reading its value. The first statement in that line sets it up for counting between 1 and some random number between 1 and 13. The NEXT statement for this loop is at the end of line 40. The READ statement falls right in this FOR . . . NEXT loop.

Suppose the value of RND(13) in line 40 happens to be 5. That means the READ statement reads the first five items in the DATA list, the card designations between 2 and 6. The values are sequentially assigned to P$, and P$ retains the last-read value (6 in this case) when the FOR . . . NEXT loop in line 40 is done.

In effect, line 40 assigns one of the DATA items to P$. The assignment, of course, is a random one.

Line 50 then causes the value of P$ to be printed along the top of the screen and near the center. The quotes enclosing a space merely places a nice space between the cards as they appear on the screen.

Line 60 is very important to the entire discussion of DATA/READ programming. The RESTORE statement is a new one as far as we are concerned, so it requires some special explanation.

Recall that a DATA line must be read in sequence, from left to right. Furthermore, the number of times a READ statement is executed must not exceed the number of items in the DATA listing. If it does, the machine generates an out-of-data error signal. READ operations do not automatically return to the first item after the last one is read.

In this particular program, the same line of data must be read five different times—one time for each card to be dealt. What the RESTORE statement does is set the READ operation back to the first item in the DATA list.

> *Principle.* RESTORE sets the READ "pointer" back to the first item in the DATA list. Such an operation is absolutely necessary whenever the same DATA is to be read more than once in a given program.

Actually, you have been using a RESTORE operation all along without knowing it. Every time you begin a program with a RUN command, any READ operations are automatically set to the first item in the corresponding DATA list.

So the READ operations are reset to the first item in the DATA line at line 60. The NEXT statement at the end of that same line loops operations back to line 30 to pick up another randomly selected DATA item.

Operations continue cycling around in this fashion until the values of five cards are displayed on the screen. After that, line 70 carries the cursor down to the bottom of the screen. (Having a question mark after the list of cards looked odd, so line 70 moves it to the lower right-hand corner of the screen.)

Line 80 lets the player deal another hand by simply striking the ENTER key.

There is a minor "glitch" in this program, but it doesn't cause much trouble in actual practice. The problem is that there is a remote possibility of dealing five identical cards. Chances of that happening are on the order of one in 13^5—probably less than the chances of running into a human poker player who has a couple of extra cards tucked up a sleeve. It's left to the programming purists to work out the little bug in this program.

11-3 Combining Numerical and String Data

Numerical and string data can be mixed together in the same DATA line as long as the corresponding READ statements assign the correct type of variable. The numerical items in the DATA list, if they are to be manipulated mathematically, must be read by means of READ *numerical variable*. String items must be read with a READ *string variable* statement.

Incidentally, numerical values that are never manipulated mathematically can be treated as either a numerical or string item.

Here is an example of a program combining numerical and string variables in the DATA lines:

EXAMPLE 11-5

```
10 CLS:PRINT"QTY","STOCK NO.","COST EA.","COST":PRINT
20 FOR N=1 TO 5
30 READ Q,S$,CE
40 PRINT Q,S$,CE,Q*CE
50 NEXT
60 END
100 REM ** DATA **
101 DATA 1,1E24,.25
102 DATA 2,1E456,1.75
103 DATA 5,1A34,.75
104 DATA 2,1DE456,1.39
105 DATA 1,23R4,2.50
```

This program prints out a typical mail-order list. The heading specified in line 10 shows columns of data for quantity, stock number, cost per unit, and total cost for each item ordered. The data, listed in lines 101 through 105, includes the quantity, stock number, and cost per unit.

The data are printed by the statement in line 40. Q is a numerical variable representing the quantity of each item, S$ is the stock number, CE is the cost per item, and, of course, the product of quantity and cost per item (Q*CE) is the total cost for each item ordered.

The point of the discussion is that the numerical and string variables contained in the data lines are read in line 30 by assigning the appropriate types of variables in the same order they appear in the data lines. The quantities are read first, so a numerical variable must appear first in the READ statement. Stock numbers are read next, and since they contain both numerical and alphabetical terms, they must be expressed as string variables. Thus the second item in the READ statement has to be a string variable. The cost per item appears last in the DATA lines, so the third item in the READ statement must be another numerical variable.

During the five FOR . . . NEXT loops specified by line 20, the READ statement calls for reading a numerical, string, and numerical variable—in that order. And indeed, those kinds of variables appear—in that order—in the DATA lines.

Principle. The DATA can be composed of mixed numerical and string variables as long as the corresponding READ statement assigns the appropriate types of variables in the same sequence.

Running the program in Example 11–5, you will see a display that looks much like this on the screen:

QTY	STOCK NO.	COST EA.	COST
1	1E24	.25	.25
2	1E456	1.75	3.5
5	1A34	.75	3.75
2	1DE456	1.39	2.78
1	23R4	2.5	2.5
READY			
>_			

So the scheme untangles the mixed variable types in the DATA lists quite nicely.

The formatting of the COST EA. and COST columns leaves something to be desired, however. It looks a bit untidy having the decimal points "floating" around at different points in the listings. Having floating decimal points is often considered an advantage when it comes to solving mathematical problems on a computer or calculator. In instances such as this one, though, floating decimals are a nuisance.

Now the floating-decimal-point feature is not directly related to the DATA/READ scheme under discussion here—the problem arises under many different kinds of listing situations. But this is a good time to deal with it briefly.

The formatting problem brought about by the program in Example 11–5 can be solved by using something called a *field specifier*. A field specifier is a type of string operation that lets the programmer fix the exact format of printed items.

The only real problem with field specifiers is that the techniques for using them vary from one kind of computing machine to another. You should check the owner's manual for your own machine to get further insight into the matter.

To solve the formatting problem in this case, try this:

1. Modify line 40 in Example 11–5 to read:

    40 PRINT Q,S$,:PRINT USING "$##.##";CE

2. Add line 45:

    45 PRINT TAB(48) USING "$##.##":CE*Q

On the Radio Shack TRS–80, the revised version of Example 11–5 looks like this:

QTY	STOCK NO.	COST EA.	COST
1	1E24	$ 0.25	$ 0.25
2	1E456	$ 1.75	$ 3.50
5	1A34	$ 0.75	$ 3.75
2	1DE456	$ 1.39	$ 2.78
1	23R4	$ 2.50	$ 2.50

READY
>_

Lo! the dollar values are lined up so that they are neater and far less confusing. Again, this notion of using field specifiers is not directly related to the DATA/READ process, and it can be used anywhere it is necessary to line up numbers having decimal points in them.

Definition/Principle. A *field specifier* is a string operation that lets the programmer specify the exact format of printed characters. The positions of the numerals are indicated by pound signs (#), and other symbols such as dollar signs, asterisks, commas and decimal points may be included in the field specifier. Since it is a string operation, the field specifier must be enclosed in quotes. It is called by the statement

PRINT USING *field specifier; field*

The field-specifying feature on some personal computing systems is quite elaborate; on others, it is rather primitive. Check your manual for details.

11-4   Expandable Data Lists

The examples cited thus far in this chapter represent workable DATA/READ schemes. Many of them are impractical, however, in the sense that it is troublesome to add more DATA lines to the original set. Example 11-5, for instance, is set up to handle no more than five groups of data. The figure is set by the 1 TO 5 specification for the main FOR . . . NEXT loop. The program reads five sets of DATA—no more, and no less.

But what if you wanted to order more than five items using the program in Example 11-5? Of course you would extend the number of DATA lines—that probably goes without saying. But you would also have to edit the FOR . . . NEXT loop to accommodate the additional data lines. Using the FOR . . . NEXT loop, the program must cycle one time for each group of data in the DATA listing.

Whenever you want to add more data to the list, you shouldn't mind having to add the new DATA lines. But actually going into the control program and editing the FOR . . . NEXT loop is a highly undesirable state of affairs.

There simply has to be a better way to handle DATA/READ schemes; and by now, you've probably guessed that the "better way" is the topic of this section.

Take a look at this computerized address book. (Also see the flowchart in Fig. 11-1.)

EXAMPLE 11-6a

```
10 CLS:PRINT"NAME","ADDRESS";:PRINT TAB(48)"PHONE":PRINT
20 READ N$: IF N$="END" END
30 READ A$,P$
40 PRINT N$,A$;:PRINT TAB(48)P$
50 GOTO 20

100 REM ** DATA **
101 DATA JIM,27 E. LONG,221-4476
102 DATA NANCY F.,4567 B'WAY,656-2271
103 DATA JUDY,1814 E. MAIN,244-8387
104 DATA END
```

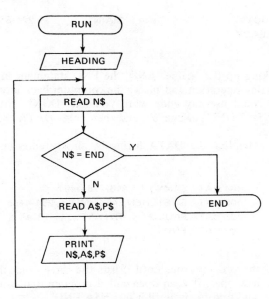

Figure 11-1 Flowchart for Example 11-6a.

Example 11-6a contains no FOR . . . NEXT loops. The program first reads N$, the individual's name. But if the first item in the DATA listing happens to be END, line 20 shows that the program itself is to be ended. So the program will print out the data (name, address, and phone number) until it reaches the DATA line in line 104. That line begins with the string expression END—and by line 20, seeing END as N$ stops the program.

In other words, this program cycles until it reaches a DATA line containing an N$ expression END. There is no limit to how many times the program can cycle and, more important, it is possible for the user to add new names, addresses, and phone numbers by:

1. Writing over the END expression in line 104 and replacing it with a new DATA line.

2. Adding as many new lines of data as desired.

3. Terminating the new DATA listing with DATA END.

If you run this example as shown, you should see something like this on the screen:

NAME	ADDRESS	PHONE
JIM	27 E. LONG	221-4476
NANCY F.	4567 B'WAY	656-2271

```
JUDY                    1814 E. MAIN                224-8387
READY
>_
```

Upon picking up the "name" END, the END statement in line 20 terminates the listing operation and places the computer back into the command
mode. You could use any code word you like—DONE, for instance. Just
substitute N$="DONE" in line 20, and then enter DATA DONE at the end
of the listing.

Now try extending the DATA listing by simply entering the following
DATA lines:

```
104 DATA SAMMY," ",416-228-4491
105 DATA GRETCHEN,345 SUMMIT, 294-4466
106 DATA PAUL,23 N. 4TH AVE.,344-1234
107 DATA END
```

This time the program runs until it lists the three original names as well
as the three new ones. It is an open-ended program that continues looping,
reading data, and printing it, until it sees N$="END".

Incidentally, you might have noticed the null-string address in line 104.
Apparently, Sammy's address isn't known. Even so, it must not be totally
omitted, else the reading scheme will get behind by one item listing; doing
terrible things such as putting Sammy's phone number in the ADDRESS
column, Gretchen's name in place of Sammy's phone number, and so on to
the end of the DATA listing. Entering the null string in place of Sammy's
unknown address causes the computer to leave a blank in the appropriate
space on the screen.

Even though you now have some insight into preparing DATA lists that
can be expanded at any later time, you might find the process a bit awkward. One way to simplify matters is by entering *all* the new information
on a single DATA line. For example, you could add the three new names,
addresses, and phone numbers this way:

```
104 DATA SAMMY," ",416-228-4491,GRETCHEN,345 SUMMIT,294-4466,PAUL
,23 N. 4TH AVE.,344-1234
105 DATA END
```

The idea is to enter the data on one line, bearing in mind that the READ
scheme has no regard at all for the line numbers. In this case, all that's
necessary is that the data be presented in the right sequence and that each
item be separated from the preceding one by a comma. At least you don't
have to type in a new line number and the statement, DATA, for each new
entry. That simplifies the task somewhat.

It's a good idea to put the END "name" on a separate line, however. That
way you know where to begin adding new DATA listings at some later time.

But everyday users who have no training in computer programming will still find the process of adding new DATA lines a very confusing one. So take a look at one of many different ways to make the process at least semiautomated:

EXAMPLE 11-6b

```
10 CLS:PRINT"NAME","ADDRESS";:"PRINT TAB(48)"PHONE":PRINT
15 N=101
20 READ N$: IF N$="END" THEN 60
30 READ A$,P$
40 PRINT N$,A$;:PRINT TAB(48)P$
45 N=N+1
50 GOTO 20
60 PRINT "LIST DONE. STRIKE 'ENTER' TO ADD NEW LISTINGS"
65 INPUT X$: CLS
70 PRINT "ENTER NEW LISTINGS BEGINNING FROM LINE"N
80 END

100 REM ** DATA **
101 DATA JIM, 27 E. LONG, 221-4476
102 DATA NANCY F.,4567 B'WAY,656-2271
103 DATA JUDY,1814 E. MAIN, 224-8387
104 DATA END
```

See the flowchart for this program in Fig. 11-2.

Upon comparing this example with Example 11-6a, you will find some new lines here: 15, 45, and 60 through 80. Lines 15 and 45 make up a DATA line counter—it keeps track of the line number of the DATA line being read. This is not important information while the program is being run, but when the listing operation is completed, N holds the value of the last-read line number. N, you see, is initialized in line 15 at the number representing the first line of data. It then increments at line 45 each time a new DATA sequence is read.

Line 20 is modified to send program control to line 60, rather than doing an END, whenever the READ operation picks up the "name" END.

And when the END "name" is reached, line 60 prints a little message to the user—LIST DONE. STRIKE 'ENTER' TO ADD NEW LISTINGS. Of course, you might want to offer some other options as well, but that is getting away from the point of this discussion.

Line 65 then allows the user to get into the new-data routine by striking the ENTER key. The screen is then cleared of all old listings.

The nice part of this routine shows up when line 70 is executed. Here the user is effectively told the line number to use for entering the first series of new data. That line number, you recall, is equal to the value of the N variable.

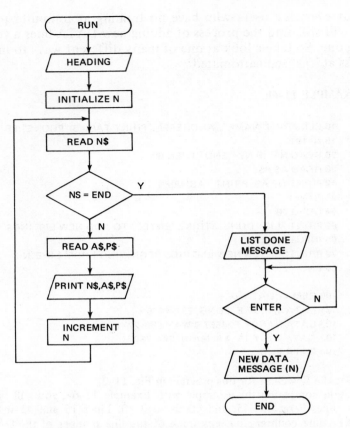

Figure 11-2   Flowchart for Example 11-6b.

Running the program in this example, you see this sort of display on the screen:

```
NAME          ADDRESS        PHONE

JIM           27 E. LONG     221-4476
NANCY F.      4567 B'WAY     656-2271
JUDY          1814 E. MAIN   224-8387
LIST DONE. STRIKE 'ENTER' TO ADD NEW LISTINGS
?_
```

Striking the ENTER key in response to this prompting message, the screen is cleared and the new display looks like this:

ENTER NEW LISTINGS BEGINNING FROM LINE 104

                        READY
                        >_

And you're ready to go. Enter

                104 DATA SAMMY," ",416-228-4491
                105 DATA GRETCHEN,345 SUMMIT,294-4466
                106 DATA PAUL,23 N. 4TH AVE.,344-1234
                107 DATA END

The next time you run the program, the entire list of names appears on the screen. And if you strike the ENTER key to add new data, the prompting message will read

        ENTER NEW LISTINGS BEGINNING FROM LINE 107.

It's one way of making the task of entering new DATA lines somewhat simpler and less prone to operator errors. The only drawback is that each set of data—name, address, and phone number—must be entered on separate program lines, and those lines must be presented in succession. (There are ways to get around this particular drawback, but the techniques are beyond the scope of the present discussion.)

The next step in the DATA/READ scheme is to see how the data can be manipulated and reorganized, doing something more than simple listings and a bit of mathematical manipulation. That is the subject of the next chapter.

EXERCISES

11-1 How many READ operations must be performed to read all the data in the following DATA lines?

   (a) DATA 2,4,6,8,10

   (b) DATA 1.2,3.14,1,000, 10.24

   (c) DATA MIKE, J, SAM, L,EDWARD, J, PAGE 3

   (d) DATA MIKE,20, SAM L. -- 200, J. PAGE

11-2 The DATA line in Example 11-1a has six items in it. Explain how all six are read with a single READ D statement in line 40.

11-3 How is the statement READ A:READ B: READ C$ operationally different from READ A,B,C$?

11-4   Which of the following READ statements could conceivably be used in conjunction with DATA 1, RALPH, 1∅, ED?

(a) READ A,B,C,D

(b) READ A$,B,C,D

(c) READ A, A$,B,B$

(d) READ A$,B$,C$,D$

(e) READ A,B,C$,D$

11-5   Under what condition(s) can a numerical quantity in a DATA line be assigned to string variable in the corresponding READ statement?

11-6   Why is it so important that the number of READ operations not exceed the number of items in the corresponding DATA listing? What would happen if the number of READ operations happened to be less than the number of items in the available DATA listing?

11-7   State the purpose of the RESTORE statement and describe the conditions that dictate its use in a program.

11-8   List the situations that make it necessary to enclose DATA items within quotes.

11-9   Referring to Example 11-4, explain how "using lists of string DATA can save a lot of translation work in some cases."

11-10   Explain the general purpose of field specifiers. Look up the use of PRINT USING statements in the manual for your own computer system.

CHAPTER
12

Putting DATA and READ
to Work
in Larger Programs

Statement introduced in this chapter:

LEFT$

Chapter 11 was really just an introduction to the workings of the DATA/READ scheme. For the most part, the programs in that chapter demonstrated the interaction of DATA and READ, calling for a rather straightforward printing of the DATA list on the screen.

This chapter deals with the same commands, but builds them into larger programs that allow the user to manipulate the listings to perform some sorting and correlating tasks. To do this sort of job, you will be working with two programs, composing, entering, and debugging them from scratch.

The first program is built around a listing of student names, courses they have taken in school, course hours, and grades. It is the sort of data processing program that might be found in the academic office of your school. The program demonstrates how it is possible to sift through the DATA listings, organizing them according to a user-specified plan.

The second program described in this chapter is one that is taking on a reputation for being a classic in BASIC programming—a personal checking-account program. You will be able to list all your ordinary checking-account transactions, keep a running balance, and, when necessary, search the listings for certain check numbers, total amounts written to a specified party, and so on.

12-1 Planning the STUDENT COURSE/GRADE Program

The basic idea behind the STUDENT COURSE/GRADE program is to give the computer operator immediate access to information regarding student names, courses, course hours, and grades. Just how the data are handled and presented on the screen depends on what the operator wants to do. Here are the options:

1. Display a complete listing of the DATA file.
2. Show a listing of courses, class hours, grades, and point-hour ratio for a specified student.
3. Show class rosters—a listing of students taking a specified course.
4. Provide a convenient means for adding new student information to the DATA list.

The students' names should be written as a last name, followed by the first initial and a period. Remember that including a comma between the last and first names would call for enclosing each student's name in quotes—and that's messy, so we won't do it here. At any rate, the students' names will have to be assigned a string variable in the corresponding READ statement.

The course names will be specified as a single letter followed by three numerals. Course M101, for instance, might mean Mathematics 101. The fact that the course designation includes a letter makes it necessary to read it with a string variable.

Course hours, generally representing the weight of the course in terms of the number of hours it meets each week, will be a numerical value. And since that value will be used to compute total class hours and point–hour ratios for individual students, it must be assigned to a numerical variable in the corresponding READ statement.

Finally, course grades will be specified as an integer between 0 and 4 inclusively. Zero in this case represents the lowest possible grade, while 4 indicates the highest possible grade for a course. Like the course hours' figure, the grades will be treated mathematically, and thus must be assigned to a numerical variable.

Putting this all together, the sequence of items in the DATA listings ought to follow this pattern:

DATA *student name, course, course hours, grade*

It actually makes no difference in what order these items are written, just as long as they are written in the same order each time. This is the sequence used throughout this particular demonstration.

The corresponding READ statement should then assign variables to the items in the DATA lines:

READ N$,C$,H,G

where N$ and C$ are the string variables for student name and course, and H and G are the numerical variables for course hours and grade.

In the process of composing the program, you will have to establish the form of several mathematical equations. Perhaps the total number of course hours for a given student seems important. Getting that figure is a matter of summing all the H values for a given student. Let's call the total class hours HT.

Although you might not consider it important to display the HT value as such, it is required for calculating the point–hour ratio. That figure is generally computed by the equation

$$PH = \frac{H_1 G_1 + H_2 G_2 + H_3 G_3 + \cdots + H_n G_n}{HT}$$

Determining the point–hour ratio is a matter of multiplying the course hours times the grade for each course, summing them all together, and then dividing the results by the total number of course hours. You should note that this equation is not written in a formal BASIC format—maybe you can call it "semi-BASIC." When necessary, you will be solving the equation by means of an algorithm.

12-2 Subroutines for the STUDENT COURSE/GRADE Program

Since it is important that the program be written to give the operator a choice of tasks, the most efficient approach to composing the program is by means of subroutines—one subroutine for each task. The first job in this case, however, is to create a temporary data file. It doesn't have to be a very extensive file, but it ought to contain enough information to make the program testing routines meaningful. Presumably, the ultimate user will be entering a more extensive file.

So for the sake of getting the programming task under way, enter this temporary data file:

EXAMPLE 12-1

```
1000 REM ** DATA **
1001 DATA ADAMS R.,B 101,4,3
1002 DATA ADAMS R.,E 301,4,3
1003 DATA ADAMS R.,M201,2,3
1004 DATA JONES  S .,B 101,4,4
1005 DATA JONES  S .,A 202,1,4
1006 DATA JONES  S .,M201,2,3
1007 DATA JONES  D.,B 101,4,0
1008 DATA JONES  D.,M101,4,1
1009 DATA JONES  D .,E 301,4,1
1010 DATA SMITH  E .,B 101,4,3
1011 DATA SMITH  E .,M101,4,4
1012 DATA SMITH  E .,E 301,4,2
1013 DATA END
```

The items in each data line are presented in a specific order as described earlier: student name, course, course hours, and grade. There is, however, no rationale behind the order of the DATA lines as they are presented here—the items for SMITH E. could appear first instead of last. In fact, the DATA lines for SMITH E. could be scattered throughout the list. You are working with something that is technically known as a *random data file.*

The operator will be able to enter data in any order, following only two rules that you, as the programmer, are imposing. First, the four items for each data entry must be written in the specified order, and second, each list of four items must be assigned a separate line number. The latter "rule" is necessary only because of the nature of one of the tasks described later in this section.

The first task available to the user is a simple listing of the data. This is the sort of job represented by most of the DATA/READ examples in Chapter 11. The subroutine and associated flowchart for this particular task appear in Example 12-2 and Fig. 12-1.

EXAMPLE 12-2

```
100 REM ** WHOLE LIST **
105 LET L=0
110 CLS: PRINT"NAME","COURSE","GRADE":PRINT
120 READ N$
130 IF N$= "END" RETURN
140 READ C$,H,G
```

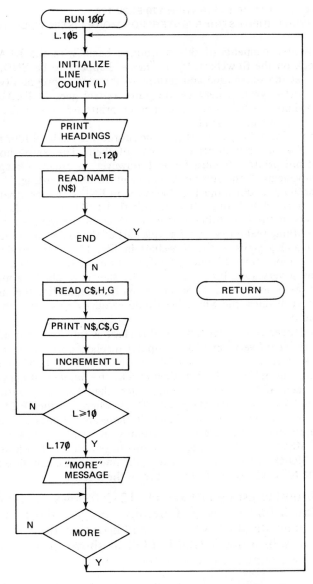

Figure 12-1 Flowchart for the WHOLE LIST subroutine in Example 12–2.

```
150 PRINT N$,C$,G
160 LET L=L+1: IF L>=10 THEN 170 ELSE 120
170 PRINT"INPUT:STRIKE 'ENTER' FOR MORE LISTING";:GO TO 105
```

The essential elements of this subroutine begin with the READ NAME (N$) block on the flowchart. If the "name" happens to be END, the computer leaves the subroutine and returns to the master program (which you haven't written yet). Otherwise, program control goes to READ C$,H,G; and immediately after that, the computer prints N$, C$, and G—the student's name, course, and grade.

Now note from the flowchart that the subroutine reads all four items on a given DATA line, but prints only three of them. The course hours (H) is read, but not printed. It must be read, however, in order to keep the item pointer advancing to the appropriate place in the DATA listing.

So basically, the subroutine first looks for an END statement that indicates the end of the data listings. If it doesn't find END, it reads the remaining three items in the DATA line and prints three of the items on the screen. There is nothing really new as far as this part of the job is concerned.

The remaining steps in the flowchart in Fig. 12-1 have to do with displaying no more than 10 lines of information on the screen at one time. Displaying a very long list of data on the screen would be a meaningless operation as far as the user is concerned. Without separating the display into blocks of 10 listings, the whole list would scroll by so rapidly that no one could read it.

The first operational step on the flowchart is thus one that initializes a line counter (L). Every time the computer displays a new line of data, this counter is advanced by the block labeled INCREMENT L. The conditional block following INCREMENT L then checks the number of lines presently on the screen. If the number of lines is less than 10, the N output carries operations back up to READ NAME (N$), where another READ/PRINT cycle is initiated. On the other hand, if there are 10 lines of information already presented on the screen, the system stops reading data and outputs a "MORE" MESSAGE. And if the user wants to see another block of information, the MORE conditional is satisfied, the line count is initialized, and the READ/PRINT cycles begin from the top of the screen.

The subroutine listing in Example 12-2 follows the flowchart in a rather straightforward way. Carefully compare the two, making certain you understand what they do and how they do it.

Enter the subroutine WHOLE LIST as shown in Example 12-2 and then write a temporary test routine:

EXAMPLE 12-3

```
10 CLS:GOSUB 100
15 PRINT: PRINT "END OF LISTING"
20 END
```

Upon entering RUN, line 10 in this test routine clears the screen and sends operations down to the WHOLE LIST subroutine. The screen should then look like this:

NAME	COURSE	GRADE
ADAMS R.	B 1Ø1	3
ADAMS R.	E 3Ø1	3
ADAMS R.	M2Ø1	3
JONES S.	B 1Ø1	4
JONES S.	A 2Ø2	4
JONES S.	M2Ø1	3
JONES D.	B 1Ø1	Ø
JONES D.	M1Ø1	1
JONES D.	E 3Ø1	1
SMITH E.	B 1Ø1	3

STRIKE 'ENTER' FOR MORE LISTING?_

Sure enough, the first 10 DATA listings are shown on the screen. Everything is there in each case except the number of hours per course. The "MORE" MESSAGE near the bottom of the screen tells the operator there are more data to be seen.

So striking the enter key resumes the listing and, in this case, terminates it as well.

NAME	COURSE	GRADE
SMITH E.	M1Ø1	4
SMITH E.	E 3Ø1	2

END OF LISTING
READY
>_

During this second phase of the listing operation, READ N$ encounters an END statement in the DATA listing, the system broke away from the WHOLE LIST subroutine and returned to line 15 of the test program.

Line 15 is responsible for printing the END OF LISTING message and returning the system to its command mode of operation. Of course, if there had been hundreds of DATA listings, instead of just 12 of them, the operator would have viewed the information in blocks of 10 lines for quite some time before getting the END OF LISTING message.

That takes care of the first task assigned to the overall project. Now look at the second one—displaying the schedule and grades for a specified student.

This subroutine, listed in Example 12-4 and flowcharted in Fig. 12-2, lets the operator enter the name of a specific student. The program searches the DATA listings for that student's name, prints the class schedule, and compiles the individual point-hour ratio.

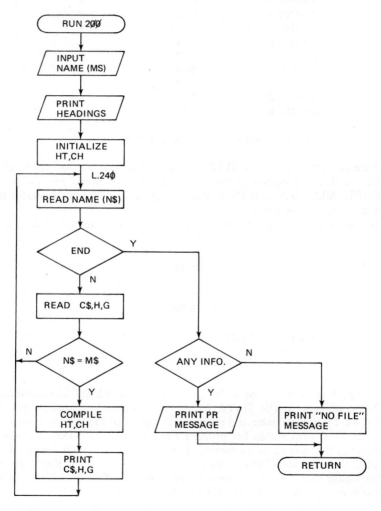

Figure 12-2 Flowchart for the LIST NAME subroutine in Example 12-4.

EXAMPLE 12-4

```
200 REM ** LIST NAME **
210 INPUT"WHAT NAME";M$
220 CLS: PRINT M$:PRINT,"COURSE","HOURS","GRADE":PRINT
230 HT=0:CH=0
240 READ N$
250 IF N$="END" THEN 290
260 READ C$,H,G
270 IF N$<>M$ THEN 240
272 HT=HT+H:CH=CH+G*H
275 PRINT,C$,H,G
280 GOTO 240
290 IF HT=0 THEN 297
295 PRINT:PRINT "POINT-HOUR RATIO="CH/HT:RETURN
297 PRINT:PRINT "THIS NAME NOT ON FILE":RETURN
```

Upon running this subroutine, the system first requests a student's name from the operator. This operation is reflected in the INPUT NAME (M$) block on the flowchart and line 210 of the subroutine itself.

The system then prints the appropriate headings, including the specified student name, and then initializes the relevant elements for calculating the student's overall point-hour ratio.

The next step is to read the first name in the DATA listing. If that first name isn't an END statement, the program calls for reading the remaining items in the DATA line—C$, H, and G.

The next step is an important one to this particular task: The system compares the student name in the DATA listing (N$) with the student name entered at the beginning of the subroutine (M$). If indeed they are the same, the system compiles the relevant terms for the point-hour ratio and then prints the course, hours, and student grade. The program then returns to READ NAME (N$), where the computer looks at the next name on the list.

The program also returns to READ NAME(N$) if the two names don't match at the N$=M$ conditional block.

So the system continues looking for names that match the one entered by the operator, printing out the relevant information whenever the names are the same. Things change only when READ NAME (N$) finds the END statement at the end of the DATA listing. That operation satisfies the END conditional statement, and the next conditional determines whether the computer found any of the specified name. If not, it prints a THIS NAME NOT ON FILE and returns to the master program. If, on the other hand, the system found some matching names, the system calculates the student's point-hour ratio by CH/HT, prints the figure, and returns to the master program.

Compare the subroutine listing and flowchart, making sure you understand everything. Then enter this short test routine:

EXAMPLE 12-5

```
10 CLS: GOSUB 200
20 PRINT: PRINT "END OF LISTING"
30 END
```

Naturally, you have to enter the LIST NAME subroutine in Example 12-4 before running the program. Suppose you do that. The first thing you see on the screen is

WHAT NAME?_

Suppose that you respond by typing and entering SMITH E. The resulting display looks something like this:

SMITH E.

COURSE	HOURS	GRADE
B 101	4	3
M101	4	4
E 301	4	2

POINT-HOUR RATIO= 3

END OF LISTING
READY
>_

And there you have it—the course schedule, grades, and overall PHR for a student named SMITH E. Try running the test routine for all the students in your data file: ADAMS R., JONES S., JONES D., and SMITH E.

Before you can consider your testing procedure complete, you must try entering an invalid name—one that is spelled wrong or does not exist in the present data file. For instance, do a RUN and respond to WHAT NAME? by entering RALPH F. You should see this display:

RALPH F.

COURSE	HOURS	GRADE

THIS NAME NOT ON FILE

END OF LISTING
READY
>_

And that's what is supposed to happen whenever the computer cannot make a perfect match between the name you specify and the N$ names in the DATA listings.

The third task in the project is to specify a course number and then see a printout of the students taking that course. It is a search-and-print subroutine much like LIST NAME. In this case, however, the computer attempts to match course numbers rather than student names. The subroutine listing and flowchart for this part of the job are shown in Example 12-6 and Fig. 12-3.

EXAMPLE 12-6

```
300 REM ** CLASS ROSTER **
310 INPUT"WHAT COURSE";M$
320 CLS:PRINT "COURSE; "M$
325 E=0
330 READ N$: IF N$="END" THEN 370
340 READ C$,H,G
350 IF C$=M$ THEN 360 ELSE 330
360 PRINT,N$:E=E+1: GOTO 330
370 IF E>0 RETURN
380 PRINT:PRINT"COURSE "M$" IS NOT IN FILE":RETURN
```

Notice that the flow of operations is pretty much the same as the LIST NAME subroutine. This one is a bit simpler because it doesn't include the point-hour algorithm.

The program first prompts the operator to enter a course designation. That expression is assigned to string variable M$. As usual, the system looks at the name N$ in the DATA listing to see if it represents the end of the data. If not, the system reads C$, H, and G (block READ C$, H, G on the flowchart) and checks for a match between the specified course number (M$) and the course number at hand in the data (C$). If there is a good match, PRINT N$ prints the student's name and operations return to READ NAME (N$) to look for the end of the DATA list or another match between C$ and M$.

The purpose of the counter, E, is to tell whether or not the computer finds any listings at all for the specified course. This counter is set to zero early in the subroutine [at INITIALIZE COUNTER (E)] and incremented whenever the system finds a course match and prints the corresponding student name (at INCREMENT COUNTER).

When the computer reaches the end of the listing, as determined by the

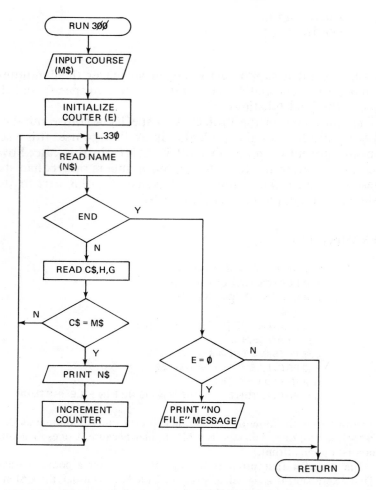

Figure 12-3 Flowchart for the CLASS ROSTER subroutine in Example 12-6.

END conditional block, it tests the value of E at the E=Ø conditional. If it so happens that E has been incremented from zero by finding one or more course matches, the system simply returns to the master program. But if there are no matches between C$ and M$ (perhaps because the specified course isn't in the listing), the system prints COURSE *whatever* IS NOT IN FILE before returning operations to the master program.

Enter the CLASS ROSTER subroutine from Example 12-6 and write a test routine that goes like this:

EXAMPLE 12-7

```
1Ø CLS:GOSUB 3ØØ
2Ø PRINT: PRINT "END OF LISTING"
3Ø END
```

Then RUN the program. You should first see the prompt message WHAT
COURSE? Respond by entering one of the course designations, say B1Ø1.
The resulting display looks like this:

```
COURSE: B1Ø1
                    ADAMS R.
                    JONES  S.
                    JONES  D.
                    SMITH  E.

END OF LISTING
READY
>_
```

Run the subroutine for each of the course designations in the DATA listing: B1Ø1, M2Ø1, E3Ø1, A2Ø2, and M1Ø1. In each case you should see a
listing of the students taking the specified course. Finally, try entering a
course designation that is not in the file—maybe something like X2, for
instance. The display will respond this way:

```
COURSE: X2

COURSE X2 IS NOT IN FILE

END OF LISTING
READY
>_
```

Hang in there, there is just one more subroutine to go. It's a short
one that lets the operator enter more data to the DATA listing. You
have already studied such a routine in Chapter 11, so there is no need
for extensive commentary on it. The flowchart and subroutine listing
for this NEW LIST are shown in Fig. 12-4 and Example 12-8.

EXAMPLE 12-8

```
4ØØ REM ** NEW LIST **
41Ø CLS: LET L=1ØØ1
42Ø READ N$
43Ø IF N$="END" THEN 45Ø
```

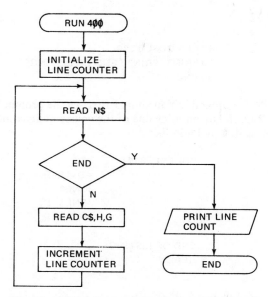

Figure 12-4   Flowchart for the NEW LIST
subroutine in Example 12-8.

440 READ C$,H,G: LET L=L+1: GOTO 420
450 PRINT "BEGIN NEW LISTING AT"L
460 END

The program simply counts the number of DATA lines, and upon finding
the END statement in the data, the system prints the line number containing that END statement. That is where the next line of data is to be placed.
The line counter, in this case, is initialized at 1001, because that is the first
line of data in the DATA listing.

So if you build a test program such as this:

EXAMPLE 12-9

10 CLS: GOSUB 300

and do a RUN, you will see this on the screen:

BEGIN NEW LISTING AT 1013
READY
>_

Consult your DATA listing or Example 12-1, and you will find that DATA END is at line 1013.

Notice that the NEW LIST subroutine does not return to the master program. It concludes with an END statement that puts the computer into its command mode. Why is this done? It is done so that the operator can begin typing in new DATA lines with no further hassle. Try it.

```
1013 DATA SCHULTZ X.,B10,4,1
1014 DATA ADAMS R., A202,1,3
1015 DATA END
```

That set of new listings adds a new student to the file, SCHULTZ X., and gives ADAMS R. an additional course. To see if these new listings have indeed been added to the DATA listing, either do a LIST command to display lines 1000 through 1015, or write the test routine in Example 12-3 and run it.

Now all the subroutines for the STUDENT/COURSE project are in the machine. The next job is to write the master program that ties things together.

12-3   Master Program
for the STUDENT COURSE/GRADE Program

The master program does little more than automate the subroutine-selection process and, at the same time, prompt the operator to do things right. Basically, the master program first prompts the operator to select one of the four available tasks: (1) COMPLETE LISTING, (2) STUDENT RECORD AND PHR, (3) COURSE ROSTER, or (4) INPUT NEW LISTINGS.

After the operator selects one of the tasks, the program sends operations to the appropriate subroutine. And after the subroutine is executed, control is usually returned to the master program, where the END OF LISTING message is generated. The only exception to this returning process is the NEW LISTING subroutine, which, you recall, concludes by shifting the system over to the command mode.

After printing END OF LISTING, the system then wants to know if the operator desires the same task to be run again. If so, the system runs the same subroutine as before. If not, the operator is again presented with the four choices.

The master program for doing this work is presented in Example 12-10.

EXAMPLE 12-10

```
10 CLS:PRINT "ENTER DESIRED TASK"
20 PRINT:PRINT TAB(10)"1 -- COMPLETE LISTING"
22 PRINT TAB(10)"2 -- STUDENT RECORD AND PHR"
24 PRINT TAB(10)"3 -- COURSE ROSTER"
26 PRINT TAB(10)"4 -- INPUT NEW LISTINGS"
30 INPUT T
40 CLS: RESTORE
45 IF T<1 OR T>4 THEN 10
50 ON T GOSUB 100,200,300,400
55 PRINT:PRINT "END OF LISTING"
60 PRINT:PRINT:INPUT "SAME TASK AGAIN";T$
70 IF T$="YES" THEN 40 ELSE 10
```

Enter the program and do a RUN. You should be greeted with this display.

```
ENTER DESIRED TASK

        1 -- COMPLETE LISTING
        2 -- STUDENT RECORD AND PHR
        3 -- COURSE ROSTER
        4-- INPUT NEW LISTINGS


    ?_
```

Respond to this request with a number between 1 and 4. If your entry is less than 1 or greater than 4, line 45 picks up that fact and causes a re-printing of the entire opening display. Otherwise, the ON T GOSUB *subroutine numbers* in line 50 sends operations to the specified subroutine.

A very important point that might appear lost in the main program is the presence of the RESTORE statement in line 40. Recall that this statement returns the DATA item pointer to the first item in the DATA listing. Such a statement is absolutely necessary in this program, ensuring that every subroutine begins its DATA-handling operations with the first item in the listing.

Study Example 12-10 carefully, comparing the listing against the events you see on the screen.

12-4   A Time for Reflection

The STUDENT COURSE/GRADE program described in the first three sections of this book requires a bit of polishing before it takes on a truly professional look. For instance, when the operator first runs the program, there ought to be a brief introductory note that explains the purpose of the program. Then, too, the operator ought to have the option of selecting a detailed description of how to use it. These elements are lacking.

What's more important, however, is that the STUDENT COURSE/GRADE program lacks a high level of elegance. With a bit of work, at least two of the subroutines could be combined into one, and the result would be a somewhat simpler program in terms of the number of program lines.

Then there is the problem of cumbersome methods for entering new data. The notion of having to write program line numbers and typing DATA at the beginning of each one is an intolerable situation in a professional sense. The problem in this regard is not readily solved with the programming tools described thus far in this book. Some new statements presented in Chapters 13 through 15 will solve the difficulty quite nicely.

This is not to say there isn't a place for DATA/READ schemes; it's just that certain kinds of problems and situations are better handled in different ways.

So what is going on here? Why are you being forced to study less-than-ideal programs in these chapters? By studying this book, you are presumably in a position of wanting to learn more about computer programming in a BASIC context; and hopefully you have seen by now that there is more to BASIC programming than simply learning the definition of commands and statements.

Simple, rote memorization of the BASIC language won't get you anywhere. What is more important than the language is the type of thinking that goes into composing programs that perform the intended task, and that often means presenting programs that emphasize certain programming procedures at the risk of losing some programming elegance.

None of the programming examples presented here are intended to be the ultimate answers to the situations they portray. Rather, they use ideas in ways intended to make you think about methods and procedures.

The CHECKBOOK TRANSACTION program outlined in the remainder of this chapter is similar to the STUDENT COURSE/ GRADE program. CHECKBOOK TRANSACTION, however, is tightened up a bit, and unless you study it very carefully, some of the reasons for using certain steps are going to elude you. In this case, composing a tight and efficient program will take precedence over clarity. Take a deep breath and get ready for a real challenge. Mastering it will mean you are just about ready to deal with some high-class BASIC programming.

This program basically represents a computerized register for a personal checking account. The idea is to record all transactions, deposits, check numbers, dates, recipients, and amounts, as data in a DATA file. You should then be able to access the information, organizing it in several different ways on the CRT monitor screen. Of course, you could also arrange a line printer to print the checks, themselves, but that is beyond the scope of what we are trying to do here.

So each line of DATA is going to be made up of four different items. The first item, N$, will be a transaction designation: a check number, the term DEPOSIT, or a passcard withdrawal against the checking account called VISA. You are free to add any other such transaction designations after working through the examples and seeing how they perform.

The second item in each DATA line will be the date of the transaction, D$. For our purposes here, the date will be printed as a number for the month, a hyphen, and a number for the day of the month. For example, 6-27 will specify June 27. The year will not be included, although it can be added without causing much difficulty.

The third item will be the recipient designation, P$. In the case of checks written against the account, the recipient can be any name or series of words and characters. Examples are RENT, DR. SMITH, RADIO SHACK, and so on. When it comes to deposits, you can specify how the money was deposited—24-HOUR, TELLER, SAVINGS XFER, and the like.

The final item in each DATA line will be the amount of the transaction, A. This is the only item in the listing that must be represented by a numerical variable.

Each DATA line thus takes this form

DATA *transaction, date, recipient, amount*

The corresponding READ sequence will be

READ N$,D$,P$,A

The operator will be able to select any one of five different ways to manipulate the data:

1. Input a new listing of data.

2. Show the last 10 transactions and the running balance in the account.

3. List all transactions having a specified transaction designation.

4. List all transactions for a specified date.

5. List all transactions for a specified recipient.

You can probably think of some other things you would do with a checkbook program, but these five represent a nice set of useful and challenging programming procedures.

12-6   Programs for CHECKBOOK TRANSACTION

Since this particular program has been devised to illustrate a rather tightly written program, it is difficult to follow the general pattern of explanation used elsewhere in this book. Rather than showing how the program goes together in a step-by-step fashion, it is necessary here to look at relatively large segments at one time. It is an approach that is suitable for analyzing existing programs written by someone else.

Begin the analysis with a look at the main program.

EXAMPLE 12-11

```
10 REM ** CHECK MASTER **
15 R$="+####.##" : S$="####.##"
20 CLS:PRINT "WHICH TASK:"
22 PRINT TAB(10)"1 – NEW LISTINGS"
24 PRINT TAB(10)"2 – LAST TEN TRANSACTIONS AND CURRENT BALANCE"
25 PRINT TAB(10)"3 – LIST BY TRANSACTION"
26 PRINT TAB(10)"4 – LIST BY DATES OF TRANSACTIONS"
27 PRINT TAB(10)"5 – LIST BY RECIPIENT"
28 INPUT T: IF T<1 or T>5 THEN 20
30 RESTORE: ON T GOSUB 100,200,300,300,300
40 PRINT:PRINT "END OF LISTING"
50 PRINT: INPUT "SAME TASK AGAIN (Y OR N)";X$
60 IF X$="Y" THEN 30 ELSE 10
```

Entering and running this portion of the program makes the display on the screen look something like this:

```
WHICH TASK:
          1 – NEW LISTINGS
```

```
2 - LAST TEN TRANSACTIONS AND CURRENT BALANCE
3 - LIST BY TRANSACTION
4 - LIST BY DATES OF TRANSACTIONS
5 - LIST BY RECIPIENT
```
?_

The display is the result of executing lines 20 through 27 and the INPUT statement in line 28. At this point, however, the program "blows up" if you try entering one of the numbers—the subroutines called by these numbers do not yet exist in the computer's program memory.

This program is quite similar to the master program for the STUDENT COURSE/GRADE version in Example 12-10. In principle, they're identical. Example 12-11 has a couple of lines that require special attention, however.

Line 15 in Example 12-11 specifies two field variables. They aren't used in the main program here, but they are used in all the subroutines. So rather than using separate field-specifying statements in each subroutine, they are established, once and for all, early in the master program.

Once these printing fields are established, they can be called at any later time by statements such as PRINT USING R$ and PRINT USING S$. In the first instance, the R$ field specifier forces a numerical value to have a plus sign in front of it, followed by character spaces for four numerals, a decimal point, and two more numerals. In the context of dollar values, the R$ specifier in line 15 can print any dollar value from +$\emptyset.\emptyset\emptyset$ to +9999.99 dollars.

The S$ field specifier in the second part of line 15 accomplishes the same thing, but without preceding the printing with a plus sign.

Line 30 contains an ON . . . GOSUB *line numbers* statement. There is nothing unusual about the statement in itself—you've already studied it in an earlier chapter. What is somewhat different from anything described earlier is the fact that the last three subroutine lines specified in the statement are identical. What are the implications of that fact?

Well, first notice that the operator sets the value of T in response to the INPUT statement in line 28. The numerical value of T determines which one of the five possible tasks will be performed.

So if the operator sets T equal to 1, the ON . . . GOSUB statement in line 30 sends control to a subroutine beginning at line 100. If the operator selects task number 2, T is equal to 2, and tne ON . . . GOSUB statement turns over program control to a subroutine beginning at line 200. But if the operator selects task 3, 4, or 5, line 30 sends program control to the same subroutine—the one starting at line 300.

There must be something about tasks 3, 4, and 5 that make them quite similar—so similar, in fact, that they can be run by the same subroutine. Apparently, tasks 1 and 2 are not sufficiently similar to warrant using the same subroutine for running them.

Now it's time to look at the subroutines. Unfortunately, it is rather difficult to describe the subroutines in separate, bite-sized pieces. The difficulty arises from the fact that they are written more for overall efficiency than ease of description.

Subroutines 100 and 200, shown in Example 12-12, are rather different in many respects; but it is hard to understand some of the statements in subroutine 100 without referring to 200, and in fact, subroutine 200 cannot even be run without having access to 100.

EXAMPLE 12-12

```
100 REM ** NEW LISTING **
110 CLS:L=1001
120 READ N$: IF N$="END" THEN 140
130 READ D$,P$,A: L=L+1: GOTO 120
140 IF T=2 RETURN
150 PRINT "BEGIN NEW LISTING AT"L
160 END
200 REM ** LAST TEN **
210 CLS:B=0:P=1001:GOSUB 100
211 PRINT "TRANS";:PRINT TAB(10) "DATE";:PRINT TAB(20) "RECIPIENT";
212 PRINT TAB(35) "AMOUNT";: PRINT TAB(50)"BALANCE":PRINT
215 RESTORE
220 READ N$:IF N$="END" RETURN
230 READ D$,P$,A: P=P+1
240 IF LEFT$(N$,5)="DEPOS" THEN 250
245 B=B-A:F$=S$: GOTO 260
250 B=B+A:F$=R$
260 IF P>=L-9 THEN 270 ELSE 220
270 PRINT LEFT$(N$,5);:PRINT TAB(10)D$;:PRINT TAB(20) LEFT$(P$,8);
275 PRINT TAB(35) USING F$;A;: PRINT TAB(50) USING S$;B
280 GOTO 220
```

The master program calls line 100, NEW LISTING, whenever the operator selects task 1—NEW LISTINGS. This subroutine merely counts the number of DATA lines in the file, and prints out the line number for the next line of data. The idea is to tell the operator where to begin tacking on a series of new checkbook transactions.

The DATA listings will begin at line 1001, and for that reason the line counter is initialized at 1001 in line 110. As the program reads through the data, L is incremented, and this line-counting loop between lines 120 and 130 continues until N$ reads END in the data.

When N$ is read as END, the IF . . . THEN conditional statement in line 120 sends program control down to line 140. And that's where subroutine 200 becomes relevant. To get through this analysis, it is a good idea to ignore line 140 for the time being, assuming it is not satisfied and that the system does not break out of subroutine 100.

Assuming line 140 is not satisfied, program control then goes to line 150, and that line is responsible for displaying BEGIN NEW LISTING, followed by the current value of L, the line-number counter. The operator now knows where to begin entering new checkbook data, and the system returns to the command mode by virtue of the END statement in line 160.

All that happens whenever the operator selects the first task—NEW LISTINGS.

But suppose the operator selects task 2. In that case, the ON . . . GOSUB statement in line 30 of the master program calls the subroutine at line 200, the LAST TEN subroutine.

The purpose of LAST TEN is to run through all available DATA listings, keeping track of the checkbook balance and printing the full list of information for the last 10 transactions—presumably the 10 most recent transactions.

In order to know when to begin printing those last 10 transactions available in the DATA listing, the system has to know how many lines of DATA are available in the first place, then count lines, printing nothing, until it reaches line L-9. L minus 9? What is L?

L is the number of lines counted by the NEW LISTING subroutine. Little wonder, then, that LAST TEN cannot be run without running NEW LISTING first. NEW LISTING provides some essential information.

Here's how it works. The first operational steps in LAST TEN are in line 210. It first clears the screen and then initializes two numerical variables, B and P. Variable B will turn out to be the checkbook balance. Before starting to read the first transaction, it figures that the checkbook balance ought to be zero; so B=∅ from the start.

Variable P is a separate line counter for LAST TEN. It works just like the L variable in NEW LISTING.

Line 210 concludes with a GOSUB 1∅∅ statement. This subroutine 200 actually calls another subroutine, and now you are dealing with some nested subroutines. That is the step responsible for determining the total number of DATA lines on file.

Now you are in a position to appreciate the meaning of line 140. Subroutine 100, you see, is actually called from both tasks 1 and 2. If task 2 is in the works, subroutine 100 is called from subroutine 200, rather than the master program. In either case, subroutine 100 counts DATA lines by looping between lines 120 and 130, incrementing the value of L as it goes along. But when things get down to line 140—and assuming the subroutine has been called by LAST TEN—there is no need to print out the value of the last line number. Line 140, in that case, returns control back to line 211 of LAST TEN. The important thing is that the value of L is carried along with it.

In a manner of speaking, the GOSUB 1∅∅ statement in line 210 is responsible for initializing the value of L—using subroutine 100 to set L equal to the number of DATA lines in the file.

Lines 211 and 212 merely go through some messy, but necessary, steps for setting up the heading for the display. If you work your way through these two lines, you can see that the display should look much like this:

TRANS   DATE   RECIPIENT   AMOUNT   BALANCE

Ultimately, these will be headings for listed displays of transaction designations, dates, names of recipients, amounts of the transactions, and current checking-account balance.

Line 215 is absolutely essential. The RESTORE statement is necessary here because the earlier execution of subroutine 100 caused the READ pointer to move all the way to the last item in the DATA listing. So before it is possible to begin reading the data for another listing, the READ pointer must be returned to the first item in the first DATA line. That is what RESTORE does.

Lines 220 and 230 ought to seem fairly routine by now. The program is simply reading the data, looking for the END statement, and incrementing counter P with each reading of a line.

Skip over lines 240 through 250 for the time being. They are all included in the reading operation, but it's more important now to see how the system knows when to begin printing more information on the screen.

Each time the program reads a line of DATA, counter P is incremented and it is compared with the value of L in line 260. If P is less than L–9, the conditional statement in line 260 is not satisfied and the logical ELSE operator sends program control back to line 220 to begin the reading of another DATA line.

But when P finally increments to a point where it is just 9 readings short of L, the conditional statement in line 260 is satisfied and it sends the system to line 270. Why 9 readings short of L, instead of 10? Remember that L is also going to count the DATA END statements in the final line of the file. Since that line should not appear on the screen when running LAST TEN, it has to be subtracted out of the count. Indeed, you will find 10 listings on the screen when you run this subroutine later.

Now line 270 calls for a printing of the DATA items in the current line. Actually, the printing begins on line 270 and concludes with line 275. Yes, there are some strange-looking statements in those lines, but skip them for now. Just take it for granted that these lines are going to print information concerning the transaction, date, recipient, amount of the transaction, and account balance. These things line up under the corresponding headings printed at lines 211 and 212.

When the printing job is done, line 280 sends the system back to line 220 to begin another DATA reading operation. This READ, PRINT loop continues until N\$=END by the second statement in line 220. Upon seeing that END statement, the computer knows it has reached the end of the DATA listing, and control is returned to the master program.

In the process of describing how LAST TEN knows when to begin listing data and when to end, you have been asked to skip over some statements. One of the reasons is that the program includes a statement not yet introduced: LEFT\$(*string, number*)

The LEFT\$ is a truncating statement. It looks at a string value—combinations of characters, words, spaces, and so on—and lops off all but the first few character spaces. In the LEFT\$(*string, number*) statement, *string* specifies the string to be truncated in this fashion, and *number* specifies the number of characters to remain, as read from the left.

Suppose, for example, that A$=WEBSTER. Doing a LEFT$(A$,5) will make WEBSTER into WEBST. The first five characters from the left remain, and the rest are dropped.

Principle. LEFT$(*string,n*) truncates *string* by leaving only *n* characters from the left and dropping the rest.

You can find a LEFT$ statement in line 240. In this case it is used as part of an IF . . . THEN conditional statement. IF the first five characters of N$ is equal to DEPOS, THEN go to line 250. DEPOS, you see, is a truncated version of DEPOSIT; and whenever this string appears as the N$ item in a DATA line, it means the user made a deposit to the checking account. This is quite a significant fact, because it means the amount of the current transaction (a deposit) is added to the balance rather than subtracted from it. See line 250 called by satisfying the conditional statement in line 240.

You will also find two LEFT$ statements in line 270. These truncate the transaction and recipient designations to make certain everything fits onto the screen. Without using the LEFT$ statements in this way, a long recipient name could shove the amount and balance figures far to the right and off the screen. (Actually, those figures would "fold over" to the left side of the screen; but that would be messy, too.)

Do you remember the filed specifiers listed in line 12? You can find references to them in lines 245 and 250. Aside from making certain the dollar amounts in the AMOUNT and BALANCE columns line up neatly, the use of R$ in line 250 automatically inserts a plus sign at the beginning of AMOUNT figures for deposits. The operator does not have to specify + amounts for deposits and − amounts for checks written against the account.

That's nice, isn't it? It's up to you to figure out exactly how it works, though.

The next step in this analysis is to look at the subroutine that handles tasks 3, 4, and 5. Recall that the purpose of these tasks is to list relevant checkbook information regarding a certain, user-specified criteria. Task 3, for instance, lists all the register information and balances for any specified type of transaction, including DEPOSIT and valid check numbers. Task 4 lists the same kind of information, but according to a certain date specified by the user. And finally, task 5 lists the register information according to the name of the recipient.

These three tasks are basically the same: Given a certain criterion, list all register information related to that criterion. It really isn't a very difficult task, either. The subroutine, FIND, is given as Example 12–13.

The first major task of this subroutine is to sort out which one of the three tasks (3, 4, or 5) is being run. This is necessary because the three tasks attempt to match three different variables with the DATA items. Task 3 looks for a match between a transaction designation and an N$ item, task 4 looks for a match between a date and a D$, and task 4 looks for a match between a specified recipient designation and a P$ item in the DATA listing. Lines 305 through 320 handle the job of getting the user's task-oriented variable into the works.

EXAMPLE 12-13

```
300 REM ** FIND **
305 CLS: M=0: ON T-2 GOTO 310,315,320
310 PRINT: INPUT "WHAT TRANSACTION";T$: GOTO 325
315 PRINT: INPUT "WHAT DATE (MONTH-DAY)";T$: GOTO 325
320 PRINT: INPUT "WHAT RECIPIENT";T$
325 T$=LEFT$(T$,5): B=0
330 PRINT: PRINT "TRANSACT";: PRINT TAB(10) "DATE";
332 PRINT TAB(20) "RECIPIENT";: PRINT TAB(40) "AMOUNT";
334 PRINT TAB(50) "BALANCE": PRINT
335 LET L=0
340 READ N$: IF N$="END" THEN 400
345 READ D$,P$,A
350 IF LEFT$(N$,5)="DEPOS" THEN 360
355 B=B-A: F$=S$: GOTO 365
360 B=B+A: F$=R$
365 ON T-2 GOTO 370,375,380
370 IF LEFT$(N$,5)=T$ THEN 385 ELSE 340
375 IF D$=T$ THEN 385 ELSE 340
380 IF NOT(LEFT$(P$,5)=T$) THEN 340
385 PRINT N$;: PRINT TAB (10) D$;: PRINT TAB(20) LEFT$(P$,8);
387 PRINT TAB(40) USING F$;A;: PRINT TAB(50) USING S$;B
390 LET L=L+1: IF L<10 THEN 340
395 PRINT: INPUT"STRIKE 'ENTER' KEY TO SEE MORE";X$
397 M=M+1:CLS: GOTO 330
400 IF NOT(M=0 AND L=0) RETURN
405 PRINT "NO SUCH LISTING": RETURN
```

This part of the job begins with the ON . . . GOTO statement in line 305. A numerical value is assigned to variable T way back in the first part of the master program, when the operator selects a task. This FIND subroutine, however, is called only when T is equal to 3, 4, or 5. The T-2 expression in line 305 reduces these numbers to 1, 2, or 3, thus making them fit the GOTO *line numbers* statement. If you were to write this statement as ON T

GOTO . . . , you would have to insert two "dummy" lines in front of line designations 310, 315, 320.

The ON . . . GOTO statement in line 305 thus sends program control to one of three INPUT lines, depending on the designated task. And those lines request the appropriate kind of criteria for the search: WHAT TRANSACTION, WHAT DATE (MONTH-DAY), and WHAT RECIPIENT, respectively.

When the operator responds to one of these INPUT statements, the response is assigned to string variable T$. T$ thus carries the criteria for the matching operation throughout the entire subroutine.

That match-criteria variable—representing the type of item the computer is going to seek out—is truncated to its first five characters in line 325.

Lines 330 through 334 merely print the headings for the information to be listed on the screen:

TRANSACT   DATE   RECIPIENT   AMOUNT   BALANCE

After all that, the reading operations finally begin at line 340. After checking for the END statement in the DATA list, and assuming for the time being that the statement is *not* satisfied, the computer reads the remaining items in the DATA line, D$ (date), P$ (recipient), and A (amount of the transaction).

Skipping down to line 365, it is time to sort things according to the task being run. This is the second, and final, time this happens. Here is another ON T-2 GOTO . . . statement. If T=3, control is sent to line 370, where T$ is compared with a truncated version of the N$ item previously read in line 340. Doing task 3, in other words, forces the system to attempt a match between T$ and N$—transaction designations.

If the operator has specified task 4, line 365 causes the system to check the match between D$ and T$ (dates) at line 375. But if task 5 is being run, line 365 tells the system to attempt a match between a truncated version of the P$ item and T$ (recipients).

If there is a good match in any one of these three cases, control goes to line 385, where the checkbook information, including the compiled balance, is listed on the screen under the appropriate headings generated by lines 330 through 334. But if there is no match, the ELSE operators return control to line 340, where the system begins reading the next DATA line.

The system continues reading DATA lines and printing information whenever there is a match up until one of two things happens: either the system displays 10 lines of information on the screen or READ N$ finally finds an END statement in the DATA list.

You don't want to list more than 10 lines of information on the screen. Allowing that to happen would run the risk of having some of it scrolled off the top of the screen. So the subroutine in this example includes a mechanism for counting the number of lines of information that is printed. The counting variable in this case is L. L is set to zero at line 335 and incremented by the first statement in line 390—directly after each line-printing operation. Also, by line 390, if L is less than 10, the system continues cycling through its match-search routine. But the moment L becomes equal to or greater than 10, the second statement in line 390 defaults to line 395.

Upon executing line 395, all searching and printing operations come to a halt, and the operator is prompted to STRIKE 'ENTER' TO SEE MORE. When the operator has a chance to study the lines of information on the screen, striking the ENTER key makes operations pick up at line 397. The screen is cleared, and by going back to line 330, the system prints a fresh heading and resets the printed-line counter, L, back to zero. The search then continues where it left off.

Eventually, the READ N$ statement in line 340 is going to encounter and END statement at the end of the DATA listing. The IF . . . THEN conditional in that line is thus satisfied and control goes to line 400.

Line 400 is a logic statement that, in effect, tests to see whether or not any relevant information has been found. If L=∅, for instance, the implication is that there are no lines of information printed on the screen. Perhaps none was found in the entire searching operation. But there is a chance that the screen might have been filled with lines and that the operator struck the ENTER key to see more—but there was no more, and L=∅. There has to be some provision for covering this case. That's the purpose of the M-variable counter.

M keeps track of the number of times an overloaded screen is cleared and restarted. Note that M is set to zero at the very start of the subroutine (line 305) and is incremented whenever the operator must strike the ENTER key to see another block of match-ups.

So if M and L are zero at the same time, it means no match-ups were found in the entire DATA listing. The logic statement is negated by NOT, however. So if M and L are both zero at the same time, control goes to line 405, causing the message NO SUCH LISTING to appear on the screen. In either case, the system breaks away from the subroutine and returns to the master program.

Earlier in this discussion of the FIND subroutine, you were asked to skip over lines 350 through 360. They should look rather familiar, because the same sequence of operations appeared in the subroutine in Example 12-12. All they do is keep a running tally of the checking-account balance and make provisions for inserting a plus sign in front of AMOUNTS figures for deposit-type transactions.

It certainly takes a lot of time, thinking, and knowledge of BASIC programming to understand this program. If you can understand it completely by reading about it just one time, you have a great future in computer programming. Most of us would have a hard time getting even the general ideas the first time through the analysis. It would be helpful to go through the entire analysis again, making notes and jotting down questions as you go. Run through the explanations several times, revising the notes and trying to answer your questions for yourself.

Eventually, you will get the impression you understand what is happening and, in the process, become a more knowledgeable and experienced BASIC programmer. Making up a flowchart for this program is left as an exercise at the end of this chapter. It's doubtful you can master the analysis without making up some sort of a flowchart as you study it, however.

No matter how you feel about the program when you're finished studying it, you should eventually load it into your computer and try it for yourself. Of course, you'll have to enter some DATA listings before the program can be run. Here is a suggested listing. It isn't long enough to cover all the features of the program, but it is adequate for demonstrating the basic principles.

EXAMPLE 12-14

```
1000 REM ** DATA **
1001 DATA DEPOSIT, 6-12,24-HR,625.50
1002 DATA 1222,6-12,GAS CO.,37.29
1003 DATA 1223,6-12,SEARS,25.00
1004 DATA 1224,6-12,DR. SMITH,10.00
1005 DATA VISA, 6-14,FRANK'S,14.95
1006 DATA DEPOSIT,6-14,TELLER,25.00
1007 DATA 1225,6-14,VOID,0
1008 DATA 1226,6-14,BILL G.,125.45
1009 DATA 1227,6-15,RENT,450.00
1010 DATA DEPOSIT,6-15,24-HR,230.19
1011 DATA 1228,6-17,CARRYOUT,15.15
1012 DATA 1229,6-18,RADIO SHACK,32.45
1013 DATA END
```

12-7 Running CHECKBOOK TRANSACTION

Assuming you have loaded the program and data as listed in Examples 12-11, 12-12, 12-13 and 12-14, it is time to run some of the task options. Do a RUN and enter task number 1. You should see this on the screen:

```
BEGIN NEW LISTING AT 1013
READY
>_
```

Enter RUN again and select task 2. The listing will look like this:

TRANS	DATE	RECIPIENT	AMOUNT	BALANCE
1223	6–12	SEARS	25.00	563.21
1224	6–12	DR. SMIT	10.00	553.21
VISA	6–14	FRANK'S	14.95	538.26
DEPOS	6–14	TELLER	+25.00	563.26
1225	6–14	VOID	0 .00	563.26
1226	6–14	BILL G.	125 .45	437.81
1227	6–15	RENT	450.50	-12.69
DEPOS	6–15	24–HR	+230.19	217.50
1228	6–17	CARRYOUT	15 .15	202.35
1229	6–18	RADIO SH	32 .45	169.90

END OF LISTING

SAME TASK AGAIN (Y OR N)?_

This display is the result of running task 2. It is the user's 10 most recent checking transactions. Notice the information in the TRAS column is truncated after five characters, and that RECIPIENT information is truncated after eight characters. Both are the result of LEFT$ statements, and the point is to let the user write in designations of any length without worrying about the possibility of shoving a line of information out of alignment with the headings.

Also notice the plus signs for deposits in the AMOUNT column. This feature makes it easier for the operator to spot deposits, and it is generated by the special "+####.##" field specifier in the program.

Can you clearly see that the user overdrew the account by $12.69 on June 15? A subsequent deposit on that same day covered the check, however.

Now enter N to get back to the main heading and select task 3. You will see the message WHAT TRANSACTION? To get a summary of deposits, enter DEPOSIT. The figures on the screen should look like this:

WHAT TRANSACTION? DEPOSIT

TRANSACT	DATE	RECIPIENT	AMOUNT	BALANCE
DEPOSIT	6–12	24–HR	+625.50	625.50
DEPOSIT	6–14	TELLER	+25.00	563.26
DEPOSIT	6–15	24–HR	+230.19	217.50

END OF LISTING

SAME TASK AGAIN (Y OR N)?_

Enter Y to get the screen cleared and a reprint of WHAT TRANS-ACTION? Respond to the question by entering check number 1225.

WHAT TRANSACTION? 1225

TRANSACT	DATE	RECIPIENT	AMOUNT	BALANCE
1225	6–14	VOID	0.00	563.26

END OF LISTING

SAME TASK AGAIN (Y OR N)?_

In the first case, the operator requested and got a complete de-posit history contained in the DATA file. In the second instance, the operator requested information about check number 1225—which happened to be a voided check.

Enter N to get back to the main heading and then request task 4. You should see a message, WHAT DATE (MONTH–DAY)? Respond by entering 6–12.

TRANSACT	DATE	RECIPIENT	AMOUNT	BALANCE
DEPOSIT	6–12	24–HR	+625.50	625.50
1222	6–12	GAS CO.	37.29	588.21
1223	6–12	SEARS	25.00	563.21
1224	6–12	DR. SMIT	10.00	553.21

END OF LISTING

SAME TASK AGAIN (Y OR N)?_

And there are all the transactions and relevant information for June 12.

Enter N again, and select task 5. The message in this case is WHAT RECIPIENT? Look at RADIO SHACK.

WHAT RECIPIENT? RADIO SHACK

TRANSACT	DATA	RECIPIENT	AMOUNT	BALANCE
1229	6–18	RADIO SH	32.45	169.90

END OF LISTING

SAME TASK AGAIN (Y OR N)?_

So the user wrote check number 1229 to Radio Shack on June 18. The amount of the check was \$32.95 and that left a balance of \$169.90 in the checking account.

Get back to the main heading, specify task 1, and enter some checking information of your own choosing. Be sure to end the listing with DATA END. Run the program any way you want, and have fun.

If you want to adapt the program for your own checking account, simply start writing your own DATA items at line 1001. You will be writing over the material from Example 12-14 as you go along.

Of course you must have some provisions for storing the information—on cassette tape, or, better yet, a floppy disk system.

EXERCISES

12-1 Construct a flowchart for the master program for STUDENT/COURSE GRADE in Example 12-10.

12-2 Each DATA line in Example 12-1 must be read with exactly four READ operations. Account for the four READ operations as applied in Example 12-2.

12-3 What is the purpose of the L variable in Example 12-2? Why is such a a variable not used in Example 12-4? How does the application of the L variable in Example 12-2 compare with that of the E variable in Example 12-6?

12-4 Explain how the use of variables H, G, HT, and CH in Example 12-4 relate to the equation for finding point–hour ratios in Equation 12-1.

12-5 What is the purpose of the M\$ string variable in Example 12-6? What is the meaning of the expression C\$=M\$ in line 350 of that example?

12-6 What is the purpose of line 45 in Example 12-10?

12-7 Explain the significance of the following ON . . . GOTO statements:

(a) ON S GOTO 5Ø,5Ø,6Ø,5Ø

(b) ON S-2 GOTO 1Ø,2Ø,3Ø,3Ø

What is the valid range of values for S in statement (a)? in statement (b)?

12-8   Explain the difference, if any, between the following examples using field specifiers:

   (a) PRINT USING "##.##";A

   (b) LET F$="##.##" : PRINT USING F$;A

12-9   Specify the result of running the following statements:

   (a) N$="NOW YOU DID IT!" : PRINT LEFT$(N$,5)

   (b) M$="MONEY":E$=LEFT$(M$,2) : PRINT E$

   (c) N$="SAMUEL":O$=LEFT$(N$,3) : PRINT O$ " IS SHORT FOR "N$

12-10   Each DATA line in Example 12-14 must be read with four READ operations. Account for those four operations in Example 12-12 and 12-13.

12-11   What is a *random file*? The opposite of a *random file* is a *sequential file*— what do you suppose characterizes a sequential file?

CHAPTER 13

Easing into Data Arrays with Subscripted Variables

Statement introduced in this chapter:
DIM

Until now, you have had to select numerical and string variables in a rather conscious fashion. You have been consciously selecting the variables, fitting them into a program and making some provisions for assigning the right kinds of values to them.

There are instances that call for using a great many numerical or string variables, and what's more, there are situations where the number of variables you must specify changes with the operation of the program. Running a program at one time might call for assigning values to 20 variables, but running the same program under slightly different conditions at a later time might call for using 50 variables. This can be a very tricky situation if you are tied down to the notion of selecting all the variable names in advance.

There has to be a better way. And there is—using *subscripted variables*. It is rather pointless to establish a formal definition of subscripted variables at this time because it probably wouldn't mean much to you. To get headed in the right direction, consider some tinkering with the computer in its command mode. Try this sequence:

```
READY
>LET T(1)=4
READY
>PRINT T(1)
 4
READY
>_
```

The operator first set up the computer for the command mode of operation, then entered the statement LET T(1)=4. The next step was to enter the command PRINT T(1), and the computer responded by printing the numeral 4. T(1) in this example is a subscripted variable. Now look at this sequence:

```
READY
>T(1)=9:T(2)=8:T(3)=7
READY
>PRINT T(1),T(2),T(3)
 9                8                        7
READY
>_
```

In this instance, the operation first specified values for subscripted variables T(1), T(2), and T(3). The next command called for a printing of the values of those same subscripted variables—and there they are. Or consider this:

```
READY
>D$ (2)="MUGGINS"
READY
>PRINT D$ (2)
MUGGINS
READY
>_
```

You see, there is such a thing as a subscripted string variable.

A subscripted variable thus takes the general form *variable(n)*, where *variable* can be any valid variable name and *n* is any integer or mathematical operation that results in an integer value.

Nice, but what is to be gained by this? These examples treat subscripted variables just as though they are the usual sorts of variables. And that is indeed a valid observation—but of course there's much more to the matter.

The key to appreciating the purpose of subscripted variables can be summarized in one sentence: *The n subscript in* variable (n) *can be generated automatically within the program.* There is no way that new variables of the usual sort can be named and specified once a program is running.

13-1 Some Preliminary Experiments with Subscripted Variables

Enter the program of Example 13-1 into your computer.

EXAMPLE 13-1

```
10 CLS: For N=1 TO 10
20 PRINT "ENTER ITEM NUMBER"N: INPUT X
30 T(N)=X
40 NEXT
50 PRINT "ENTRY PHASE DONE"
60 INPUT "STRIKE THE 'ENTER' KEY FOR DISPLAY";X$
70 CLS: FOR N=1 TO 10
80 PRINT "ENTRY"N"="T(N)
90 NEXT
100 PRINT "DISPLAY DONE"
110 END
```

First note the FOR . . . NEXT loop between lines 10 and 40. Ten times, you are prompted to enter an item X. And each time you enter the item (a numerical value), it is assigned to the subscripted variable T. So by the time the program gets down to line 50, you have stored 10 item values in memory, each assigned a subscribed variable between T(1) and T(9).

And after the system executes lines 50 and 60, it waits for you to strike the ENTER key. The display to this point looks like this:

```
ENTER ITEM 1 ? 00
ENTER ITEM 2 ? 99
ENTER ITEM 3 ? 88
ENTER ITEM 4 ? 77
ENTER ITEM 5 ? 66
ENTER ITEM 6 ? 55
ENTER ITEM 7 ? 44
ENTER ITEM 8 ? 33
ENTER ITEM 9 ? 22
ENTER ITEM 10 ? 11
ENTER PHASE DONE
STRIKE 'ENTER' FOR DISPLAY?_
```

Of course, this display was built from the top and downward, adding a new line every time you enter a new item. The items in this instance happen to be a sequence 00, 99, 88, . . . , 11. You can respond to the question marks with any number you choose.

Responding to the STRIKE 'ENTER' . . . message, another FOR . . . NEXT begins. This one, however, runs between lines 70 and 90, printing out the information stored in the first phase. The display ought to look something like this:

```
ENTRY 1 = 00
ENTRY 2 = 99
ENTRY 3 = 88
ENTRY 4 = 77
ENTRY 5 = 66
ENTRY 6 = 55
ENTRY 7 = 44
ENTRY 8 = 33
ENTRY 9 = 22
ENTRY 10 = 11
DISPLAY DONE
READY
>_
```

The program worked its way through all 10 subscripted variables and printed out their respective values that were assigned in the first phase of the program.

How would you compose a program for doing this same job if you did not have the benefit of subscripted variables? The first phase of the job would have to look like this:

EXAMPLE 13-2

```
10 CLS: FOR N=1 TO 11
20 PRINT "ENTER ITEM NUMBER"N
30 ON N GOTO 40,41,42,43,44,45,46,47,48,49,50
40 INPUT T1:NEXT
41 INPUT T2:NEXT
42 INPUT T3:NEXT
43 INPUT T4:NEXT
44 INPUT T5:NEXT
45 INPUT T6:NEXT
46 INPUT T7:NEXT
47 INPUT T8:NEXT
48 INPUT T9:NEXT
49 INPUT T0:NEXT
50 PRINT "ENTRY PHASE DONE"
60 INPUT "STRIKE 'ENTER' KEY FOR DISPLAY";X$
```

That is a lot of work for the programmer, and what's more, it is terribly inefficient in terms of the amount of program space it occupies in the system's memory. Considering Example 13-2 represents only the first phase of the job in Example 13-1, you are looking at a compelling case for using subscripted variables.

So it ought to be clear that using subscripted variables allows the creation of highly efficient programs when those programs call for specifying the values of a lot of variables. But there is more.

What about instances where the number of variables required is not known in advance? Example 13-1 fixes the number of variables at 10, by virtue of the FOR . . . NEXT statement. Look at the same task modified to accommodate any number of input items.

EXAMPLE 13-3

```
10 CLS:N=1
20 PRINT "ENTER ITEM NUMBER"N;: INPUT X
30 T(N)=X
40 IF X=9999 THEN 60
50 N=N+1: GOTO 20
60 PRINT "OK. DONE FOR"N-1 "ITEMS"
70 INPUT "STRIKE 'ENTER' KEY FOR DISPLAY";X$
80 CLS: FOR M=1 TO N-1
90 PRINT "ENTRY" M"="T(M) :NEXT
100 PRINT "LISTING DONE":END
```

This is an open-ended program that allows the user to enter any number of numerical values, X. With each entry, counting variable N is incremented at line 50, generating a looping action that is similar to the FOR . . . NEXT loop in Example 13-1, but unending.

The operator signals the end of the data-entry operation by specifying 9999. Whenever X is set to 9999, line 40 sends operation down to line 60, and the operator sees the message OK. DONE FOR so many ITEMS. Using 9999 as an entry for signaling the end of the data-entering process is a rather arbitrary move that assumes 9999 will never be one of the items to be saved as a subscripted value.

The display phase of the job begins at line 80, using the number N-1 as the end point for the FOR . . . NEXT operation. Other than that little variation, the display phase is virtually identical to the version already described in connection with Example 13-1.

The main point of this example, however, is that the operator is free to enter any number of values. The scheme automatically specifies the subscripted variables—something that cannot be done with ordinary variables.

Suppose you run the program. The display generated through the first, data-entry phase might look like this:

```
ENTER ITEM NUMBER 1 ? 12
ENTER ITEM NUMBER 2 ? 23
ENTER ITEM NUMBER 3 ? 34
ENTER ITEM NUMBER 4 ? 45
ENTER ITEM NUMBER 5 ? 9999
OK. DONE FOR 4 ITEMS
STRIKE 'ENTER' KEY FOR DISPLAY?_
```

In this example, the operator responded to the requests for item numbers with the sequence 12, 23, 34, 45, and then terminated the operation by entering the "magic number" 9999. The computer responded to that last entry by printing a couple of relevant messages.

After striking the ENTER key, the display changes to this:

```
ENTRY 1 = 12
ENTRY 2 = 23
ENTRY 3 = 34
ENTRY 4 = 45
LISTING DONE
READY
> _
```

The same sort of operations can be applied to entering string values—words and combinations of alphanumeric characters and symbols. Look at this example:

EXAMPLE 13-4

```
10 CLS: N=1
20 PRINT "ENTER ITEM"N;: INPUT X$
30 T$(N)=X$
40 IF X$="DONE" THEN 60
50 N=N+1: GOTO 20
60 PRINT "OK. DONE FOR"N-1"ITEMS"
70 INPUT "STRIKE 'ENTER' KEY FOR DISPLAY";X$
80 CLS: N=1
90 IF T$(N)="DONE" THEN 110
100 PRINT "ENTRY"N"="T$(N): N=N+1: GOTO 90
110 PRINT "LISTING DONE":END
```

This program runs much the same way as that in Example 13-3, the only differences being that Example 13-4 accepts string expressions and the entry phase is ended by entering DONE. Note the use of the subscripted string variable T$(N) and input variable X$, in place of T(N) and X shown in Example 13-3.

The flowchart for this example appears in Fig. 13-1.

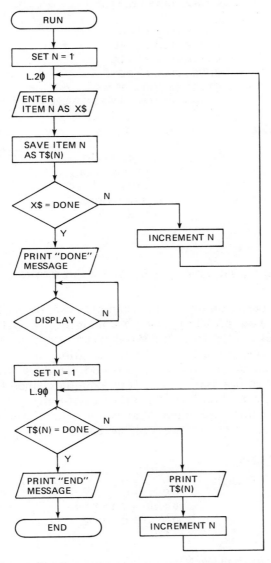

Figure 13–1 Flowchart for a program that lets the operator enter string variables into subscript memory space, and then list the results. See the program in Example 13–4.

A typical entry sequence for this example looks like this:

```
ENTER ITEM 1 ? BIC
ENTER ITEM 2 ? TAB
ENTER ITEM 3 ? MUG
ENTER ITEM 4 ? DONE
OK. DONE FOR 3 ITEMS
STRIKE 'ENTER' KEY FOR DISPLAY?_
```

Upon striking the ENTER key:

```
ENTRY 1 =BIC
ENTRY 2 =TAB
ENTRY 3 =MUG
LISTING DONE
READY
>_
```

13-2   Allocating More memory Space for Subscripts

If you have been running these examples exactly as they are pre-sented here, you probably haven't run into any system-generated error messages related to running out of subscript range. Most home computers allow at least 10 memory locations for subscripts. That means you can use up to 10 subscripted variables within any pro-gram. And since none of the previous examples called for more than 10 subscripts, you haven't run into the out-of-range problem.

Here is a short experiment that lets you determine exactly how much subscript memory is normally available.

EXAMPLE 13-5

```
10 CLS:N=1
20 T(N)=N: PRINT T(N)
30 N=N+1: GOTO 20
40 END
```

The idea is to build an N counter, using the values of N to specify the sub-script as well as its value. So whenever N=5, for instance, T(5)=5. As the values are assigned in the first statement in line 20, the second statement in that line prints them on the screen.

The program is essentially an unending counting loop, but you will run out of available string space before the program counts very far. The result of this experiment, as run on Radio Shack's Level II TRS-80, looks like this:

```
RUN
1
2
3
4
5
6
7
8
9
10
?BS ERROR IN 20
READY
>_
```

After assigning values to 10 subscripted variables, T(1) through T(10), the system ran out of its allocated memory space for subscripts. The error message, printed by the computer itself, will be slightly different from one kind of computer to another, but the message will be clear: You're out of the allocated memory space for subscripts, my friend.

Now that's a real jolt! Things have been looking pretty good until now.

But there's a nice way to get around the problem. The amount of memory space set aside for string variables can be specified by the user. It so happens that Radio Shack allows 10 spaces if you don't specify anything different, and if you want more space, you simply tell the computer about it.

Modify this example by entering a new line:

5 DIM T(100)

Now run the program and watch what happens. Ah-ha! The thing counts like crazy up to 100—and then you get the error message. The statement DIM T(100) allocated 100 memory spaces for subscripted variable T(n).

How large can you make the memory space? That depends on the system you have. A system featuring a 4K memory cannot allocate as much subscript space as an 8K or 16K system. An out-of-memory error will signal that you have assigned more subscript space than the system can handle.

Principle. DIM *variable name(n)* allows you to specify the amount of computer memory set aside for storing subscripted variable, *variable name.* The amount of memory space, n, can be any integer between 1 and some relatively large number determined by the memory capacity of your machine.

Incidentally, *the DIM statement must not be executed more than one time during the running of any one program.* For that reason, DIM statements are usually placed very early in the program.

If you do not specify a DIM in the program, the computer automatically does its own DIM for some amount of subscript space—$n = 10$ in the case of the Radio Shack TRS–80.

So a DIM statement sets aside a block of memory space for storing values of subscripted variables. And thinking further along this line, it is often convenient and quite helpful to view subscripted variables as designations for memory locations, rather than variables per se. S(12), for example, need not be considered just another variable, but memory location 12 in memory block S. In a sense, it is a memory address—an expression that specifies the memory location of some specific piece of information.

You can *write* information into that memory location by means of a statement such as S(12)=2. That statement stores number 2 in memory block S, location 12. At any later time, you can *read* that information by means of a statement such as PRINT S(12).

13-3   Manipulating Information Specified as Subscripted Variables

All of the examples presented in the first part of this chapter merely list the information entered in an earlier phase of the program. The point was to show that subscripted variables can accept numerical or string values, store it, and then read it out at a later time. But, of course, it is also possible to manipulate the information as it is read out of the memory, doing things such as mathematical operations, sorting, and even program control operations.

The program in Example 13–6 allows the operator to enter up to 100 numbers and then get a printout of those numbers and a figure representing their average value. A flowchart for the program is illustrated in Fig. 13–2.

EXAMPLE 13-6

```
10 DIM A(100):CLS:N=1
20 PRINT"TYPE A BUNCH OF NUMBERS (UP TO 100 OF THEM),"
30 PRINT"DOING 'ENTER' AFTER EACH ONE OF THEM."
40 PRINT:PRINT"ENTER 9999 TO END THE ENTRY OPERATION."
50 INPUT A(N): IF A(N)=9999 THEN 70
60 N=N+1: GOTO 50
```

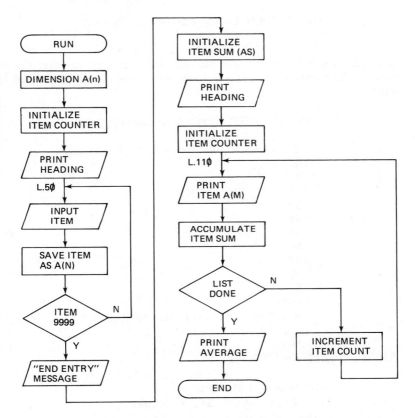

Figure 13-2 Flowchart for a program that sorts user-specified numbers and prints their average value. See the program in Example 13-6.

```
70 PRINT "OK, ENTRY PHASE DONE FOR"N-1"NUMBERS"
80 INPUT "DO 'ENTER' TO DISPLAY";E$
90 CLS: AS=0:
100 PRINT"YOUR" N-1 "NUMBERS WERE:"
110 FOR M=1 TO N-1: PRINT A(M)",";:AS=AS+A(M):NEXT
120 PRINT:PRINT "THE AVERAGE VALUE OF YOUR"N-1 "NUMBERS IS"AS/
(N-1)
130 END
```

Upon entering RUN, you are greeted with this message on the screen:

TYPE A BUNCH OF NUMBERS (UP TO 100 OF THEM),
DOING 'ENTER' AFTER EACH ONE OF THEM.

ENTER 9999 TO END THE ENTRY OPERATION
?_

The question mark and cursor indicate that it is time to enter the first number. Upon entering a "bunch of numbers," the display might look like this:

DOING 'ENTER' AFTER EACH ONE OF THEM.

ENTER 9999 TO END THE ENTRY OPERATION.
? 0
? 11
? 22
? 33
? 44
? 55
? 66
? 77
? 88
? 99
? 9999
OK, ENTRY PHASE DONE FOR 10 NUMBERS
DO 'ENTER' TO DISPLAY?_

And after striking the ENTER key:

YOUR 10 NUMBERS WERE:
0 , 11 , 22 , 33 , 44 , 55 , 66 , 77 , 88 , 99 ,

THE AVERAGE VALUE OF YOUR 10 NUMBERS IS 49.5
READY
>_

Lines 10 through 30 of the program in Example 13-6 are the ones that let the operator enter the "bunch of numbers." Line 50 directly inputs the value of subscripted variables, checks for 9999 "magic number," and if the 9999 is not specified, sends operations down to line 60. Line 60 then increments the value of N and loops the program back up to line 50.

This looping operation between lines 50 and 60 continues until the operator specifies 9999. When that happens, control is sent to line 70.

The second phase of the program picks up at line 90, clearing the screen and initializing an ordinary variable, AS. Line 100 prints a simple message that includes the number of numbers included in the entry process; and after that, line 110 begins reading the values of the subscripted variables, printing them, and accumulating a sum of the values, AS.

When all the subscripted values have been read—as determined by the completion of the FOR . . . NEXT loop in line 110—the system prints the final message, which includes the average value. That average is calculated by dividing the sum of the values by the number of values: AS/(N-1).

Information that is stored as subscripts can be manipulated mathematically in much the same fashion as items in a DATA list are handled.

Now this is a good time to try a sorting operation, using a batch of subscripts as the data source. The program in this instance uses the same entry phase as the program in Example 13-6. Instead of calculating the average value of the numbers, however, Example 13-7 searches the list for the largest value and prints it on the screen.

EXAMPLE 13-7

(Use lines 10 through 80 from Example 13-6 here.)

```
90 CLS: PV=0
100 PRINT "YOUR"N-1"NUMBERS WERE:"
110 FOR M=1 TO N-1: PRINT A(M)",";
120 IF A(M)>PV THEN PV=A(M)
130 NEXT
140 PRINT: PRINT"THE LARGEST OF YOUR"N-1"NUMBERS IS"PV
150 END
```

The idea here is to examine all the subscripted information, one element at a time, saving the largest value as ordinary variable PV. This is done by first setting PV to zero in line 90, looking at the value of A(1), and if that is larger than PV, saving the value of A(1) as PV. The FOR . . . NEXT loop then causes the system to compare A(2) and PV. If A(2) happens to be smaller, PV is not changed; but if A(2) is larger, its value replaces the smaller one in PV.

This comparison operation continues through the entire list of subscripts, the current largest value of A(N) being held as value PV. Line 140 then prints the final value of PV, which, of course, has to be the largest of all the A(N) numbers.

The complete flowchart for this program is shown in Fig. 13-3. Load the program and run it for yourself. You'll see that it prints out the largest of all the numbers you enter during the first phase of the program.

Before going to bigger and better things, you ought to have a chance to work with a program that combines operations on both numerical and string subscripted variables. Example 13-8, in fact, uses three subscripted variables that are treated in parallel. Two of them are strings and one is a numerical variable.

The purpose of the program is to let an operator enter some data

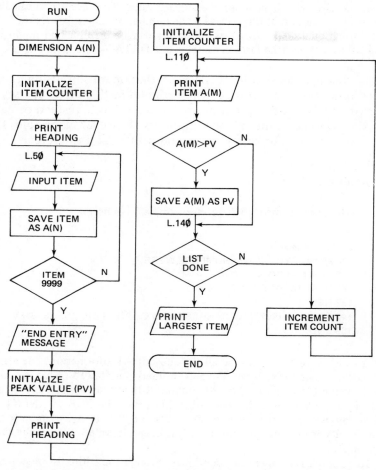

Figure 13-3 Flowchart for a program that sorts user-specified numbers and prints the value of the largest one. See the program in Example 13-7.

regarding wind speed and the times the speeds occurred. After entering the time/speed information, the program then lists the information, figures the average wind speed for the period of time the data represent, and sorts out the maximum speed.

The flowchart for Example 13-8 is shown in Fig. 13-4.

EXAMPLE 13-8

```
10 CLS:N=1;DIM H$(100): DIM M$(100): DIM S(100)
20 PRINT"INPUT THE TIME AND WIND SPEED AS HR,MIN,SPEED"
```

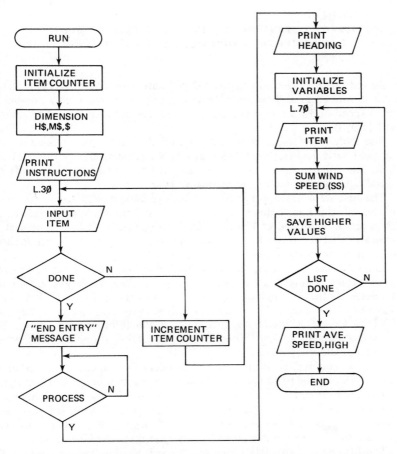

Figure 13-4 Flowchart for a program that lets the operator enter wind speeds and the times of day they occur. The program then compiles the list, printing the average wind speed for the interval as well as the peak wind speed and the time of day it occurred. See the program in Example 13-8.

```
25 PRINT"ENTER DONE,Ø,Ø WHEN FINISHED"
3Ø INPUT H$(N) ,M$(N) ,S(N): IF H$(N)="DONE" THEN 5Ø
4Ø N=N+1: GOTO 3Ø
5Ø CLS:PRINT"ENTRY TASK DONE FOR"N-1"ITEMS."
55 INPUT"DO 'ENTER' FOR DATA PROCESSING";X$
6Ø PRINT:PRINT"TIME","WIND SPEED":PRINT
65 SS=Ø:SP=Ø:HP$="":MP$=""
7Ø FOR M= 1 TO N-1:PRINT H$(M)":"M$(M) ,S(M)
8Ø SS=SS+S(M): IF S(M)>SP THEN 9Ø ELSE 1ØØ
9Ø SP=S(M) :HP$=H$(M) :MP$=M$(M)
```

```
100 NEXT
110 PRINT: PRINT"THE AVERAGE WIND SPEED IS"SS/(N-1)
115 PRINT"THE PEAK WIND SPEED IS"SP"AT "HP$":"MP$
120 END
```

As indicated by the informative PRINT statement in line 20, the information is entered as an hour, minute, and speed—separated with a comma. A wind speed of 10 knots occurring at 12:30, for instance, would be entered as 12,30,10.

The INPUT statement in line 30 assigns these three values to separate subscripted variables, $H\$(N)$, $M\$(N)$, and $S(N)$, respectively. Notice that the hour and minute figures have been assigned to string variables, while the speed figure is assigned to a numerical variable.

The first steps in the program, line 100, gets things initialized: the screen is cleared; the item counter, N, is set to 1; and the three subscripted variables are dimensioned at 100 memory locations each. The latter procedure indicates that the program is capable of accepting up to 100 combinations of hour, minute, and speed.

Lines 20 and 25 in Example 13-8 are merely tutorial messages. The real work begins at line 30. The first statement in line 30 assigns subscripted variables to the information the operator is entering from the keyboard. The use of a multiple INPUT statement does away with having to strike the ENTER key after specifying each one of the three essential items. The second statement in line 30 looks for the DONE statement that signals the end of the entry phase.

The list counter, N, is incremented in line 40 and control is returned to line 30, thus giving the operator a chance to enter another set of three items.

Whenever the entry phase is done, as detected by the conditional statement in line 30, the program picks up at line 50. And after printing out a couple of incidental messages (lines 50 and 55), the system lets the operator get into the data processing phase by simply striking the ENTER key.

The first part of the data processing phase is to print a set of headings for the figures. See line 60.

Line 65 initializes the variables used in this second phase of the program. Ordinary variable SS, as you will see shortly, accumulates the sum of the wind speeds, while SP picks up the highest wind speed read at any given moment. String variables HP$ and MP$ pick up the hour and minute specifications for the highest-read wind speed. Note that these two string variables are initialized by setting them equal to the null string value—nothing.

Line 70 begins the reading operations, calling for a printing of the time and speed figures. Note that the hours and minutes elements are compiled with a colon inserted between them. A time originally entered as 12,30, for example, will appear here as 12:30.

Variable SS in line 80 accumulates the sum of all the wind speeds read at the time, and the second statement in that line searches for wind speeds that are larger than any read at the moment.

Upon finding a wind speed that is greater than any read before, line 90 saves the peak speed and time it occurred.

Line 100, of course, loops the operation back to line 70 for fetching another series of time/speed information.

The FOR . . . NEXT looping operation continues until all the available items have been read, printed, and manipulated by the operations between lines 70 and 100. When that part of the job is done, lines 110 and 115 compile and print the results.

Load the program in Example 13-8, and RUN it. You will see this on the screen at first:

```
INPUT THE TIME AND WIND SPEED AS HR,MIN,SPEED
ENTER  DONE,0,0 WHEN FINISHED
?_
```

Then try entering this series of data:

```
? 12,00,10
? 12,15,12
? 12,30,15
? 12,45,15
? 13,00,8
? 13,15,8
? 13,30,6
? DONE,0,0_
```

After striking the ENTER key, you will see this:

```
ENTRY TASK DONE FOR 7 ITEMS.
DO 'ENTER' FOR DATA PROCESSING?_
```

Following the instructions and striking the ENTER key again causes this information to be added to the display:

```
TIME              WIND SPEED

12:00             10
12:15             12
12:30             15
12:45             15
13:00             8
13:15             8
13:30             6

THE AVERAGE WIND SPEED IS 10.5714
THE PEAK WIND SPEED IS 15 AT 12:30
READY
>_
```

That's a nice little list. It could be a lot longer—up to 100 items. Also note that the peak wind speeds in this particular listing occurred at two different times, 12:30 and 12:45. The program is written to save the earliest-occurring peak, whenever there are multiple peak wind speeds of equal value.

13-4 Making DATA/READ and Subscripted Items Work Together

Much of the work in data processing involves sorting through lists of data, searching for some prescribed relationships between the elements of the data, and then presenting it in a neat, well-organized display or printout.This sorting task simulates a human file clerk who is using some rational criteria for compiling a list of names or whatever. The data all exist in a room full of file cabinets, and the trick is to get your hands on the few files you really need.

In the case of computer filing and searching, the files can be kept in the form of DATA statements. The DATA items are then read and compared to some prescribed criteria. If the criteria are not met, the computer looks at the next DATA item, but if the criteria are satisfied, that item is saved somewhere in memory until the searching task is done and the desired items are compiled in that special section of memory.

Of course, that "special section of memory" can be some space allocated to subscripted variables. And what's more, the items "pulled" from the DATA files can be further manipulated, arranging them in alphabetical order and the like.

Indeed, the notion of using DATA files and subscripted variables in the same program is an extremely useful and important one.

The example cited in this section will be a program for a poker-hand dealing operation. Unlike the simpler version in Chapter 11, this one displays the suit as well as the face value of the card.

The DATA file consists of all 52 playing cards. The items will be string values such as 3H, KC, and 10S, representing the 3 of hearts, king of clubs, and 10 of spades, respectively.

The file will be read at random, and the selected card will be saved as a subscripted string variable—provided the same card hasn't been "dealt" before. So the program picks a card from the file of card names, checks to see whether or not it has been dealt already, and if the card hasn't been dealt, saves the card value in the player's subscript "hand." If the new card has been dealt already, the program simply returns to the DATA file to pick another one.

The program then runs until the player has a hand of five different cards. The cards are displayed on the screen, and the player evaluates the hand. It is possible to devise a subroutine for evaluating the hand automatically, but that would add needless complexity to the whole affair, risking the chance of losing the point of the example. Devising such a subroutine is left to poker buffs who want to try their hand at composing a very challenging program.

The improved version of the poker-dealing program is listed in Example 13-9. The corresponding flowchart is shown in Fig. 13-5.

EXAMPLE 13-9

```
10 DIM C$(5)
20 CLEAR:CLS:CD=1
30 RESTORE
40 FOR NC=1 TO RND(52): READ S$: NEXT
50 FOR CS=1 TO 5: IF C$(CS)=S$ THEN 30
60 NEXT
70 C$(CD)=S$: IF CD>5 THEN 90
80 CD=CD+1: GOTO 30
90 FOR CS=1 TO 5: PRINT C$(CS);" ";:NEXT
100 PRINT:PRINT:INPUT X$: GOTO 20


500 DATA 2H,3H,4H,5H,6H,7H,8H,9H,10H,JH,QH,KH,AH
505 DATA 2D,3D,4D,5D,6D,7D,8D,9D,10D,JD,QD,KD,AD
510 DATA 2S ,3S ,4S ,5S ,6S ,7S ,8S ,9S ,10S ,JS ,QS ,KS ,AS
520 DATA 2C ,3C ,4C ,5C ,6C ,7C ,8C ,9C ,10C ,JC ,QC ,KC ,AC
```

In this card-dealing game, subscripted string variable $C\$(n)$ is the card designation, and since five cards are to be dealt, that variable has five memory locations set aside for it. See the DIM C$(5) statement in line 10. (Actually, it isn't necessary to specify such small segments of subscript memory, because most systems automatically set aside more space than that. The DIM statement is included here to remind you that such a statement is often necessary, however.)

Line 20 includes both a CLEAR and a CLS statement. Recall that CLEAR sets the values of all string and numerical variables to zero. Now you should add subscripted variables to that list of items set to zero by CLEAR. The step is necessary when requesting another dealing operation. CLS, of course, merely clears old information from the screen.

Variable CD represents the card being dealt. The variable is initially set to 1 in line 20, but you'll see that it increments to 5 before the program sequence is completed.

Line 30 resets the READ pointer back to the first item of DATA (2H in line 500) whenever it is time to READ the DATA for another card designation.

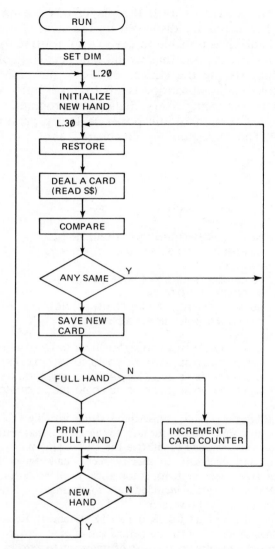

Figure 13-5 Flowchart for an improved poker-hand dealing program—the same card cannot be dealt twice. See the program in Example 13-9.

Line 40 causes the system to READ the data from the first item to an item determined by RND(52). After executing line 40, string variable S$ holds the value of a card randomly selected from the DATA file.

Line 50 then searches the list of card designations already assigned to the "hand"—the values already assigned to C$($n$). And if there is a match between a newly selected card, S$, and one of the cards already saved in the subscript memory, C$($n$), the system is restored and another card is pulled from the file. The point of all this is to make certain that no two cards in the hand are identical.

The new card is assigned to the "hand" by the first statement in line 70. If the hand already contains more than five cards, control goes down to line 90, where the values of the cards are printed out on the screen. Otherwise, the card counter, CD, is incremented at line 80, and control goes back to line 30 for picking another card.

By line 100, any number of fresh hands can be dealt by simply striking the ENTER key.

13-5 A First Look at Bubble Sorting

One of the most powerful applications of subscripted variables is that of sorting items of data into alphabetical or numerical order. Items of data are often entered into the system in a random fashion, but at some later time it is desirable to read out all that data in a particular order.

The most popular technique for arranging data in alphabetical or numerical order is called *bubble sorting*. There are alternative techniques available, but bubble sorting is most effective and efficient for smaller computer systems.

To see how bubble sorting works (and perhaps get some insight into how its peculiar name came about), imagine a small list of numbers that have been entered into the system. Maybe that list is something such as

12,24,2,18

The bubble-sorting procedure first looks at the first two items, comparing their values. In this example, 12 is compared with 24. If the first item happens to be smaller than the second, nothing changes. The list remains as

12,24,2,18

But then the system compares the second and third items—24 and 2.

In this instance, the second is smaller than the first, and the system responds by exchanging their places in the list. So now the list looks like this:

12,2,24,18

The next operation is to compare the third and fourth items—24 and 18. And since the fourth one is smaller than the third, the system exchanges their places, and the new list takes this form:

12,2,18,24

Notice how the largest number in the list "bubbles" to the top of the list. That always happens on the first pass through the list.

Obviously, the task of setting these items into numerical order is not done yet—the 12 and 2 are still out of order. So the whole job is done again.

Looking at the first two items, the computer sees that they are out of order, and responds by exchanging their positions. The list then looks like this:

2,12,18,24

The job is actually done at this point, but the computer doesn't know that. It continues running through the list, comparing successive pairs of items, until it runs through the complete list without making any exchanges. *Then* the computer has the information it needs to signal the end of the program.

Getting down to specifics, assume the computer has some memory space containing subscripted numerical variables $A(1)$ through $A(20)$; and further assume those 20 variables have been assigned random numbers between 1 and 99. The idea of the bubble-sort program is to rearrange the list so that the numbers are in numerical order.

As the program progresses, the system inspects the values of two successive subscript locations, say $A(I)$ and $A(I+1)$. $A(I)$ represents any one of the values, and $A(I+1)$ represents the next one along the line.

Now values $A(I)$ and $A(I+1)$ are compared, and if $A(I)$ is smaller than $A(I+1)$, the two are already in numerical order and there is no need to exchange their locations in memory. But when it turns out that $A(I)$ is greater than $A(I+1)$ the numbers in those two locations must be exchanged, and the exchanging process goes like this:

1. Assign the value of A(I) to an ordinary variable,

    S=A(I)

2. Assign the value of A(A+1) to A(I),

    A(I)=A(I+1)

3. Retrieve the original value of A(I) from S, and assign it to the A(A+1) memory location,

    A(I+1)=S

This process is shown in diagram form in Fig. 13-6. The squares represent memory locations. Location S is that of an ordinary numerical variable, whereas locations A(I) and A(I+1) are two successive subscript locations. Notice how values are copied into these memory locations and, at the end of the process, values *a* and *b* have switched locations in the subscript memory. The fact that a *b* value remains in S at the end of the process is not relevant.

Writing this exchanging process in formal BASIC:

EXAMPLE 13-10

140 S=A(I):A(I)=A(I+1):A(I+1)=S

Sure enough, the value originally assigned to A(I) ends up in location A(I+1), and the value originally residing in A(I+1) turns up in location A(I). That's the exchange process.

The fact that the process calls for swapping information around in variable spaces made it difficult to introduce the idea earlier in this book. But rest assured, you have not seen the end of it now.

The following examples make up a complete bubble sorting program. It starts out with a list of 20 randomly generated numbers that are assigned to an equal number of spaces in the subscript memory. The idea is to rearrange the list so that the values are in numerical order.

The actual sorting routine is presented as a subroutine in Example 13-11. Two additional subroutines in Example 13-12 are responsible for generating the list of random numbers and printing the results of both the random and ordered lists. The subroutines are then pulled together into a working program by the main program in Example 13-13. The whole business is presented as a flowchart in Fig. 13-7.

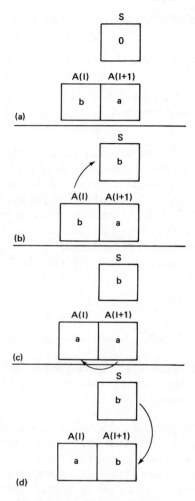

Figure 13-6 Block diagrams of memory elements involved in the exchange portion of a bubble sorting program. (a) Original status. (b) A(I) is saved in S. (c) A(I+1) is moved to A(I) space. (d) S is moved to A(I+1) space.

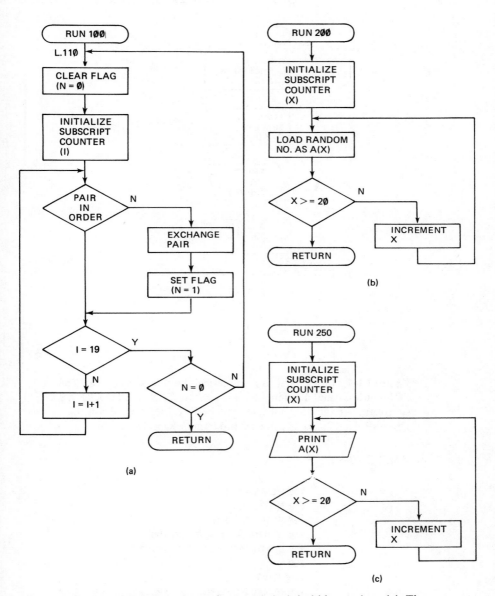

Figure 13-7 Flowcharts for numerical bubble sorting. (a) The SORT subroutine—Example 13-11. (b) The GENERATE ARRAY subroutine—Example 13-12. (c) The PRINT ARRAY subroutine—Example 13-12. (d) The master program—Example 13-13.

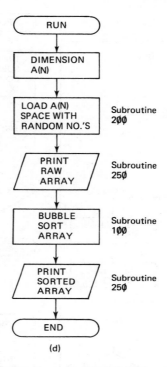

(d)

Figure 13-7 Flowcharts for numerical bubble sorting. (a) The SORT subroutine—Example 13-11. (b) The GENERATE ARRAY subroutine—Example 13-12. (c) The PRINT ARRAY subroutine—Example 13-12. (d) The master program—Example 13-13.

EXAMPLE 13-11

```
100 REM ** SORT **
110 N=0
120 FOR I=1 TO 19
130 IF A(I)<=A(I+1) THEN 155
140 S=A(I): A(I)=A(I+1):A(I+1)=S
150 N=1
155 NEXT
160 IF N=0 RETURN
170 GOTO 110
```

The statement in line 120 sets up the system for searching through the A(n) subscript memory, one item at a time. Although there will be 20 items in the list, the FOR . . . NEXT loop will not be executed more than 19 times. If you were to write line 120 as FOR I=1 TO 20, you would be greeted with a machine-generated out-of-data error at line 130. The term A(I+1) in that line would request the value stored at location 20+1, or 21—and there are only 20 items available. For that reason, the FOR . . . NEXT loop searches $n - 1$ spaces. The fact that it looks at A(I+1) takes care of the nth space, you see.

So the values contained in spaces A(I) and A(I+1) are called and compared in line 130. If it happens that A(I) is less than, or equal to, A(I+1), the two values are already in numerical order and there is no need to exchange them. Control is subsequently sent to line 155 and, after that, the value of I is incremented by the FOR . . . NEXT loop.

If the conditional statement in line 130 is *not* satisfied, it means the two values are out of numerical order and must be exchanged by the procedure in line 140. This procedure has already been described in detail. See Example 13-10, Fig. 13-6, and the text associated with them.

After the exchange of values takes place in line 140, a variable N is set to a value of 1. In this subroutine, N is being used as a *flag* that signals whether or not any exchange of values has taken place. N is equal to zero if there has been no exchange, but is set to 1 whenever there is an exchange.

The FOR . . . NEXT looping operations continue through all available subscript locations until it is satisfied—I=19, in this case. [Remember that the twentieth location is checked when I=19 by the expression A(I+1).] The conditional in line 160 is then executed. If N=∅, the implication is that the list of numbers is arranged in numerical order—no exchanges were necessary. That line concludes the bubble sorting operation if, indeed, N=∅.

But if there have been one or more exchanges during the FOR . . . NEXT looping phase, N=1, and line 160 defaults to line 170. Line 170 restarts the whole FOR . . . NEXT looping phase again, but only after resetting the exchange flag, N, back to zero in line 110.

The subroutine in Example 13-11 assumes that 20 items are already residing in a block of subscript space, A(n), where n is an integer between 1 and 20 inclusively. The subroutine cannot be run without those values available, so subroutine 200 has to be entered into the system.

EXAMPLE 13-12

```
200 REM ** GENERATE ARRAY **
210 FOR X=1 TO 20 A(X)=RND(99): NEXT
220 RETURN
250 REM ** PRINT ARRAY **
260 FOR X=1 TO 20: PRINT A(X)","::NEXT
270 RETURN
```

Subroutine 200 simply assigns random integers between 1 and 22 to 20 successive subscript spaces designated A(1) through A(20). After filling those spaces with number values, the RETURN statement in line 220 returns operations to the master program. So that's where the program will be getting the data to be sorted. It can come from a lot of different kinds of sources, but this random source is a nice one for the sake of demonstration.

Subroutine 250, included in Example 13-12, simply scans the existing subscript space and prints the values contained therein.

Finally, here is the master program:

EXAMPLE 13-13

```
10 CLS: DIM A(20)
20 GOSUB 200
30 PRINT "RAW ARRAY:":PRINT
40 GOSUB 250
50 GOSUB 100
60 PRINT:PRINT:PRINT"SORTED ARRAY:":PRINT
70 GOSUB 250
80 END
```

Line 10 in Example 13-13 clears the screen and sets the dimension of the subscript memory at 20 elements. Line 20 then calls subroutine 200 to fill that space with random numbers.

When subroutine 200 completes this task, line 30 of the main program prints RAW ARRAY:, followed by a complete listing of the random numbers residing in the subscript memory space. The printing of these numbers is handled by subroutine 250, as called by line 40 in the main program.

After printing out the original number list, line 50 calls for the sorting subroutine. The numbers are thus arranged in numerical order, using the bubble-sorting algorithm in subroutine 100. And upon returning to the main program, line 60 prints SORTED ARRAY:, followed by a printing of the revised array of numbers. If all has gone as planned, the second list of numbers will be in numerical order.

Upon running this program, you will note a considerable time delay (something on the order of 6 seconds) between the printing of the original list and the sorted list. The time delay is caused by the sorting algorithm, and the more scrambled the values in the list, the longer it takes to sort them into numerical order.

The program can be run any number of times, each run starting out with a different list of scrambled numbers in the subscript memory space.

The next example of a bubble-sorting program, Example 13-14, highlights three other features: (1) sorting a list of names into alphabetical order, (2) using a DATA list as the source of original information, and (3) using a little trick to shorten the sorting time. Any one

of these three features can be used without reference to the other
two, however.

Load the program in Example 13–14 and give it a try.

EXAMPLE 13–14

```
10 CLS: DIM A$(100): N=0
15 N=N+1
20 READ A$: IF A$="DONE" THEN 35
30 A$(N)=A$: GOTO 15
35 CY=N-1
40 NF=0
45 FOR Q=1 TO CY
50 IF A$(Q)<=A$(Q+1) THEN 80
60 S$=A$(Q):A$(Q+1):A$(Q+1)=S$
70 NF=1
80 NEXT
90 CY=CY-1
100 IF NF=0 OR CY=0 THEN 110 ELSE 40
110 FOR X = 1 TO N-1: PRINT A$(X): NEXT
120 END
500 REM ** DATA **
510 DATA DAVID,JUDY,PAUL,CARMEN,PUMPKIN,TABATHA,MUGGINS,HERM
AN,HARRIET,MABEL,EDWARD,MARGARET,STANLEY,DONE
```

The first task in Example 13–14 is to get the listed information out of the
DATA listing and into subscript space A$(*n*). The information residing as
DATA in line 510, you see, cannot be organized at that level. It is fixed by
the fact that it is a program line. Once the same information is copied into
subscript space, however, it can indeed be shuffled, sorted, and reorganized.
*The original DATA base in line 510 will remain unchanged by the sorting
operation.*

Lines 15 through 30 in Example 13–14 are responsible for copying the
DATA items into A$(*n*) subscript space. This is a counting loop that reads
an item of data, assigns it to ordinary string variable A$ (first statement in
line 20), and then checks to see whether or not it is reading the last item in
the DATA listing, DONE. If that item is not DONE, the item counter, N
is incremented in line 15 and the copying operations are repeated.

This copying loop continues until READ A$ turns up a DONE. And that
is how one goes about transferring items in a DATA list to subscript space
where it can be sorted.

Basically, the next phase of the operation is to bubble-sort the names, re-
arranging the string statements in the list into alphabetical order. Lines 50
and 60 are largely responsible for this part of the job. Line 50 tests to see
whether or not a given name falls alphabetically ahead of the next name on
the list. Recall that inequality operators, as applied to string variables, test

the alphabetical sequence (as opposed to numerical sequence for numerical variables).

If it so happens that the two successive string variables are indeed out of sequence, line 60 does the exchanging operation on them. The flow of operations is identical to that already described earlier in this section.

Now lines 35 and 90, and the CY variable in lines 45 and 100, can be eliminated without affecting the operation of this program in any basic sense. The use of the CY variable is related to one of the special features of this program—shortening the sorting time.

Each time the program makes a set of exchanges on the available data, the largest value always "bubbles" to the top of the list. That being the case, there is no need to test the value of the last variable on the list on subsequence search-and-exchange operations. The CY variable marks the end of the list-searching loop, and by line 90, the number of loops necessary to complete the cycling operation grows shorter.

CY forces each search-and-exchange cycle to be one item shorter than the one before, letting the larger values "bubble" to the end of the list and remain untested after that.

The reshuffling part of the program comes to a conclusion under one of two conditions specified in line 100: Either the system makes a search and finds no exchanges are necessary (flag NF=∅) or the system exchanges the first two items after having a chance to "bubble up" all the others in alphabetical order (CY=∅).

Line 110 then calls for a printing of the revised list, which, of course, ought to be the original DATA items arranged in alphabetical order.

You can expand or modify the DATA listing in line 510 any way you like, but in this case the final printout on the screen looks like this:

```
                    CARMEN
                    DAVID
                    EDWARD
                    HARRIET
                    HERMAN
                    JUDY
                    MABEL
                    MARGARET
                    MUGGINS
                    PAUL
                    PUMPKIN
                    STANLEY
                    TABATHA
                    READY
                    >_
```

If you want to get some appreciation of how the CY variable shortens the sorting time in Example 13–14, first time the program as it is shown. The execution time will be on the order of 4 seconds or so. Then delete 90 and time the program again. You should find that it takes 1 or 2 seconds longer.

Of course, a difference of a second or two doesn't mean a whole lot to the operator. But what if the DATA listing had perhaps a thousand items in it. Those extra milliseconds for each seek-and-exchange loop add up rather quickly to many minutes of extra execution time.

Much of the finesse in data processing these days is coming up with ways to shorten the execution time of lengthy algorithms, and that is mainly done by systematically eliminating unnecessary steps.

EXERCISES

13-1 Explain how ordinary variables and subscripted variables differ (a) in appearance in a program and (b) in their application.

13-2 What is the purpose of the DIM statement when it comes to using subscripted variables? What factor is mainly responsible for limiting the maximum DIMension of subscript space?

13-3 A DIM statement must be specified only one time within the running of a program. What is the best way to be certain a DIM statement will never be included in a looping operation?

13-4 For each of the examples listed below, list all variables, describing them as (1) ordinary numerical or string varibles or (2) subscripted numerical or string variables. Describe the purpose of each variable in terms of its place in the program.
   (a) Example 13-6
   (b) Example 13-8
   (c) Example 13-9

13-5 Sketch a flowchart illustrating the bubble-sorting algorithm as it applies to (a) numerical values and (b) string values.

13-6 Explain why DATA items to be bubble-sorted must first be copied into subscript memory space.

CHAPTER 14

Working with Multidimensional Arrays

Statements introduced in this chapter:
STR$ VAL

Recall from basic algebra and geometry that a point on a straight line can be specified by a single number. A straight line can be viewed as a one-dimensional coordinate system, and a single number is adequate for specifying a point on it.

A plane, however, is a two-dimensional figure that requires two numbers to specify any point on it. One of the numbers represents the horizontal coordinate of the point, and the second specifies the vertical coordinate.

These notions carry over directly to arrays in computer memory. Chapter 13 dealt with one-dimensional arrays—arrays whose separate elements could be specified or addressed by means of a single number. A piece of information stored in one-dimensional subscript space can be accessed by means of a term such as $A(n)$, where n is any integer between 1 and some larger number that falls within the dimension—size—of the array.

In a one-dimensional array, you can store information in location $A(5)$, for example, by doing a statement such as $A(5)=numerical$ *value*. And you can retrieve that information later by means of a statement such as *numerical variable*$=A(5)$. The term $A(5)$ can be considered the fifth element in memory block A.

A memory block for a typical one-dimensional array is illustrated in Fig. 14–1.

A two-dimensional array is one composed of a bunch of memory elements that are systematically arranged so that any one of them is accessed by two numbers. Putting some information into a two-dimensional array is a matter of applying a statement such as A(3,5)= *numerical value*. That same value can be retrieved at any later time by doing something such as *numerical variable*=A(3,5). A(3,5) in this instance represents a subscripted memory location found by looking at the third row and fifth column of a rectangular two-dimensional memory array.

Put your computer into its command mode of operation and try these two examples:

EXAMPLE 14–1a

```
READY
>A(1)=1Ø
READY
>A(2)=2Ø
READY
>A(3)=3Ø
READY
>A(4)=4Ø
PRINT A(1),A(2),A(3),A(4)
>1Ø          2Ø          3Ø          4Ø
```

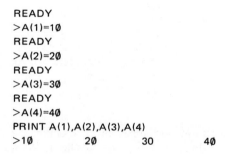

(b)

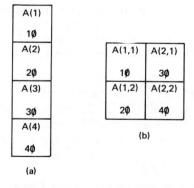

(a)

Figure 14–1 Memory configurations. (a) A one-dimensional array—Example 14–1a. (b) A two-dimensional array—Example 14–1b.

```
READY
>_
```

There should be nothing new about Example 14–1—it represents one-dimensional subscript operations of the kind featured in Chapter 13. You merely assigned values to subscripted variables A(1) through A(4) and told the computer to print them on the screen. Note, however, the memory configuration of this one-dimensional array as illustrated in Fig. 14–1a

Now try the same project, but specifying a two-dimensional array:

EXAMPLE 14–1b

```
READY
>A(1,1)=1Ø
READY
>A(1,2)=2Ø
READY
>A(2,1)=3Ø
READY
>A(2,2)=4Ø
READY
>PRINT A(1,1),A(1,2),A(2,1),A(2,2)
   1Ø          2Ø          3Ø          4Ø
READY
>_
```

From all outward appearances, Example 14-1b does the same job as Example 14-1a. The only difference lies in the way the elements are organized in the memory. Compare Fig. 14-1a and b.

In the two-dimensional case, 1Ø is stored in a location specified as A(1,1)—a memory element found in the first column, first row. Number 2Ø is stored in the first column, second row, as specified by A(1,2). Number 3Ø is stored in the second column, first row, and number 4Ø was stored in the second column, second row.

Now doesn't it seem a bit more awkward to use the two-dimensional specifications? If they do the same job, why bother with the more complicated arrangement? You will find the answers coming through quite clearly in the next section of this chapter. Before getting into that interesting matter, consider arrays that are dimensioned beyond two.

What, for instance, does the statement PRINT M(1,2,3) mean? It means print the value stored in a three-dimensional array. A point in three-dimensional space, you see, must be specified by three coordinates.

What about C$(4,19,2Ø,4)="DARLING"? That means "store

the word DARLING in a four-dimensional string array at location 4,19,2∅,4." Of course, it is virtually impossible to visualize the memory space for four dimensions, but your computer does not know that—it can handle the notion quite easily.

All of this can be summarized in the following principle. If you can understand exactly what it is saying, you are getting pretty good at this business. If you don't understand it, copy it down on a sheet of paper and show it to some of your friends—they will be impressed with how smart you are.

Principle. An *n*-dimensional array is specified by *variable name* $(e_1, e_2, e_3, \ldots, e_n)$, where *variable name* is any valid numerical or string variable, and e_k is any integer between 1 and the maximum dimension of that element space.

14-1   Why Use Multidimensional Arrays? An Example

Suppose that you are the chairperson of a local beauty contest and want to computerize a list of contestants' names, including the color of eyes and hair, heights, addresses, and telephone numbers.

Now you will probably want to enter the list of items as DATA in the program itself, thus making it possible to save the list on cassette tape. (It is altogether possible to save just the list, using a home computer equipped with a disk operating system, but such a feature is generally an option most users cannot yet afford.)

So you enter the information like this:

EXAMPLE 14-2

```
1000 REM ** GIRLS **
1001 DATA HELEN,BLUE,BLONDE,5'4,2175 E. MAIN,334-5591
1002 DATA JANICE,BROWN,BROWN,5'8, 16 CRESCENT,286-2551
1003 DATA ANNE,BLACK,BLACK,5'3,1226 N. FOURTH,291-4478
1004 DATA SUSAN,GREEN,RED,5'10,980 KING,334-9909
1005 DATA SALLY,BROWN,BROWN,4'11,123 SUMMIT, 291-4567
1006 DATA DONE
```

That is a rather short list, but it will serve the purpose. Note the sequence of items in each line: name, eye color, hair color, height, address, phone number.

You want to be able to manipulate, sort, and reorganize these data, and as you learned in the previous chapter, this means that some or all of the information has to be pulled out of the DATA file and transferred into subscript space. And that means reading through the data list, systematically assigning the items to some subscript space.

Using the procedures for one-dimensional subscripts in the previous chapter, you could do the job by assigning a one-dimensional array to each of the items in the list. Names, for instance, could be assigned to N(n), eye color to E(n), hair color to H(n), and so on. You would end up with a set of six subscripted string variables, one for each of the DATA items—name, hair, eyes, height, address, and phone number. And if you used the same n value at any given moment, the six subscripts would all relate to one girl. For instance, setting $n=2$, you would get N(2) for JANICE, H(2) for her BROWN eyes, H(2) for her BROWN hair, and so on. Changing n to 3 would then set all the one-dimensional arrays to elements relevant to ANNE.

This parallel application of several one-dimensional arrays isn't really too bad. You could make it work quite nicely for the DATA in Example 14-2. The program might be a little bit cumbersome in places. Consider how you would have to dimension those six different arrays: DIM N(100):DIM E(100): DIM H(100), and so on through DIM P(100). You need six DIM statements to set the dimensions of the arrays—to 100 elements in this case.

But you will have to agree that the DATA list in Example 14-2 is a very simple one. What if you had 100 different items related to each name on the list? Let your own imagination play around with 100 different parameters for these girls—the point is that working with 10, 25, 50, 100, or more items on each line isn't that unusual in the data processing business.

With so many items on each DATA line, you would have to assign a lot of subscript variable names yourself. And then there are programs that call for item lists of varying length.

Now, doesn't this sound a lot like the opening sections of Chapter 3, where the use of subscripted variables is clearly better than the use of ordinary variables? You are facing the same sort of predicament here—one-dimensional variables are getting cumbersome. It would be nice if the computer could assign subscripts to the subscripts, thereby eliminating the need for having to specify the variable names in the program itself.

Well, the computer does that sort of work, and that is where multidimensional arrays enter the picture. The DATA list, as shown in Example 14-2, can be handled quite easily with a two-dimensional array.

You will need only one subscript variable name; and since this project has a lot to do with girls, make that name G$. The minimum dimension of the array can be specified as five rows (girls' names) by six columns (items for each girl). An expression such as G$(1,4)$ would thus specify $5'4''$—first girl (HELEN) and fourth item (height $5'4''$). In fact, everything related to HELEN can be summarized by the expression G$ $(1,n)$, where n is an integer between 1 and 6 inclusively. By the same token, the information for SUSAN can be specified by G$(4,n)$.

There is only one variable specifier, G$, as opposed to six that would be required if using one-dimensional arrays. Working with all the elements in the subscript space is a matter of playing around with the two numbers that, in a sense, indicate the coordinates of each element in the two-dimensional memory space.

The illustration in Fig. 14–2 shows a convenient way to organize the DATA from Example 14–2 into a two-dimensional subscript space. The information could be organized in a lot of other ways, but this seems to be the most straightforward one.

Now put together a program for drawing the items out of the DATA list and putting it into the subscript space we have just defined.

EXAMPLE 14–3

```
1Ø CLS: DIM G$(5Ø,6): N=Ø
2Ø N=N+1: READ I$: IF I$="DONE" THEN 4Ø
3Ø G$(N,1)=I$
35 FOR L=2 TO 6: READ I$: G$(N,L)=I$:NEXT: GOTO 2Ø
4Ø PRINT "TRANSFER DONE FOR"N-1"GIRLS";INPUT"STRIKE 'ENTER'";X$
5Ø CLS: FOR C=1 TO N-1: FOR R=1 TO 6
6Ø PRINT G$(C,R)"/";:NEXT:PRINT:NEXT
7Ø END
```

	Col G$(m, 1)	Col G$(m, 2)	Col G$(m, 3)	Col G$(m, 4)	Col G$(m, 5)	Col G$(m, 6)
Row G$(1,n)	G$(1,1) HELEN	G$(1,2) BLUE	G$(1,3) BLONDE	G$(1,4) 5'4	G$(1,5) 2175 E'.MAIN	G$(1,6) 334-5591
Row G$(2,n)	G$(2,1) JANICE	G$(2,2) BROWN	G$(2,3) BROWN	G$(2,4) 5'8	G$(2,5) 16 CRESCENT	G$(2,6) 286-2551
Row G$(3,n)	G$(3,1) ANNE	G$(3,2) BLACK	G$(3,3) BLACK	G$(3,4) 5'3	G$(3,5) 1226 N.FOURTH	G$(3,6) 291-4478
Row G$(4,n)	G$(4,2) SUSAN	G$(4,2) GREEN	G$(4,3) RED	G$(4,4) 5'10	G$(4,5) 98Ø KING	G$(4,6) 334-99Ø9
Row G$(5,n)	G$(5,1) SALLY	G$(5,2) BROWN	G$(5,3) BROWN	G$(5,4) 4'11	G$(5,5) 123 SUMMIT	G$(5,6) 291-4567

Girls' names:	Col G$(m,1)	Helen's Info:	Row G$(1,n)
Hair colors:	Col G$(m,2)	Janice's Info:	Row G$(2,n)
Eye colors:	Col G$(m,3)	Anne's Info:	Row G$(3,n)
Heights:	Col G$(m,4)	Susan's Info:	Row G$(4,n)
Addresses:	Col G$(m,5)	Sally's Info:	Row G$(5,n)
Phone numbers:	Col G$(m,6)		

Figure 14–2 Memory configuration for a 5 × 6 array, G$($m,n$)— see the program in Example 14–3.

That is all. Enter the program along with the DATA in Example 14-2. When you first RUN the program, you will see this:

TRANSFER DONE FOR 5 GIRLS
STRIKE 'ENTER'?_

Hit the ENTER key and you see this:

HELEN/BLUE/BLONDE/5'4/2175 E. MAIN/334–5591
JANICE/BROWN/BROWN/5'8/16 CRESCENT/286–2551
ANNE/BLACK/BLACK/5'3/1226 N. FOURTH/291–4478
SUSAN/GREEN/RED/5'1Ø/98Ø KING/334–99Ø9
SALLY/BROWN/BROWN/4'11/123 SUMMIT/291–4567

The program in Example 14-3 is dimensioned to 50 × 6, meaning the list can handle up to 50 names, each carrying 6 different items of information.

As in so many of the preceding examples, the first operational step is to see if the system pulls a DONE out of the DATA list. If that is the case, control goes down to line 40, where the transfer operation is terminated. If the first item read is *not* a DONE, however, line 30 assigns the item to G$(N,1) subscript space. According to the diagram in Fig. 14-2, any argument (characters enclosed in parentheses) having a 1 in the second place designates a NAME position. Thus line 30 assigns I$—a name at this point—to that slot in the subscript memory.

Line 35 is then responsible for reading the five remaining pieces of information to be associated with that name. In the statement G$(N,L)=I$, N does not change, but L changes in incremental steps from 2 to 6. So as the values of I$ come pouring into the memory via the READ I$ statement in that line, the values are assigned to G$(N,2). G$(N,3), . . . , G$(N,6). That sequence of statements in line 35 transfers all the data associated with name N to subscript positions.

Line 35 then concludes with a GOTO statement that ultimately causes the system to look at the next name in the DATA list, check it for DONE; and if the conditional is not satisfied, load the name and its associated information into the next row of the array.

When I$ finally picks up the DONE at he end of the DATA list, the operator gets the TRANSFER DONE message and initiates a printout of the entire listing—from subscript space this time—by striking the ENTER key.

Line 50 sets up a pair of nested FOR . . . NEXT loops, causing the six items of information for each name to be printed on separate lines on the screen. In this case the individual items are separated by a slash(/).

So why use multidimensional arrays? In instances where you have some data that are organized with a lot of items falling into a number of different categories, the alternatives are intolerable. Assigning an ordinary variable to each and every item in the data list is unbearably awkward and time consuming, and assigning a one-dimensional array to each category of information isn't a whole lot better.

Using multidimensional arrays opens the door for handling large amounts of categorized information in fairly large blocks. The whole list of data, no matter how extensive and detailed it might be, can be handled with a single variable name.

14-2 Getting the Elements Into a Multidimensional Array

Example 14-3 in Section 14-1 shows how items in a DATA list can be transferred into a two-dimensional array. A READ statement picks up an item from the DATA listing, and a set of nested FOR . . . NEXT loops place that item into the array.

The FOR . . . NEXT loops generate a systematic pattern of row–column coordinates. And if the READ operation is properly synchronized with the operation of the nested FOR . . . NEXT loops, each item is deposited into a well-defined position in the array's memory space.

That was just one example illustrating how items in a DATA list can be transferred into array space. An array can also be loaded from the keyboard as shown in the next example. The scheme still uses nested FOR . . . NEXT loops to access the elements in the array in a systematic fashion, but the items are entered via INPUT statements rather than READ statements.

Example 14-4 demonstrates this particular process, using a student grade summary as its objective.

EXAMPLE 14-4

```
10 CLS: DIM F(50,11)
20 INPUT "HOW MANY STUDENTS (1 TO 50)";NS
30 PRINT "HOW MANY GRADES (1 TO 10) FOR EACH OF THE"NS"STUDENTS";:
INPUT NG
40 FOR ROW=1 TO NS
50 CLS: PRINT "ENTER ID NUMBER (NUMBERS ONLY) FOR STUDENT" ROW "
OF" NS: INPUT ID
60 F(ROW,1)=ID
70 FOR COL=2 TO NG+1
80 PRINT "ENTER GRADE" COL-1 "FOR STUDENT" ID;: INPUT G
90 F(ROW,COL)=G
100 NEXT:CLS:NEXT
```

```
110 CLS: PRINT "ENTRY JOB DONE": INPUT X$
120 FOR ROW=1 TO NS: CLS: PRINT"STUDENT ID";:PRINT TAB(20) "GRAD
E SUMMARY"
130 PRINT:PRINT ID;
140 FOR COL=2 TO NG+1:PRINT TAB(20) F(ROW,COL): NEXT
150 INPUT X$: NEXT
160 PRINT:PRINT"THAT WAS THE LAST STUDENT SUMMARY"
170 INPUT"SEE SUMMARY AGAIN (Y OR N)";X$
180 IF X$="Y" THEN 120
190 END
```

The entry operations for this program occupies lines 10 through 110. The general idea is to enter a student ID number (variable ID) and a set of grades for that student (variable G). The number of students to be entered into the scheme is set by the operator in line 20 (NS), and the number of grades for each student is set by line 30 (NG). The two-dimensional array for this information is dimensioned to 50 × 11, meaning that the program can accept up to 50 rows of names having up to 10 columns of grades associated with each name.

The statement DIM F(50,10) in line 10 also infers that the program is going to work with only numerical expressions. If the program included string expressions (which it doesn't, the dimensioning statement would have to read something such as DIM F$(50,10).

Once the operator establishes values for NS and NG, line 40 sets up the "outside" FOR . . . NEXT loop for the ROW operations—rows 1 through NS. Line 50 then requests a student ID number to be placed in the first row position, and that value is entered in that row and column 1 by the expression in line 60: F(ROW,1)=ID. So if ROW happens to be equal to 1 at the moment, the value of the first student's ID goes into array position (1,1).

The next step is to enter that student's grades, one at a time, into the succeeding columns of that row. And since the first column in that row already contains the student's ID number, the grade-entry process must begin at column 2. Hence the "inner" FOR . . . NEXT loop specified in line 70 begins with COL=2. It should then cause an INPUT looping operation that runs to the NG+1 position in the array. So if there happens to be five grades entered for each student, this loop specifies columns 2 through 6.

The request for a grade is generated by line 80, and the grade that is INPUT on that same line is then assigned to coordinate (ROW,COL)=G by line 90.

Line 100 then specifies the return points for both of the FOR . . . NEXT loops, causing the entry phase to continue until all grades for all students have been entered. After that, the system (by line 110) prints the message ENTRY JOB DONE and waits for the operator to strike the ENTER key to get a printing of the results.

Figure 14-3 shows the layout of this particular array, assuming that the information has all been entered.

The next phase of the task is to print out the contents of the array. This is

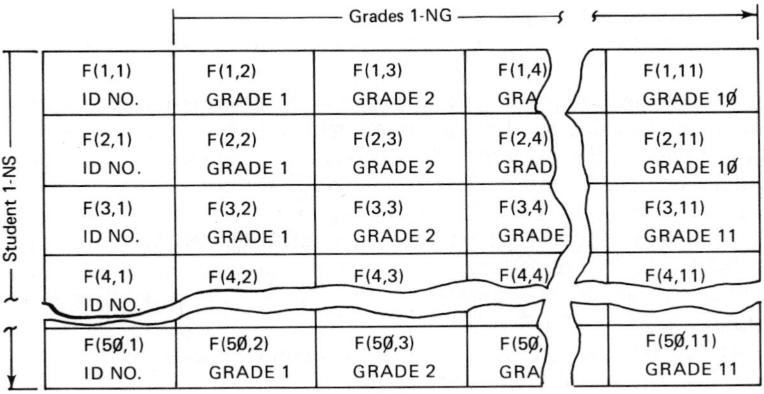

	Grades 1-NG				
F(1,1) ID NO.	F(1,2) GRADE 1	F(1,3) GRADE 2	F(1,4) GRA		F(1,11) GRADE 1∅
F(2,1) ID NO.	F(2,2) GRADE 1	F(2,3) GRADE 2	F(2,4) GRAD		F(2,11) GRADE 1∅
F(3,1) ID NO.	F(3,2) GRADE 1	F(3,3) GRADE 2	F(3,4) GRADE		F(3,11) GRADE 11
F(4,1) ID NO.	F(4,2)	F(4,3)	F(4,4)		F(4,11)
F(5∅,1) ID NO.	F(5∅,2) GRADE 1	F(5∅,3) GRADE 2	F(5∅, GRA		F(5∅,11) GRADE 11

Student 1-NS

Figure 14-3 Memory configuration for a 50 × 11 array, F(m,n)—see the program in Example 14-4.

done with another set of nested FOR . . . NEXT loops. The loops in this instance print out the contents of the array, rather than load the array with keyboard information.

The FOR . . . NEXT loop established in line 120 is responsible for keeping track of the student names—the row specifiers for the array. Upon selecting a new row, the PRINT statement in line 20 sets up a heading on the screen:

    STUDENT ID   GRADE SUMMARY

Line 130 then prints the ID number of the student selected by the outer, row-selecting FOR . . . NEXT loop. Immediately after that, line 140 sets up the inner FOR . . . NEXT loop that systematically picks and prints the column information concerning that student's grades.

Line 150 is picked up when the grade-printing operation is done and the operator strikes the ENTER key to get the grade summary for the next student. Note that the NEXT statement in line 150 loops operations all the way back to line 120, where the row count is incremented by that outer, ID-specifying loop.

The operator is greeted with the message THAT WAS THE LAST STUDENT SUMMARY when all grades have been viewed on the screen. The operator then has the option of viewing the entire sequence of grade summaries again, or ending the program.

Consider the entire program, using just one student and four grades. In a practical sense, the project is too simple to be of any use, but you can enter more names and see the scheme work in a more realistic sense.

Upon doing a RUN, the first message on the screen is: HOW MANY STUDENTS (1 to 5∅)? For this demonstration, respond by entering 1. Then the system prints the request: HOW MANY GRADES (1 to 1∅)? The reply in this case should be 4. So this point, the screen shows:

HOW MANY STUDENTS? 1
HOW MANY GRADES (1 TO 10) FOR EACH OF THE 1 STUDENTS? 4_

Although the grammar in that second line of information leaves something to be desired, it is good programming technique to confirm the entry made in response to the request in the first line. The grammar is alright when you enter a number for more than one student, however.

After striking the ENTER key, the system requests the ID number for the first student: ENTER ID NUMBER (NUMBERS ONLY) FOR STUDENT 1 OF 1. The "1 OF 1" phrase is a trick that lets the operator keep track of which student is being considered. If you had specified 10 students, the phrase would be "1 OF 1∅".

At any rate, respond to the request with an ID number such as 1234, and ENTER. The screen then looks like this:

ENTER ID NUMBER (NUMBERS ONLY) FOR STUDENT 1 OF 1
? 1234
ENTER GRADE 1 FOR STUDENT 1234?_

Entering that grade, you will see a request for the second grade, and the process continues until you've entered the number of grades specified earlier in the program. For example:

ENTER ID NUMBER (NUMBERS ONLY) FOR STUDENT 1 OF 1
? 1234
ENTER GRADE 1 FOR STUDENT 1234 ? 8∅
ENTER GRADE 2 FOR STUDENT 1234 ? 85
ENTER GRADE 3 FOR STUDENT 1234 ? 9∅
ENTER GRADE 4 FOR STUDENT 1234 ? 95_

And that completes the grade-entering process for a student having an ID number 1234. What you are actually doing is filling out a row of elements in the array. It is row 1 in this instance, and the five elements are: ID, grade 1, grade 2, grade 3, and grade 4.

Since you have specified just one student for the purposes of the demonstration, entering that fourth grade results in an end-of-entry message: ENTRY JOB DONE. Striking the ENTER key, the display shows a summary of grades:

STUDENT ID	GRADE SUMMARY
1234	8∅
	85
	9∅
	95

And because this listing represents the last student in the file, striking the ENTER key yields the message

THAT WAS THE LAST STUDENT SUMMARY
SEE SUMMARY AGAIN (Y OR N)?_

That ends the main operating cycle. Again, the demonstration is so simple that it is almost trivial, but you can enter your own, more extensive list to see the thing really go to work for you.

In summary, elements can be entered into a multidimensional array in a serial (one-at-a-time) fashion, with nested FOR . . . NEXT loops specifying the location of the element at any given moment. Likewise, elements of a multidimensional array can be retrieved in a serial fashion with the help of nested FOR . . . NEXT loops.

The source of information can be a DATA listing (Example 14-3) or the keyboard (Example 14-4). Other sources can include disk files, graphics on the screen, and similar input schemes, most of which require a study of your own machine's features and capabilities.

14-3 Working with Mixed Variable Types in Arrays

The arrays presented so far in this chapter are defined as either string or numerical arrays. The DIM G$(5∅,6) statement in line 10 of Example 14-3 clearly specifies string information, and in that example all the information had the characteristics of string variables.

By the same token, the DIM F(5∅,11) statement in line 10 of Example 14-4 specifies numerical elements. No string elements were allowed.

There is no problem as long as all the information in the array is either string or numerical information. Simply dimension the array accordingly. But, of course, there are many situations where it is necessary to work with both string and numerical values within the same array. In the grade-summary program of Example 14-4, for example, it would be nice if the first column in each row could carry the student's name, instead of an ID number. That would call for a string specification in that column. If you want to manipulate the grades as numerical values—doing something useful such as averaging them—the grade columns must carry numerical designations.

The array must be specified as string or numerical, never both. So how do you reconcile a contradiction of variable types?

The key to the answer is that a string variable can be made up of numbers as well as any other combination of alphanumeric characters and special keyboard symbols. So you could rewrite the grade-summary program in Example 14–4, specifying F$(ROW,COLUMN)— that allows you to enter the students' actual names. The grades can be entered as string variables, and when the time comes, they can be translated into their numerical counterpart. The translation of a string number to a numerical value is accomplished by means of a rather simple operator, VAL(*string number*).

An expression such as F=VAL(F$) translates a string-specified number, F$, into its numerical counterpart, F.

Principle. A statement such as *numerical variable*=VAL(*string variable*) translates a number originally specified as a string variable into the corresponding numerical variable.

A complementary operation, *string variable*=STR$(numerical variable) translates a number specified as a numerical value into its string equivalent.

The following program is a reorganized version of the one already described in connection with Example 14–4. The input operations have been reclassified as string-variable inputs, thereby making it possible to enter student identification by name, rather than a simple (and usually meaningless) ID number. The grades are also entered as string values.

And the grades remain string values throughout the program except at line 140, where they are translated into numerical equivalents for the purpose of averaging them. Note the VAL operator in line 140 of Example 14–5.

EXAMPLE 14–5

```
10 CLS: DIM F$(50,11)
20 INPUT "HOW MANY STUDENTS (1 TO 50)";NS
30 PRINT "HOW MANY GRADES (1 TO 10) FOR EACH OF THE"NS"STUDENTS"
;: INPUT NG
40 FOR ROW=1 TO NS
50 CLS: PRINT "ENTER STUDENT'S LAST NAME AND FIRST INITIAL FOR S
TUDENT"ROW"OF"NS: INPUT ID$
60 F$(ROW,1)=ID$
70 FOR COL=2 TO NG+1
80 PRINT "ENTER GRADE" COL-1"FOR "ID$;: INPUT G$
90 F$(ROW,COL)=G$
100 NEXT:CLS:NEXT
110 CLS: PRINT "ENTRY JOB DONE": INPUT X$
```

```
120 FOR ROW=1 TO NS: CLS:PRINT "STUDENT";:PRINT TAB(20)"GRADE S
SUMMARY"
130 GS=0:PRINT:PRINT ID$;
140 FOR COL=2 TO NG+1:PRINT TAB(20)F$(ROW,COL):GS=GS+VAL(F$(ROW,
COL)):NEXT
150 PRINT:PRINT "AVERAGE GRADE IS"GS/NG:INPUTX$:NEXT
160 PRINT:PRINT "THAT WAS THE LAST STUDENT SUMMARY"
170 INPUT"SEE SUMMARY AGAIN (Y OR N);X$
180 IF X$="Y" THEN 120
190 END
```

The operating procedures are identical to those of Example 14–4. As far as the operator is concerned, the difference between the two versions of this grade summary is that the latter version requests the students' names and includes an average grade with the summary for each student.

The main point of the demonstration is that programs calling for both string and numerical variables in an array ought to treat all variables as strings. And wherever it is necessary to manipulate some of the numbers mathematically, simply convert them into a numerical type by means of the VAL operation. *All values in the array remain string values, however.*

14-4 Sorting Multidimensional Arrays

The final major point concerning multidimensional arrays is that of sorting such arrays. To get some appreciation of the problem, return to the list of girls' names spelled out in Example 14–2 and imagine what is involved in doing a bubble sort on the names—arranging them into alphabetical order.

Now doing a bubble sort was not much of a problem in Chapter 13, where the array was a simple one-dimensional list of subscripted string or numerical variables. Using multidimensional list, sorting just one classification of elements (the girls' names, for instance) runs the risk of getting the names disassociated with the corresponding items on the list.

If you were to bubble-sort the girls' names in Example 14–2 and failed to provide some means for carrying the hair and eye color, height, addresses, and phone numbers along with the names, the list is going to turn out rather badly. Anne, for example, would end up with Helen's specifications. That is not so good.

Whenever the original data base exists as DATA lines in the program, the simplest way to sort a multidimensional array is to bubble-sort the names first and then work through the revised, sorted list of names one at a time. Each time the system picks a new name on the list, it searches the DATA listing for that particular name and then loads the items properly associated with it. The following programs assume the DATA listing in Example 14-2 is loaded into program memory.

EXAMPLE 14-6

```
10 CLS: DIM G$(50,6):N=0
20 N=N+1: READ I$: IF I$="DONE" THEN 50
30 G$(N,1)=I$
40 FOR L=2 TO 6:READ I$: NEXT: GOTO 20
50 PRINT "MEMORY LOADED FOR"N-1"GIRLS":INPUT "STRIKE 'ENTER' FOR
LISTING";X$
60 NF=0
70 FOR L= 1 TO N-2
80 IF G$(L,1)<=G$(L+1) THEN 110
90 S$=G(L,1):G$(L,1)=G$(L+1,1):G$(L+1,1)=S$
100 NF=1
110 NEXT L
120 IF NF=1 THEN 60
130 PRINT: FOR L=1 TO N-1:PRINT G$(L,1):NEXT
140 INPUT "ENTER FOR MORE INFO";X$
150 CLS: FOR L=1 TO N-1
160 RESTORE
170 READ I$: IF I$=G$(L,1) THEN 190
180 FOR S=2 TO 6: READ I$: NEXT: GOTO 170
190 FOR S=2 TO 6: READ I$: G$(L,S)=I$:NEXT:NEXT
200 FOR L=1 TO N-1: FOR S=1 TO 6: IF S=6 THEN 220
210 PRINT TAB(S-1)*8)G$(L,S);: GOTO 230
220 PRINT TAB(50)G$(L,S)
230 NEXT:NEXT
240 END
```

The program in Example 14-6 is divided into three phases. The first phase, represented by lines 10 through 50, loads the first item in each DATA line—the girls' names—into the first column of the two-dimensional array. The second phase, lines 60 through 140, bubble-sorts the names, shuffling them around so that they are in alphabetical order in the array.

The final phase runs through the sorted list of names in the array, returning to the DATA list to select the information related to the name being searched. The program ends when each name has the appropriate information arranged beside it in the two-dimensional array. The final steps are responsible for printing this reorganized information.

Doing a run on the program in Example 14-6, you see this first on the screen:

MEMORY LOADED FOR 5 GIRLS
STRIKE 'ENTER' FOR LISTING?_

Upon striking the ENTER key, you see this:

ANNE
HELEN
JANICE
SALLY
SUSAN
ENTER FOR MORE INFO?_

There are the names arranged in alphabetical order. This display marks the end of the second, bubble-sorting phase. The system has not yet sorted the DATA to attach the appropriate information to each of the names.

So striking the ENTER key one more time you get:

ANNE	BLACK	BLACK	5'3	1226 N. FOURTH	291-4478
HELEN	BLUE	BLONDE	5'4	2175 E. MAIN	334-5591
JANICE	BROWN	BROWN	5'8	16 CRESCENT	286-2551
SALLY	BROWN	BROWN	4'11	123 SUMMIT	291-4567
SUSAN	GREEN	RED	5'10	980 KING	334-9909

That is the same information shown in Example 14-2. Here, however, the names are arranged in alphabetical order.

It is possible to do the same job easier and more efficiently using the program in Example 14-7. The better procedure, however, is conceptually a bit more difficult. It calls for pulling *all* information from the DATA lines into subscript memory, bubble-sorting the names, and carrying all the relevant information along with the names. So when the program exchanges a pair of names to put them into alphabetical order, it exchanges the associated information—all of it—at the same time.

Bubble-sorting a lot of information at one time requires the help of an additional subscript space. Back in Example 14-6, the system exchanged names only by placing one of them in a temporary memory slot, S$. See line 90 in that example. Instead of shifting the data to be exchanged into a space designated by an ordinary string variable, the following example shifts a whole line of information into a one-dimensional subscript space designated S$(E)—line 90 of Example 14-7.

EXAMPLE 14-7

```
10 CLS: DIM G$(50,6):DIM S$(6); N=0
20 N=N+1: READ I$: IF I$="DONE" THEN 50
30 G$(N,1)=I$
40 FOR L=2 TO 6: READ I$:G$(N,L)=I$:NEXT:GOTO 20
50 PRINT "MEMORY LOADED FOR"N-1"GIRLS";INPUT "STRIKE 'ENTER' FOR
LISTING";X$
60 NF=0
70 FOR L=1 TO N-2
80 IF G$(L,1)<=G$(L+1,1) THEN 110
85 FOR E=1 TO 6
90 S$(E)=G$(L,E):G$(L,E)=G$(L+1,E):G$(L+1,E)=S$(E)
95 NEXT
100 NF=1
110 NEXT L
120 IF NF=1 THEN 60
130 CLS:FOR L=1 TO N-1:FOR E=1 TO 6: IF E=6 THEN 150
140 PRINT TAB((E=1)*8)G$(L,E);:GOTO 160
150 PRINT TAB(50)G$(L,E)
160 NEXT:NEXT
170 END
```

The flow of the program in Example 14-7 follows that of the previous version. Items from the DATA list (Example 14-2) are read into the two-dimensional space specified and dimensioned in line 10, DIM G$(50,6). That part of the job is completed at line 50.

Lines 60 through 110 take care of the bubble-sorting algorithm, working with the entire listing this time. And lines 130 through the end simply print out the sorted list of information in an orderly fashion. The final display is identical to the one shown for the program in Example 14-6.

Incidentally, the program in Example 14-7 also shows that it is possible to use more than one subscript space within a given program. This one happens to use a two-dimensional array, G$, as well as a one-dimensional array, S$.

EXERCISES

14-1   Suppose that a one-dimensional array is defined as $Z(n)$. What is the meaning of the term $Z(2)$?

14-2   You are planning to use a two-dimensional array composed of 12 names and six items associated with each name. What is the appropriate dimensioning statement for that array?

14-3 If a two-dimensional array is specified at $U(m,n)$, which one of the three terms represents column information? row information?

14-4 How would you go about adding more names and relevant information to the DATA listing in Example 14-2 without having to write a program routine?

14-5 Referring to the program in Example 14-3, how many girls' names *could be* included in the DATA listing?

14-6 Why is it necessary to transfer DATA listings (such as the one in Example 14-2) to an array before the information can be sorted or manipulated in some sorting fashion?

14-7 Why is the array in Example 14-4 dimensioned to 50 × 11 when later statements in the program limit the number of grades to 10? Why not dimension to 50 × 10, in other words?

14-8 What puts an upper limit on the size of an array?

Answers to Selected Exercises

CHAPTER 1

1-8 (a) ZZZZZ

(b) Cannot be answered because the numerical value of ZZ has not been defined.

(c) Z

(d) 1Ø

(e) –2

(f) Z-Z-Z

CHAPTER 2

2-11 (a) Clearing the screen, followed by:

```
               16
               READY
               >_
```

(b) The end result is READY and prompt. Character 16 appears as line 20 is executed, but line 30 clears it away in a fraction of a second. The program is virtually useless.

(c) Clearing the screen, followed by

```
        THE ANSWER IS 16
```

```
                              READY
                              >_
```

(d) Clearing the screen, followed by

```
                    2 TIMES 8
                    THE ANSWER IS 16
                    READY
                    >_
```

CHAPTER 4

4-2 (a) Unconditional

(b) Conditional

(c) Conditional

(d) Conditional because preceding FOR . . . TO statement is assumed.

4-3 (a) 10   (b) 1   (c) 1   (d) 11   (e) 1   (f) 1

(g) 10   (h) 10   (i) 11   (j) 10

CHAPTER 5

5-4
```
10 CLS: INPUT "CHARACTER";C$: CLS
20 FOR N=0 TO 9: PRINT: NEXT
30 PRINT TAB(31)C$
40 GOTO 40
```

5-5
```
10 CLS: INPUT "CHARACTER,X,Y";C$,X,Y
20 CLS
30 FOR N=1 TO Y: PRINT: NEXT
40 PRINT TAB(X)C$
50 GOTO 50
```

5-6
```
10 CLS: FOR X=0 4: PRINT: NEXT
20 PRINT TAB(28)"#########"
30 PRINT TAB(27)"#   -   -   #"
40 PRINT TAB(26)"&#   *   * #&"
50 PRINT TAB(27)"#   '  '   #"
60 PRINT TAB(28)"#   -0-  #"
70 PRINT TAB(28)"( ( ( ( ) ) ) )"
80 PRINT TAB(30)"( (   ) )"
90 GOTO 90
```

CHAPTER 6

6-1 (a) 2   (b) 5   (c) 67   (d) 67

6-2 b, c, and f

6-4   I=RND(11)-6

6-11   (a)   GOTO line 100   (b)   GOTO line 140   (c)   GOTO line 160
      (d)   THE DOG SLIPPED AND SQUASHED THE LAKE AND ALL ITS
          CONTENTS

CHAPTER 8

8-2   THESE ARE NESTED   10
     SUBROUTINES   70
                                          80
                                        20
                                        90
                                      100
                                        30
                                        50
                                        60
                                        40

8-3   START AT 1Ø
     AT SUB 1ØØ
     AT SUB 2ØØ
     AT SUB 3ØØ
     AT SUB 4ØØ
     AT SUB 5ØØ AND RETURNING
     AT SUB 4ØØ AND RETURNING
     AT SUB 3ØØ AND RETURNING
     AT SUB 2ØØ AND RETURNING
     AT SUB 1ØØ AND RETURNING
     AT THE START AND ENDING
     DONE
     READY
     >_

CHAPTER 9

9-1   (a)   16   (b)   16   (c)   1   (d)   1   (e)   Ø   (f)   –1
      (g)   1Ø   (h)   –66.5

9-2   (d)   VC=VØ+C*LOG(V*T-1)
      (f)   D=((V1-VØ)↑2+(W1-WØ)↑2)↑(1/2)

CHAPTER 10

10-1   (a)   A=Ø while B=1
       (b)   A=Ø while B=any value

B=1 while A=any value

(c) Any combinations of A and B *except* where A=∅ while B=1

(d) Any combinations of A and B *except* where A=∅ while B=any value, B=1 while A=any value

(e) A=∅ while B=1
 A=∅ while B=∅

(f) Same as (e)

(g) A=∅ while B=any number *except* B=1, B=∅

10-2 A numerical variable cannot logically have more than one numerical value at the same time. B would have to be equal to 1 and ∅ at the same time to satisfy this statement.

10-3 (a) IF A>=∅ AND A<=1∅

CHAPTER 11

11-1 (a) 5   (b) 5   (c) 7   (d) 4

11-3 They are operationally identical.

11-4 (c), (d)

CHAPTER 12

12-7 In example (a), S can have values of 1, 2, 3, or 4.
 In example (b), S can have values of 3, 4, 5, or 6.

12-8 The two operations are operationally identical.

12-9 (a) NOW Y   (b) MO   (c) SAM IS SHORT FOR SAMUEL

CHAPTER 14

14-1 Z(2) specifies the second element out of n possible elements.

14-2 DIM *any string variable name* (12,6)

14-3 m expresses row information; n expresses column information.

14-5 Fifty

14-6 Program statements cannot alter the arrangement of other program statements, specifically those listed as DATA items.

14-7 The first column in the series is required for the ID number.

14-8 The amount of program RAM (random-access memory) available within the machine.

Index

Index

Index